filling

her shoes

9-6-17

filling
her shoes

a memoir of an inherited family

Betsy Graziani Fasbinder

SHE WRITES PRESS

Published 2017
Printed in the United States of America
Print ISBN: 978-1-63152-198-0
E-ISBN: 978-1-63152-199-7
Library of Congress Control Number: 2016959225

For information, address:
She Writes Press
1563 Solano Ave #546
Berkeley, CA 94707

Cover design © Julie Metz, Ltd./metzdesign.com
Interior design by Tabitha Lahr

She Writes Press is a division of SparkPoint Studio, LLC.

Names and identifying characteristics have been changed to protect the privacy of certain individuals.

In memory of Janet Lundgren Fasbinder,
to whom I owe three lifetimes of
gratitude for my beautiful inherited life.

And in the end we were all just humans,
drunk on the idea that love,
only love, could heal our brokenness.

—F. Scott Fitzgerald

No Answers on The Shelves

* a prologue *

When I was about to be a mother for the first time, I did what lots of expectant moms do; I went to the bookstore to try to prepare myself. My fingers perused the spines of the books on the shelf: *The Best Baby Name Book,* and *What to Expect When You're Expecting* and dozens more. But I wasn't pregnant. I was expecting nothing like what those books described. I was about to become a parent, not by giving birth, but by marrying a man with a six-and-a-half-year-old son. So I looked to another shelf, with books all about stepparenting. I cracked open book after book and found tables of contents that had no connection to what I was going through. I saw chapters like "Managing the Ex Factor," "Two Houses, One Set of Expectations," and "Jealous of the Ex?", and topics such as spousal support, child custody battles, lawyers, resentment, conflict, and guilt. While the pregnancy and baby books didn't describe what I was facing, neither did the books on being a stepparent.

My husband-to-be had not divorced his young wife; she had died. Leukemia took Janet Lundgren Fasbinder when she was a young mother of a five-year-old. Tom was a widower at forty. And Max, their son, had lost his mother. I wasn't stepping into conflict or court battles, custody hassles, or disputed alimony payments. I was joining a family that had suffered a tragic loss.

Daunted by the prospect of facing motherhood under such unusual circumstances, I found no comfort or information on the shelves. It wasn't just the absence of self-help books relevant to my circumstances that got to me that day in the bookstore. It was the preponderance of negative images of stepmothers. Most every fairy tale I could recall and nearly every Disney movie featured an orphan of some sort, a vulnerable character whose parent, or parents, had died. Stepparents don't get very high marks in fairy tales. They're neglectful, abusive, cruel, unloving. The stepmother is an evil archetype, a much-used trope of a villain. I could find no model on the shelves for the kind of mother I wanted to be, and no instructions for how to deal with the presence of grief in our family rather than the conflict of divorce.

During the time I became Tom's wife and Max's second mother, I did what I always do to try to understand my circumstances: I wrote. I didn't find stories describing my life, providing guidance, so I wrote them. I wrote in my journal. I wrote short essays and poems. I ranted, I whined, I questioned, all through the flow of ink onto the page. And like all of the writing I did at that time, I never intended to share any of it with anyone. Writing, at that point in my life, was a private endeavor. I wrote to understand, to gain perspective, to sort things out, to express the things I couldn't find a way to say aloud. My writing helped me step back and approach mothering more thoughtfully. It let me have a private space to confess my fears and my confusions, to air my petty yearnings along with my heartbreaks without spilling them onto Tom and Max. They had enough to deal with. The stories sat for many years in a file on my computer and in fragments in various journals.

More than a dozen years after I wrote the first stories, I read one of them aloud at a writers' salon. It was spring, and the theme of the salon was mothering. To me it was a simple little story of that moment when I began to feel "motherly" love for Max. I feared that my humble story would not mean much to anyone who had not been in my precise circumstances. But listeners told me that the story moved them. They told me of their own experiences, which were different than mine, but somehow the themes were the same. I was wrong because of something that I've always known, but had forgotten. While the exact circumstances of our lives may differ wildly from one another's, love and loss, triumph and disappointment, desire and discouragement, courage and fear are the themes of everyone's stories, and it is those themes which inextricably bind us as humans, one to another.

If this book had been a screenplay, I'd have written a director's note to move the camera close for every exchange. This story is not meant to represent the entirety of what life was like for us as we became and endured as a family. Friends and family members looking for themselves in these pages may be disappointed because, but for a small few, the "characters" in this story all lived in my house.

As I read through journals and stories, looked through photographs, and allowed myself to remember, I was struck by two truths: A lot of really bad stuff happened in order for us to become a family, and a lot of really good stuff happened, too. Despite the tragedy that allowed us to become a family in the first place, much of our shared life has been absent some of the challenges that so many blended families experience. While grief and loss are recurring themes in my marriage and in our shared family experience, we've been fortunate beyond measure to be a close and loving family.

This book is a simple story of a regular family, formed in an irregular way. It is a collection of the ordinary and extraordinary moments inside our family. It is my story of love and loss living side by side in our home, as it does in so many others. It is my story of falling in love with my inherited family.

First Dates and Resolutions

I have my family because of a New Year's resolution.

When Tom called to ask me out on our first date, we'd known each other for more than sixteen years. A call directly from Tom was unexpected enough—we usually encountered each other at gatherings at my sister's house. Tom had been college friends at Purdue with my older sister, Dianne, and had been freshman roommates with Jim, who would later become Dianne's husband.

Di and Jim were part of what I've always thought of as "The Great Purdue Migration" in the mid-seventies. Realizing they were actually free to leave Indiana, they—and a whole group of their friends in the post–Summer of Love era—set their sights on the "City by the Bay." Tom was part of that migration. Tom, Di, and Jim became housemates in San Francisco.

I met Tom when I was fifteen and he was twenty-five. Tom joined my sister and her husband one Christmas when they drove from San Francisco to California's Central San Joaquin Valley town of Visalia, to share the holiday with our family.

Tom was appealing with his full beard and long hair, which were common to the mid-1970s—the kind of guy a young girl could get a crush on. Though I noticed him, my attentions were pretty focused on a guy my own age. Tom was playful, easy with a laugh, respectful to my mom, helpful in the kitchen, and instantly likable. Because he's a stand-up guy, I was not even a blip on his romantic radar then. I was his roommate's kid sister—emphasis on *kid*. Ours was then a familial kind of connection.

There is one standout moment from that Christmas in 1975 that would later take on greater significance. Tom brought gifts for my mother, my younger brother, John, and for me. This was a pretty nice gesture from a young single guy, given he'd just met us. One might expect he'd get something like mittens or bubble bath for a fifteen-year-old girl he'd never met. But when I opened Tom's gift, my breath left me. I don't know what I was expecting, but opening Joni Mitchell's *Blue* album wasn't it. I felt that sense of *wow* that you feel when someone gives you the perfect gift—a gift that feels as though they really *know* you and understand what you'd like. Had he given me mittens or bath salts, it would have been a nice enough gesture. But Joni Mitchell's *Blue* was personal and spot-on for who I was at that moment. I loved poetry even then, and Joni is nothing if not a poet. I was also emerging out of the bub-ble-gum music preferences of adolescence—The Carpen-ters, David Cassidy, Captain and Tennille—and stepping into my more womanly choices. *Blue* was the threshold.

I sat with the album on my lap, stunned. "Is it okay?" Tom asked. "If you don't like it, you can change it for something else." I mumbled something that must've been positive because he said, "Great. I thought you'd like it." The rest of the holiday was the normal hubbub, but I kept thinking about that album, looking forward to the moment when the holiday hullabaloo would settle and I could retreat to my room to listen to it.

In the time between that Joni Mitchell Christmas in 1975 and Tom's call for a first date in March of 1991, our lives had each taken their separate courses. He got married to Janet; I got married to Ernie at about the same time in 1979. Tom was twenty-nine and I was nineteen when we each got married. His wife Janet and I became casual friends, seeing one another at gatherings of the extended Purdue crowd. She and I cohosted a baby shower for Jim and Di when they were expecting their first child, my niece Megan. Ernie and I went to dinner at Tom and Janet's house; they came to ours. I sent a gift and a card when their first child was born, and observed Max move from infancy to toddlerhood at various gatherings over the next three years.

Then Janet got sick. Max was three when his mother discovered she had leukemia.

I'd see Janet now and then, wearing some kind of hat or headscarf to cover her hair loss. She had always been thin, but she got scary thin. Her skin turned gray. Radiation and chemo did their harms, but they also did good and Janet's leukemia went into remission. I got updates about

Janet's condition through my sister. Everyone in the concentric circles of friendship with Tom and Janet was hoping for the best. About that same time, my first marriage was struggling and would soon come to an end.

Janet's remission allowed her to celebrate Max's fourth birthday, though she was likely too ill to enjoy his fifth. Just after he turned five, her remission had come to an abrupt and cruel end. Her decline was rapid. While a bone-marrow transplant was being arranged, Janet died just days after Max started kindergarten.

Janet's death was shocking on so many levels. She was just thirty-four, with a small child. She'd been sick, but had gotten better. Everyone's hopes were high. Her death was, for many in our circle, the first death of a peer other than those lost in Vietnam many years before. Everyone's attention turned to Tom and to Max. It all seemed so unfair.

∽∽∽∽∽∽

About six months after Janet's passing, I asked Dianne how Tom and Max were doing. "Pretty well," she said. "You know Tom. He probably wouldn't let anybody know if it was going too badly. He's just taking care of Max. Figuring things out."

"Such a good guy," I said.

"Yeah," Di said. "You know, I can't imagine he'll stay single for a long time. Tom's a married kind of guy."

I agreed with her and we talked about what a homebody Tom was, how he preferred nights in to going out, how his form of recreation was fixing up his fixer-upper. We talked about how impossibly hard it must be to be widowed with a child. I had not one molecule of thought—nor did Dianne, she later told me—that I might in any way be part of Tom's future romantic plans. At that time, Tom likely didn't know it either. We were just sisters talking about our friend and his boy and how very sad the loss was.

At that time I was slogging through an on-again-off-again relationship with a guy I'll call "Carlos." The relationship was fraught with problems, but we were both lonely enough to hang onto it long past its expiration date. We were more companions than lovers, really. I'd turned thirty-one, and was feeling that my on-again with Carlos should be off-again . . . for good. We were perfectly wrong for each other in nearly every way. It shames me to admit this, but I was too insecure to break it off. Apparently, he was too. We had no overt commitment to one another. Both of us had dated other people, though we had a tacit understanding that we didn't really talk about that.

On January 1, 1991, I made a New Year's resolution. I got honest with myself and admitted that I wanted a relationship—a real, whole, healthy relationship. I was ready. I understood myself better than I had as a nineteen-year-old bride. I wasn't thinking marriage, just that I wanted a partner. I had dated enough to see that I was not a dating kind of a woman—that I preferred to be in a relationship. I'd been with Carlos long enough to know that there was nothing there for me. But I wasn't meeting dateable men. It was my own doing, of course. Bringing Carlos to most gatherings and spending weekends with my gay friends was not exactly setting me up to be seen as single and available for dating.

My New Year's resolution was that I was going to tell friends that I was interested in meeting someone. I'd been in graduate school and working full time. I'd developed the habit of declining invitations. I began telling friends that I'd welcome invitations. More than that, I resolved to suck it up and get out more, even to events and gatherings by myself, rather than bringing Carlos or a gay male friend as I'd usually done. I'm uncomfortable at parties, and I'd always brought someone along to avoid that awkward and alone feeling. Home with a book was so much easier, but it was clear that this wasn't the way to connect with eligible partners.

That February, I went on our annual ski trip with Di, Jim, and a bunch of friends. I'd gone for several years, but had always brought Carlos. Keeping my resolution, I went solo.

I stayed in the house shared by Di and Jim with their kids. Tom and Max were there, too. Tom, widowed for more than a year by then, was dating Judy, a friendly woman who fit easily into the larger group with her good nature and her pitch-in-with-the-cooking attitude.

"So, Judy's nice," I said to Di. "It's good to see Tom dating. And Max seems to really like her."

"Yeah. She's great," Di agreed.

We enjoyed meals and skiing, jigsaw puzzles at the house, and a lot of laughter. I left the weekend feeling so happy for Tom and Max, and happy to have met Judy. She was sunny and kind, just what I thought Tom and Max deserved. Tom looked happy, in his quiet Tom way. Max looked carefree and playful.

A few weeks later, my phone rang.

"Hi," he said on the phone. "This is Tom. Tom Fasbinder."

Tom had never, in my memory, called me directly. It caught me by surprise. "Hi," I said. "Is everything okay?"

My mind raced through the possibilities: Di and Jim were in an accident, something wrong with Max. It's funny now, looking back, that I assumed Tom could only be calling with bad news.

I instantly regretted the question. This is a guy whose wife died a year before. What could "Is everything okay?" even mean to a guy who'd gone through what he'd been through?

"Yeah, great," he said. There was an awkward cadence to his speech I'd not heard before.

We waded through small chitchat. Was I finished with school? I had finished my masters in counseling and I told him about my arduous preparations for my written licensing exams and how they were coming up in a few months. I asked about Max. Silence hung in awkward tendrils between us in our unfamiliar conversation. I still feared he was trying to warm up to give me bad news. This man I'd known for sixteen years seemed suddenly like a stranger.

"Say, I was wondering if you'd like to, you know, go out for dinner sometime. With me, I mean." I was instantly back in high school. So, it seemed, was Tom. I tried to pull up a memory of even once being alone with Tom and couldn't come up with one.

I closed my eyes trying to sort out the new information. This wasn't a bad-news call. No sick children or fatal car crashes. This was a guy asking a woman out on a date. This was *Tom* asking *me* out on a date. I'm sure he felt a few seconds of miserable silence on his end of the line while I did the complex computation of combining two and two.

"Sure," I said. "I'd like that." It wasn't until I heard myself accepting the date that I even knew I would. There was a lot at stake here. This was a friend. This was a close friend of my sister's and of her husband, Jim. If this went badly, we'd have a double scoop of uncomfortable for a long future of gatherings. Tom's circle and my circle intertwined . . . a lot. His son was a playmate of my niece and nephew, attending each other's birthday parties and play dates. Pretending none of those thoughts were going through my brain, I adjusted my voice channel to *chipper*, chatted amicably, and we made arrangements for the following Friday night.

When I set the phone receiver back in its cradle, I kept my hand there for a while. Had that just happened? Was that really Tom? Joni Mitchell Tom? Asking *me* out? It's not that I wasn't happy. I was just reshuffling all of my assumptions. I thought he was with Judy. I thought he saw me as Di's kid sister. But then, I wasn't fifteen any more; I was thirty-one. I picked the receiver up and called Di.

"I know," she said, when I told her of my surprising call.

"You know? How do you know?"

"Tom talked to me first. He said he'd been thinking about you since he saw you on the ski weekend. He said he was thinking of asking you out, but he wouldn't if Jim or I are uncomfortable with it." There was a long pause. "We're not, by the way."

Another stunner. Tom was then, and remains today, a man of few words. He is not one to expose his emotions easily. It must have been a tremendous effort for him to make not just one phone call, but two, exposing his vulnerable feelings for the sake of a date. I was flattered, but more than that, I was impressed. This was a guy that cared enough about his friendship with my sister and her husband that he didn't want to risk damaging it.

"I'm not sure how to feel about all of this," I confessed to Di. "I mean, I've always thought Tom was great, but I've never thought of him romantically before. He was too old for me when we met. Then we were both married. Then Janet. You know."

"It could be kind of great though, don't you think? We already know Tom's a good guy, right?" she said.

"Right," I conceded. "But the dating thing. I have a feeling it'll either be really weird or really right. I'm kind of nervous."

"Just relax," Di reassured. "It'll be fine. However it turns out."

ler____eel

My living situation was in flux in the days leading up to this first date. I'd just been evicted from the flat I loved, the first place I'd had all to myself. I'd decided that I'd outgrown having roommates, and had found a budget-busting flat in San Francisco's Noe Valley. On the day I moved in, the owner let me know she was putting the whole building up for sale. Great timing. After I'd lived there only seven months, the place sold and I got the boot. I'd been looking for a place I could afford to live in alone for weeks. No luck.

With Tom coming over to pick me up, I'd confined the packing chaos to the bedroom and kitchen, leaving the living room intact, hoping that this made me also appear intact despite the chaos and my impending homelessness.

He came to my door, this oh-so-familiar man, looking quite unfamiliar. Was it nerves? I noticed he'd ironed his crisp cotton shirt. I'd known Tom for the better part of two decades and didn't remember ever seeing him wearing anything other than a T-shirt or plaid flannel. Ironing his shirt seemed like a special effort. My face flushed thinking about him ironing in front of a baseball game on TV.

He drove us in his Jeep Cherokee to a French restaurant on San Francisco's Church Street. Neither of us had ever been there. He was the Tom I'd known for years, but somehow a stranger; I was seeing him in a new light. This was "Date Tom." I'd never met Date Tom, other than during his phone invitation. We ordered and chatted about the same newsy kinds of things we'd always talked about. Di and Jim and their kids. Max. How was work? He asked about my graduate school and my upcoming licensing exams. We talked about my futile hunt for an apartment I could afford on the meager salary I was getting from the outpatient mental health clinic where I worked.

Once the distraction of waiters bringing food and drink had settled, there was a quiet moment. "Do you mind if I ask you something?" Tom asked.

Caution and curiosity blended. "Sure."

"What didn't work out with Ernie? I always thought he was a pretty nice guy."

Yes. My date had known my ex-husband and Carlos, too, for that matter. I hadn't exactly thought about that before, though it was conspicuous in his question. I placed my napkin in my lap and took a fortifying sip of wine. "Ernie *is* a nice guy," I said. "A really nice guy. There was no cheating, nothing like that. But we married really young, before I knew that nice wasn't enough. Ernie is so nice he'll become anything I want him to be. I didn't want that. I wanted somebody who knows his own mind and is willing to partner with me, but won't just defer to my direction. He never had any of his own opinions. He just adopted all of mine."

I looked up, wondering if the expression I saw on Tom's face was confusion or judgment. "So *you* ended things?" he asked.

"Yeah," I admitted. I instantly raced through the options. Was he glad I'd ended it because maybe it indicated I wasn't such a pain in the ass that someone would leave me? Or did he think I was a flake for ending a marriage with a nice guy for reasons even my own mother couldn't get her head around? I decided honesty was my best answer. "I've never felt worse about anything than about breaking my promise to Ernie. This may be hard to understand." I paused to see if Tom was scoffing. He wasn't. He just looked at me as if I was giving him pieces of a puzzle and he was trying to see the picture. "I was lonely," I said. "Being with someone who will be whatever you want him to be, will think anything you say is right, who has no opinions of his own, is a lot like being alone. I really care about him, but I wanted more from a relationship. It may sound a little lofty, but I also felt like he really deserved someone that wants him exactly how he is. I'm sure there's a woman for him that likes being totally in charge of him. His mom was like that. Ernie's dad always looked to her for direction. I think that's what Ernie wants." I tried to read Tom's expression. "I know. It's kind of confusing."

"No, I get it," Tom said, wiping his lips with his napkin. "I just wanted to know."

This was my first experience with Tom questioning me about something so personal. After I'd answered, he probed no further, shifting the topic naturally. My explanation was enough for him and he required no more details. I'd learn over the next weeks and months, and the decades that we've since shared, that Tom's sense of privacy and respect caused him to ask for only what he absolutely needed to know about my past relationships in order to decide if he wanted to take the next steps with me. He's never, since that day, asked me another question about my marriage or past partners.

After that series of questions was answered, our interaction shifted. As we walked back to his car, he took my hand. I was glad he did.

Back at my apartment, sitting on my sofa we shared our first kisses, sweet and shy. I'd known that to shift my image of Tom from family friend to potential romantic partner would be either weird or wonderful; it was wonderful.

We kissed for a while, then Tom sat back. "I'd like to see you some more," he said. I could tell by the clearing of his throat that he had something more to say before he expected my reply. I was already learning to read his signals. "But I have Max. It's not easy for me to get away a lot and I don't like to leave him with sitters too much. I'd need you to understand. You know—" His voice trailed again and the silence was filled with all that he didn't say. I could see his pulse pounding in the hollow of his throat. This was risky for him. Tom was the dad of a boy who'd lost his mother, a boy who needed his dad.

The gravity of all that Tom and Max had been through made me feel heavier where I sat. I'd always known that Tom, as my sister said, was a good guy, but in that moment, my respect for him as a man, as a father, as a person who had his priorities straight swelled. I'd always liked him. In that moment I came to admire him.

"I understand," I said. "I wouldn't expect anything less from you." Paragraphs of words lodged in my throat. I wanted to say how sorry I was, how hard I knew it must be for him and for Max. I wanted to tell him how much I respected and admired how he was handling it all. But our kisses kept any of those unnecessary words from escaping my lips.

lee⎯uel

The next day I called Carlos and we went to lunch. Though we had a tacit agreement that kept us from talking about the other people we were dating, I knew I had to tell Carlos about Tom right away. Logic would have told me that such a conversation was premature after going on exactly one date with Tom. But my heart knew. That first date with Tom didn't feel like just a date—and certainly not a first date; it felt like a beginning. It also felt like a long-overdue ending. While Carlos and I didn't have any sort of formal commitment and we hadn't really been romantic partners for a long time, I felt the need to be straight with him. Tom and I had formalized nothing. We'd shared only one date, some lovely kissing, and an agreement that we'd see each other again.

lee⎯uel

My second date with Tom was dinner at Tom and Max's house in Pacifica, a coastal town just south of San Francisco. Tom fed Max first; he ate at a TV table watching *Rugrats* on Nickelodeon. Tom excused himself to check the grill and stepped out the sliding glass door, spatula in hand.

"Hey, Max," I said as I entered the family room.

"Hi," Max replied between bites. He returned his attention to the program. His body wriggled and moved as a reply to every one of the cartoon tots' exploits. He laughed easily, and his body was in near-constant motion. He turned to me, his dark brown eyes lively. "Who's your favorite?" he asked.

"My favorite what?"

"Rugrat?" he said. "I don't like Angelica at all. She's really bossy. I like Tommy a lot. But I like Dil the very best." As Max looked at the TV, I could also see that he was poking his tongue around beneath his closed lips.

"Oh, well. Hmm." I stalled. I didn't know this program, but his question felt like a test of some sort. "Why do you like Dil?" I asked.

Max looked back at me with his palms raised "Duh. His name."

"Dil?"

"Dil *Pickles*," Max said, rolling his eyes as though I had missed the most obvious of details. Clearly my Rugrats ignorance was vast.

"Ah. That is a pretty cool name."

"Check it out," he said, standing and stepping toward me. He then parted his lips and pushed his tongue, forcing a precariously dangling front tooth forward, then sideways into the blank space that had already been vacated by the next-door tooth.

"Wow. That's pretty loose. Be careful not to swallow it while you're eating."

He sat back down and looked back at the TV screen. "It's okay. I'm chewing only on the side." Max then howled in response to an ice cream cone landing on Angelica, the meanie's, head. "Ha. Serves her right!"

I'd known Max since he was an infant, but as an acquaintance, not as the son of the man I was dating. I felt strange and nervous in front of this cheerful six-and-a-half-year-old, though I worked comfortably with kids all the time, and was close to my nieces and nephew.

Tom re-entered through the sliding glass door and gave me a smile. "How do you like your steak?"

"Medium, please."

Tom glanced over at the TV. "How's Dil doing?"

"Pretty good," Max said, his cheek bulging as he chewed. He slid an oven-baked french fry through a puddle of ketchup. "He dumped ice cream on Angelica's head."

Tom put his fist out, inviting Max's knuckle bump in return. Clearly, Tom shared Max's disdain for Angelica. He slipped back outside, the fragrance of grilling steak lingering behind as he closed the door. In a few minutes he returned through the door with a platter. A drumroll sounded from the TV, followed by a melody of bells and whistles, and pictures of tumbling toddlers and toys, signaling the end of the show.

"Okay, Skib," Tom said to Max. "TV off. Time for your bath. Betsy and I are going to have our dinner while you take your bath, then it's bed time."

"Can I play Legos for a little while first? It's not a school night."

Tom looked up at the wall clock. "Bath first. Then a half an hour of Legos. Then bed. Deal?"

"Deal," Max said. He clicked the remote, picked up his plate from the TV table, and balanced his glass atop it as he brought it to the sink. "Look," he said to Tom, and did another round of tongue/tooth manipulation.

Tom shivered. "Brrrr," he said. "Let's pull that nasty thing. It's disgusting."

"Nope," Max said with a lilt in his voice. "Not ready yet."

Tom held up his hands in surrender. "Okay. But I want to look before you go to bed. I don't want you to swallow it while you're sleeping. I'll go get your water going so it won't be too hot." He looked at me with a small apology on his face. "Be right back."

"Don't worry, I'm fine," I said.

While they were gone I surveyed the family room and kitchen. The rooms of the suburban two-story home were neat and organized, nothing fancy. The style could be categorized as nothing specific, a few antiques mixed with generic furniture pieces. Simple and comfortable. Everything looked kid-friendly. I remembered that Tom and Janet had moved into this house during the months when her leukemia had been in remission. The walls had only the most basic of decorations. A clock over the mantle. A framed picture with five openings, each filled with Olan Mills studio shots of Max in a different pose. He was about three in the pictures, wearing a striped turtleneck and elastic-waist jeans, his face pudgier than it was now, and his hair much lighter, almost blonde. An image popped into my mind of Janet holding him in her arms when he was about that age.

I stepped into the dining room. It and the adjoining living room held antique oak furniture. Atop one carved cabinet sat an arrangement of Beatrix Potter figurines: rabbits and foxes and geese clad in bonnets and aprons, a frog wearing a crown. I recalled receiving Max's Beatrix Potter–themed baby announcement. On the wall near the table hung two old-time portraits of a stern-looking pair from sometime in the 19th century, a mustachioed gent and a woman in black wearing the scowlier scowl.

"Some of Janet's grumpy-looking relatives," Tom said as he descended the stairs. He shrugged, seeming not to know what else to say.

I was suddenly aware that I was in a house that Janet had selected, furnished, and arranged. Tom seemed matter-of-fact about it, but I felt a little bit like an intruder. I wondered whether Tom changed any of the décor since her passing.

"Not as good as the French restaurant," Tom said, taking a bite of his steak.

"Well, not many of us can stand up against restaurant-grade French cuisine. This is pretty good though," I said, meaning it. "And Max ate broccoli. I'm impressed. Most kids hate broccoli."

"It's his one vegetable. That and raw carrots."

Another flash of Janet came into my mind. Even before she got ill, Janet had always been exceptionally thin and I recalled her food peculiarities. Her entrée foods were limited to spaghetti, hot dogs, peanut butter and jelly, and chicken. I'd often found it odd at parties that Janet didn't partake of most of the foods served by the hosts, instead opting for her baggie full of raw carrots and raw, sliced potatoes she'd brought for herself.

"Do you cook?" Tom asked.

"I did. I like to. But I've been in grad school and working full time, so I'm afraid I've gotten in the habit of yogurt for dinner, or take-out Thai food. I've told myself I'm going to cook real food again as soon as I pass this exam."

"I've done most of the cooking for a long time," Tom said. "Janet just wasn't really into food."

"I remember."

"Is it a tough one?"

I looked at my steak. "No, it's good. Very tender."

Tom chuckled. "The test. Is it a hard one?"

"Oh. The written has a sixty-percent fail rate. Then, assuming I pass that, I get to take oral exams which have an over seventy-percent fail rate."

"Don't worry. You'll do great."

While the compliment was baseless—Tom had no idea about any academic or clinical skills that the Board of Behavioral Sciences was assessing in me—it still felt reassuring. And sweet.

As Tom poured me a second glass of wine, Max made his pajama-clad entrance down the stairs and stood beside Tom. His outgrown Teenage Mutant Ninja Turtles PJs gapped a bit, allowing a sliver of tummy to peek out from beneath the bottom of the shirt. His lips were tucked in and he cast a sideways glance to me, then flashed me a grin showing a new space where his top front tooth had dangled.

"Let's check," Tom said. He sniffed Max's damp hair, then scruffed it up.

"Hey!" Max said smoothing his sleek, dark hair back down. "I just combed that."

"Whoa," Tom said, pulling back and examining the new vacancy in Max's mouth. "Did you pull it out?"

"Nope. Fell out when I was blowing underwater bubbles."

"Ah, the old bubble extraction method." Tom poked Max in the side causing him to laugh and wriggle away.

"Tub drained?" Tom asked.

Max stood at attention. "Check."

"Towel hung?"

"Check. And teeth brushed, see." Max stretched his lips into an exaggerated smile while Tom lifted his chin.

"Good job and easier since you had fewer teeth."

"Story time."

Tom looked up with an *I warned you* apology on his face.

"No worries. You take story duty. I'll clear the table. Goodnight, Max. It was nice to see you."

"Night," he said. Then he delivered a quick hug, his small arms around my neck and his head resting briefly on my shoulders. His little hand offered two "there there" taps, like one might offer to someone who needed comforting. And it was . . . comforting. The unexpected embrace caught me off guard, but I returned it with a squeeze. Just as quickly, Max pulled away and scampered up the stairs. I watched as Tom followed him up, resting my hand on the warm spot where Max's head had rested.

⁂

The next weekend was another first date of sorts. This one included Max. We decided to go to the San Francisco Zoo. It was a sunny April day and I was nothing but optimistic. The warmth of Max's hug still lingered with me. Tom picked me up and I climbed into the front seat of the Cherokee. Max was on his booster seat, strapped into the back seat. "Hi, Max," I said.

Max's lips were turned downward, his bottom lip jutting out so far that if he'd been walking, it seemed he might trip on it. He gave me a glance, but no verbal greeting. Tom started the car and we were on our way to the zoo. Tom whistled as he drove, oblivious to the serious pout that Max was wearing. "How was school this week?" I asked. Too chipper. I was trying too hard.

Max shrugged and looked out the window toward the vast gray Pacific.

Tom asked me how my studying was going and I explained about the prep course I'd just paid six hundred dollars for. I didn't want to say what a pounding six hundred dollars did to my limited budget.

"How'd your spelling test go?" I asked, attempting to engage Max in the conversation. "Your dad said you had one yesterday." As I turned my body to look into the back seat, Tom took my hand and rested our coupled hands on my knee. A surprising feeling of being embarrassed drew heat to my face, as if a date had kissed me in front of my mother.

Max's dour expression was unchanged. He shrugged. Tom whistled along with the radio, seemingly unaware of Max's conspicuous funk. I'd been an intern in a counseling agency for two years, with much of my time conducting therapy with troubled and abused children. I knew how to charm kids, build trust, and, when appropriate, help to cheer them. I made several more attempts to be playful with Max, but he was having none of it. He replied with only one-word answers or shrugs. His bottom lip hung. His eyelids drooped. If he'd been a toddler, I'd have said he needed a nap.

I relaxed. I figured the zoo animals would cheer him. Really, what kid could stay grumpy in front of orangutans flinging their poop?

But grumpy he remained. Through howler monkeys howling. Through penguins catching fish tossed by their keepers. Through the elephant spraying water on her back with her trunk. And yes, through the orangutans flinging their poop. I didn't think there was a six-year-old boy alive who could remain unsmiling during poop tossing.

Doubt began to run through my veins, ice cold, rendering me stiff. Sure, Max had been cheerful in his home when I was just a visitor. Now I was an intruder, horning in on his time with his dad. Now I was a "date," not a friend having dinner, and I assumed his grim expression and stubborn mood were his silent commentary on my presence, on my being an intruder. Every wicked stepmother in every fairy tale I'd ever heard flew through my mind.

Tom and I had seen each other every few days for the past two weeks and talked on the phone between visits. I confessed to him that I'd formally broken things off with Carlos. He let me know that he'd done the same with Judy, though they also had no formal agreement.

"So, now it's my turn for a question," I'd said as we drove to Woodside for dinner earlier in the week. "Why didn't things work out with Judy? She seemed really nice."

Tom tilted his head from side to side. "She is nice. Really nice. But I sort of think she was more in love with Max and the idea of being his mom than she was into me. She's over thirty-five. I didn't feel right about wasting any more of her time if we weren't going to work out and she really wants to be a mom. Funny, though, it was Judy who suggested I date you."

I pulled back and let my surprise show in a slack-jawed expression. "Really? Do tell."

"After the ski trip in February. She and I were talking about whether or not things should go forward with her and me. It wasn't hostile or anything. She said that she really liked meeting you, and that you and I might be a better fit."

"When did you tell Judy about seeing me?"

Tom's face twisted with a boyish look of shyness. "The next day after the French restaurant."

"No way! That's when I called Carlos."

That New Year's resolution had taken an interesting turn.

With neither of us letting the other know, we'd both untangled ourselves from our loose romantic entanglements. We'd both known we'd found someone we felt needed to be the "only" one. I was full of the wonderful, distracting love feelings I was having with Tom and he confessed he was having them for me. I was near giddy with it.

But Max and this zoo date were beginning to worry me.

Tom and Max were a package deal. My relationship with Max would be as important as the one I was forming with Tom. What's more, if that relationship couldn't work, I knew that a future with Tom would not be one I could even consider. Though I'd felt the first glimmers of falling in love with Tom, Max's well-being would be my concern as well, if things got serious. I had no idea what the source of Max's funk was. Maybe he'd already attached to Judy, and I was horning in—in his mind anyway. While Judy had perhaps been overly focused on Max, I also knew that it would be a mistake on every level to disregard him as a vital factor in whether or not Tom and I had any kind of a future together.

Tom held my hand as we walked. He asked Max what he wanted to see and ignored, or was oblivious to, Max's moody shrugs. "How about the zoo train, Skib?" Tom asked. Max shrugged. I wondered about the origin of this odd little nickname. Later I'd learn that Tom's playful names for loved ones had no specific origin or meaning and that each morphed into dozens of permutations. Skib. Skibber. Scoop. Scooper. All applied to Max. Years later I'd be Snooch, Schnook, Schnutzelheimer, though I couldn't have known that then.

"Let's get an ice cream," Tom suggested. I appreciated his attempt to shift Max's mood. "We can eat it on the train."

Max ate only part of his ice cream before a look of utter disgust crossed his face. "Can I throw this away?" he asked Tom.

"If you don't want any more of it," Tom said, licking his own cone.

"You feeling okay, Max?" I asked. Maybe he was sick. That would explain it.

He shrugged. Tom asked, "Do you have a tummy ache?"

"No. My hands are getting all sticky." His voice, low and slow, made me think of Eeyore from Winnie the Pooh. If the stakes hadn't felt so high, I'd have laughed at his pouty mouth and his old-man grumbling.

Tom pulled a bandana handkerchief from his pocket, an old-fashioned habit I found appealing. He took Max's cone and dropped it in the trash as the train rode past and wiped Max's hand.

"Still sticky," Max complained.

"You can wash when we stop." Tom squeezed my hand. "Want to go into the reptile house?"

"No. Just want to wash my hands."

lee eel

Tom and Max emerged together from the rest room. Every bit of spring-in-the-step I hoped to see in Max I found in Tom. If Max was Eeyore, Tom was Tigger, nearly bouncing with each stride. Max walked in drag-footed steps beside him. I half expected to see a tail tacked onto Max's backside, just like Eeyore's.

"You about ready to head back?" Tom asked me.

Fuck yeah, I thought. This was the most miserable zoo day I'd ever spent. "Sure, if you guys are ready," I said with false cheer.

In the car my heart felt heavy in my chest. I was convinced if I looked in the back seat too long at Max, he'd scream and ask me to jump out of the moving car. As much as Max's mood troubled me, Tom's obliviousness also concerned me. Was he just ignoring it? Or did he really not see it? Tom fumbled in the console between the front seats and extracted a cassette tape. He inserted it in the tape player and backed out of the parking lot. Tom Petty and the Heartbreakers began to play what I feared was Max's theme for the day.

I'll probably feel a whole lot better when you're go-o-o-one.

The lyrics pounded through my head. Tom resumed his trilling whistle, a descant harmony above the pounding melody. I kept my eyes forward, willing myself not to look back, if only to avoid receiving another double dose of Max's stink-eye. Between Max's sourpuss in the back seat, and Tom's whistling in the front, I felt I'd entered an episode of *The Twilight Zone*.

"Back one song, please," Max said. It was the first almost-full sentence I'd heard him say in hours, and the first *please* all day. Tom pressed the rewind button on the tape deck and turned up the volume. The car was filled with a throbbing drumbeat and the wail of electric guitar. From the corner of my eye, I saw lively movement from the back seat. I turned to see Max's thick, dark hair swinging and his hands twitching as his fingers slid up the neck of his air guitar. Soon Tom's palm tapped an accompanying rhythm on the steering wheel while Max swung to the beat.

"I *love* this song," Max cried, as though he was declaring his devotion from the top of a mountain. Soon the chorus rang out. Tom and Max's voices joined in. *Runnin' down a dream/That never woulda come to me/Workin' on a mystery/Goin' wherever it leads/Runnin' down a dream.*

When the song ended, Max smiled and panted in mock, tongue-hanging exhaustion. He cast a snaggle-toothed grin toward me. I recognized this as the boy I'd seen wiggling his tooth with his tongue, watching *Rugrats* only a few days before. I'd feared he'd left for good.

Tom complied with Max's wishes and advanced the tape. "Zombie Zoo" rang out. Max resumed his air guitar playing. When that song was done, he panted again. "Number five, please."

"Can we just listen in order?" Tom asked.

"Nope. Skipping all the dumb ones. She doesn't want to hear the dumb ones. Do you?"

"Who me?" I said, with theatrical exaggeration. "Why would I want to listen to the dumb ones?"

"Cool," Max pronounced. He looked at me. "Five is another goodie."

"Then five it shall be," I said. Soon the car was filled with all of us singing. *And I'll probably feel a whole lot better/when you're go-o-o-one.*

"Whoa. You know this song?" Max asked.

"Sure. I know the whole album. Love Tom Petty."

"Cool."

Tom gave my hand another squeeze.

When we got back to Tom and Max's house, Max scampered to the front door, then waited for Tom to come unlock it. As we entered, Max took my hand. "Hey, you want to see my Lego collection? I've got a *lot* of Legos."

I looked at Tom, who was shuffling through the mail he'd picked up on the way into the house. I tried to signal to him. Did he see? Had he seen the transformation that had taken place? But Tom just continued sorting the mail.

Max grabbed my hand and tugged me toward the stairs. "Come on. You won't believe all of my cool space crafts I built."

"What do you say I order a pizza?" Tom said as Max and I ascended the stairs.

I looked back and nodded.

"Pepperoni and olive, please," Max said.

"And what do you like on yours?" Tom asked.

I glanced down at the eager face of the boy whose hand I held. "Pepperoni and olive is perfect."

As Max tugged me into his super-tidy room, introducing me to his toy collection, I thought about all the angst of the day. So many dramas had unfolded in my mind, none of which turned out to be real. I'd thought that this forty-pound, snaggle-toothed figure in front of me, demonstrating how his Transformer morphed from a robot into a monster, had been about to pop the love balloon I'd begun to feel for his father. I'd already begun to mourn the loss of a relationship that had barely begun. On one hand it seemed neurotic of me, taking the lousy mood of a six-year-old so seriously, so personally. But my angst was not mere insecurity. It was evidence—evidence of how much love had already begun to grow and evidence of my fear that the future of that love might be in jeopardy. I hadn't just fallen for Tom; I'd begun to love Max as well.

I hadn't made my New Year's resolution with marriage in mind, but I'd begun to allow myself to see the bud of a possible future with these two. The thought of that bud not getting the chance to blossom made my heart ache.

Max took my hand in his again and tugged me toward his toy display shelf. "Now for the best stuff," he said.

"Yeah," I said. "Let's see some of that best stuff."

⟞⟝

Today, decades after that first series of dates, Joni Mitchell's *Blue* serves as the soundtrack to the love story that is Tom and me. It's our romance music, though he gave it to me many years before our romance began. Tom Petty's *Full Moon Fever* will forever conjure the mother–son love story that I share with Max; in my mind, it's our personal soundtrack. Each time I hear a cut from either album, I'm instantly back in those early days of what would become my inherited family.

It's also true that I hold Janet as a presence in this story, but I have no soundtrack for my relationship to her. Max is the music that she left behind, the melody of her love evident in his gentleness. His appearance is her album cover, passed from her DNA. His character is the song she began, but was forced to leave as an unfinished symphony.

Max on our "first date" to the zoo. He was a lot grumpier than this photo would imply. Still cute, though.

Tom and Max, October 1991, just as we were becoming a family.

Super Power and Baby Talk

On my twenty-first birthday I decided that I would never have children. Married to my first husband for two years at that point, I was just beginning to face the reality of the trauma in my family history, how it had influenced my decision to marry so young, and what it meant for my future. The idea of perpetuating the agony of my family's dysfunction and abuse to the next generation became a palpable terror to me as I entered adulthood. At that stage of my young adulthood, I had no ability to express my fear to anyone, instead making sweeping decisions without consultation. My lack of communication included, it shames me to say, not talking things through with my husband.

Ernie was the definition of a family man. He wanted us to start a family as soon as I was done with college, less than a year away. He was four years older than I. "Let's have kids while we're young," he suggested eagerly. "We can be active with them and have lots of time to enjoy being a family together." It was a nice idea, but one I couldn't picture.

Ernie's talk of babies sent me into a dark and sticky downward spiral of panic attacks and secrecy. Fear, unnamable and unavoidable, dominated my days and haunted my dreams. I woke up with my heart hammering and sweat running down my back.

After this went on for months, and without telling Ernie about it, I went to my gynecologist and asked him to set me up for a tubal ligation that would permanently remove the fear of pregnancy. Even as a teenager, I'd always had an eerie feeling that little baby spirits were hovering around my uterus, waiting for just one slip-up on my part. I was religious—well, fanatical—about birth control, never once having the risky, unprotected sex so many of my peers confessed to. But now that Ernie was talking babies, I knew with the single-minded sureness that is only available to twenty-one-year-olds that I would not, *could not ever*, become a mother. The fear blinded me to all else, including my value for honesty with my partner. I wanted no debate. I had to take action.

My gynecologist declined my request, saying simply that I was young and healthy and that it would be unethical for him to perform permanent sterilization in such circumstances. He renewed my prescription for Ortho-Novum.

In the coming months, while Ernie's talk of babies and family continued, I sought the services of nine more gynecologists with the same request, receiving the same general response. It was the early 1980s, and all of my "second opinions" came from male doctors. On our tight budget, it was hard to squeeze out enough secret cash for all of my off-the-books gynecology appointments. Each time I went to the grocery store I wrote my check for ten dollars extra—a seemingly small amount now—pocketing the money and secreting it away in my bottom dresser drawer under scarves and miscellany until I had squirreled enough away for another appointment. My secrecy was getting pricey in terms of both my morals and our supposedly shared pocketbook. I had become both a liar and a thief.

My final approach was to a female gynecologist at Planned Parenthood, desirable for its then five-dollar co-pay for students. When I told her the procedure I wanted, her face contorted into a question mark. She rolled her chair back from her desk and drew it around the side to be nearer to me. She was the first of the eleven doctors to meet me and address my question while I had my clothes on. It was a lot more comfortable than the paper-caped conversations in the ten prior offices.

She leafed through my file. "I see that you've consulted other physicians," she said. Her eyes were warm amber. Her voice was gauzy, as if wrapped with cotton. "Can you tell me exactly *why* you want this?" She was the first to ask.

I swallowed and tried to form my face into a neutral, businesslike expression, but my attempt was in vain. Tears spilled, but I kept my voice steady. "I was raised by an abusive father," I confessed. "He was probably abused by his father. And I've been studying a lot in my masters program about how abused children grow up to be abusers. I couldn't live with myself if—" My words jammed in my throat. I hadn't uttered them aloud before, to anyone. I was stunned to hear them in my own voice.

The kind doctor leaned forward, reached across the corner of her desk, and rested her hand atop my folded ones. A very un-doctorly gesture, but it was both kind and professional under the circumstances. "I understand," she whispered. "It's an admirable thing, wanting to stop the cycle of abuse. I wish everyone took becoming a parent so seriously. Believe me."

I did. Her face said that she'd seen a lot. But I wasn't feeling so admirable, given the weeks of skulking around behind my husband's back, intending full well to make a choice for both of us without offering him a voice in the matter. My only excuse was that my drive felt involuntary, a force from which I was defenseless.

With her eyes unblinking, the doctor looked past my tears, deeply into my eyes. "We each have every right to determine our reproductive paths. Not having children at all is a perfectly viable choice. Your thoughtfulness implies to me that you might someday be a very good mother and I believe it's my duty to preserve that as a future option for you, should you change your mind. I invite you to get some counseling to deal with your family history." She then wrote a few names on her prescription pad, one of which was the woman who would ultimately become my first therapist. The good doctor had tossed a life vest across the bow into the murky sea where I was treading water. "How about this? How about I prescribe you the most dependable birth control pill on the market. You must take them faithfully for them to be fully effective."

I sniffed. "I've never missed one." My heart pounded and I feared that she could hear it from where she sat.

She then paused and studied my face. Likely my fear

was apparent. Offering to quell the last of my anxiety, she suggested using a diaphragm as a secondary barrier method to give myself the last bit of assurance I needed. "Permanent sterilization is a serious decision. But if when you're twenty-five you still feel exactly the same way, we can talk about doing a more permanent contraceptive procedure at that time."

I exhaled without having known I'd been holding my breath. *Yes.* This was what I wanted, more of a guarantee that I wouldn't be in the miniscule minority of oral contraceptive failure rate. Even miniscule felt like too much risk. I'd been having anxiety attacks for months, feeling sure I was pregnant at least a dozen times though there'd been no evidence to substantiate my worry. I couldn't imagine what I'd do if I accidentally got pregnant while married to Ernie. While I have always been politically pro-choice, abortion didn't seem like a reasonable thing to do given my circumstances. Prevention was my strategy.

After meeting this final gynecologist, I told Ernie the partial truth that I was going to use a diaphragm as birth control. For the remaining five years of our seven-year marriage, I used it faithfully, though I never told him that I was also still on The Pill. He occasionally brought up the topic of children, to my repeated response that I wasn't ready, which was the essence of the truth, though I didn't know it then.

While Ernie imagined future family camping trips and family game nights, photos at the beach, and teaching our kids to ride bikes, I had no such library of images to draw upon.

Ernie and I got along. We seldom argued. He was kind, loving, and gentle. I had married him young, thinking kindness was so exceptional a feature in men, given my early exposure to the opposite kind of man, that I'd found the only such man to love me. He was my chance for safety, as I saw it—maybe my only chance. I cared for him and loved him in a certain way. But I'd not married him because I was *in love* or because we had great passion. Having a baby together would make my wobbly, immature decision to marry Ernie irreversible. And what if Ernie was a monster-in-waiting, only to be unleashed when a baby cried too loudly or broke a cereal bowl? Even though he'd been nothing but a gentle partner, my history wouldn't let me trust that he would remain so forever. Or worse, what if I was the sleeping monster, to be awakened only by the frustrations of motherhood? I knew about monsters.

⁓

My father, the monster of my youth, was dead eight years by my twenty-first birthday. Though long buried, my memory of him was still Technicolor in its detail. Cruel. Dangerous. When not drunk, hung over. Abusive in nearly every way a father can be. My mom was generous and gentle, but was oblivious—probably out of necessity—to the worst of my father's abuses.

I remember not one image of my parents laughing, or embracing, or snuggling while they watched TV. I recall little of their exchanges but for my father yelling and my mother inhaling her thoughts as she drew deeply on her ever-present no-filter Camel cigarette and replying to him only with silence and a stream of blue smoke. The only remotely romantic gesture I recall between them was my dad lighting my mother's cigarettes with the silver lighter he always carried in his pocket. Very Bogie and Bacall. In the end, it was cigarettes that killed them both long before their time.

My way of surviving my father was a ritual that began when I was very small. I remember being six or seven, enduring another in a long series of purple-faced rages from my drunken dad. One Saturday morning, while my father was sleeping after working his night shift at the battery factory, my brother and I watched morning cartoons. Our three older siblings had already moved out of the house to college or families of their own. John and I were the second batch in my parents' brood. Stragglers at the end of the rickety caravan. We knew well enough to keep the volume down on Saturday mornings and to refrain from any wild play indoors or anywhere near the house. But I was barely seven, John was four-and-a-half. John wanted to watch *The Fantastic Four*. I was indifferent to The Human Torch and The Thing, though I was intrigued by The Invisible Girl and envied her ability to disappear when danger struck. But I still preferred *Bugs Bunny* for Saturday entertainment. It was one program or the other in the days of three channels and no way to record a show and watch it another time. A skirmish ensued and our voices got louder, as children's voices do on Saturday mornings.

Our dad blasted through his bedroom door, his eyes bloodshot and his face swollen. He was huge, with hands like slabs of rib-eye and shoulders so broad he eclipsed the light as he towered over us. "What the hell is wrong with you idiots!" he screamed.

I froze. Time slowed down. This was *my* super power, this ability to freeze time so that it unfolded one frame at a time, like a series of photographs rather than a moving picture. Between each still image I could sit motionless for a split second, assess the danger level, reposition my facial expression to something neutral and pleasant that would not belie my fear, and listen carefully to what he said so that my response would not further enrage him. My brother had no such super powers. In the same circumstances where I froze, he was often caught in fits of involuntary nervous giggling and twisted facial expressions that further infuriated our father, unable to stop the awkward responses no matter how violent the command. The results were predictable. And frequent.

This particular Saturday, John's giggles prompted a powerful, unbridled kick. My dad's thick foot hit John's tiny backside so hard that he flew from the floor, over the coffee table, and onto the cigarette-burned sofa. His skinny limbs gyrated like eggbeaters as he flew. He landed hard enough that the couch scooted back with a screech and the front legs lifted off the floor and came down with a loud bang. With a dazed look in his eyes, John's giggling was silenced. Through my child's eyes, he looked like a not-so-funny Elmer Fudd when Bugs had gotten the better of him, clouting him on the head with a giant mallet, a goose-egg rising on his head, wobbly and drunken-looking. The only thing missing was the circle of bluebirds around John's head. Today, as I look back it seems likely that my baby brother must have had a concussion. One of many, probably. Nobody ever thought to have such things checked out.

This was the moment I first remember my survival chant arriving in my mind. It was a vow that I silently made every time I was in the presence of my father's venomous anger. I didn't know from where the vow came. As a little kid, I thought it might be God talking to me. Though its origin was unclear, the voice was anything but. While my father screamed and cursed, pounded and ranted, I had one simple thought, *This is not mine. When I grow up, I'll never have this in my house.*

I created dozens of coping techniques for distancing myself from my father's danger and my own terror. My first and best choice was always to stay invisible or absent, and to limit my exposure to him. The Invisible Girl had inspired me. I was sometimes literally absent. Weekend overnights at friends' houses. Outdoor chores. Drawing and coloring in a secret hiding place in the woods near our house. Reading *Little House in the Big Woods* or *Wind in the Willows* in the closet with a flashlight, silent and out of sight. If I couldn't be absent or invisible during my father's rants, I learned to keep my expression flat. To keep my focus I'd move my tongue, touching each of my teeth one at a time, one touch for every time my father's lips came together. Or I'd count the number of times he said "it" or "the," separating myself from the content of his words, focusing instead on the sound alone. I learned to sing funny songs in my mind during his rants. *Three six nine/The goose drank wine/ Monkey chewed tobacco on a streetcar line.* I know now that my chanting, singing, counting, and slowing of time was adaptive, a necessary protection I devised to tolerate the intolerable. The rituals, though absurd and involuntary, worked. They kept me silent and still, just as my father preferred all of his children to be. This limited the number of blows I received over the thirteen years of exposure I had to my dad before he died. Unfortunately, my practice didn't keep my younger brother safe at all.

It was these early experiences that brought terror about becoming a mother into my heart. My oldest sister had her first child when I was eight, her second when I was seventeen. She, by virtue of the timing of her birth and its occurrence during my dad's most volatile years, had likely been the recipient of the worst he had to offer. She too lacked the super power of avoiding him and, as with so many abuse survivors, her first choices in men proved not to be the safe harbor she craved and deserved. One of her husbands was an absent father. The second was a wild drunk with a temper. She was on the brink of a second divorce, always broke, always exhausted, always struggling. I'd had a ringside seat to what resulted from so much struggle. Her kids were on a trajectory that would eventually prove fatal to one, disastrous for the other and though I'm sure she wanted to, she seemed unable to stop what was happening to them. I couldn't let this happen to my imagined children. I was two years into a marriage that I wasn't confident I could sustain for a lifetime. I didn't want children to come into a home I feared might become a broken one and didn't then trust myself to be the kind of parent I know every child deserves. I couldn't tolerate another iteration of this pattern in my own home.

❦

By my twenty-fifth birthday, my other sister Dianne had had her first baby. By then we both lived in San Francisco. Our eight-year age difference disappeared and we became peers and the dearest of friends. She and her husband, Jim, adored their baby Megan. I was once again at ringside, but the show was altogether different. Three years later, they welcomed Matthew. I watched them join expectant parent groups and form friendships with the other couples, with their living room often full of happy toddlers and adoring parents. They celebrated milestones of their children's babyhood with photos and videos, parties, and games. All the events I'd seen on TV, but had never experienced. They decorated their nursery with a rainbow wallpaper border and Jim carried the babies in a backpack on hikes in Golden Gate Park. There was laughter and noise, and things got broken, but no one got kicked. Their house was a wonderful mess of strewn toys and a closet filled with dress-up clothes that invited imagination. A new library of images was now at my fingertips, making what once seemed impossible not only possible, but something I yearned for. Jim was a loving, involved, protective dad. Dianne was an imaginative, playful, adoring mom. My assumption that it would be impossible to be a loving parent if raised by my father was being turned inside out. As I began to welcome the new notion that having a family was a possibility for me, the missing pieces in my marriage to Ernie grew more apparent. Turns out that choosing a guy, even a very nice guy, simply because you don't think any other nice person will ever want you, isn't the best strategy for picking a life partner. As awful as I felt about it, I knew that though I now wanted a family, I no longer wanted to be married to Ernie.

Guilt is also not a foundation for a happy marriage. I ended my marriage to Ernie when I was twenty-six. Ernie didn't want to separate and was stunned by my announcement. Once again, my immaturity cost Ernie a lot. He was in it for life, but I gave him no option. He proved every bit the nice guy I'd married and we parted as amicably as was possible, given the circumstances. While I've never regretted departing from Ernie, I've always regretted making him a promise that I was unable to fulfill. But then, he deserved to be with someone who loved him as I couldn't. He went on to find a new love and to create his own family. I'm sure he's a fabulous dad.

I used the double, fail-safe birth control method through the end of my twenties and into my very early thirties, but never sought out that kind gynecologist for the surgery she'd offered to consider.

I'd also gotten some therapy, which helped me realize that I had the power of choice in designing my own family. I'm grateful beyond words for that amber-eyed doctor at Planned Parenthood, and even for the ten less-communicative doctors before her for not making my fears into a permanent, regrettable choice.

⌇

On the first morning after the first night Tom and I spent together, he broke every pattern I'd encountered in men during my post-divorce dating years. Though I'd known him for sixteen years before our first date, and liked Tom a lot, I had no guarantee that we'd be romantically and sexually compatible. I didn't confess it then, but I'd harbored a little fear that Tom would feel more like a brother than a lover to me. Our first night together obliterated that fear.

The next morning, he'd already gotten up, dressed, and shaved. I was still lounging in the unfamiliar bed, happy that our night together had been passionate, loving, and tender. Tom sat on the edge of the bed where I lay.

He ran his fingers through my hair and kissed me sweetly. "So," he said with more buoyancy in his voice than I was accustomed to, "what do you think about having kids?"

The room was suddenly too bright for my eyes. You could've smacked me with a watermelon truck and I'd have been less surprised. We'd been dating only a few weeks. We'd just shared a bed for the first time. I had been dating for five years since my divorce, all manner of commitment-phobic, family-averse, indirect, non-conversational guys. This straightforward question made me blink rapidly and adjust the position of my head to listen better. Surely, I'd not heard what I just heard. My response was genius. "Well. Um. I, uh—" The stammering bought me only enough time to form a cogent toss-back. "I guess I'd like to hear what you think about having kids before I say."

Silence passed in heartbeats. "I'd be happy with just Max," he said. "But I also figured that if I decided to be with a woman who didn't have children, she would probably want to have a baby. But I feel like I only have the resources to manage one more if that's what you'd want. I'm already forty-one. In terms of financial commitment and time, I don't think I could take on a family larger than two kids."

I'd just chucked the last of the shady, commitment-phobic guys in my post-divorce dating train. I'd not imagined this level of candor and emotional availability. I decided it was less shocking than it was refreshing, so I dipped into my own pool of courage and candor. "I would like to be a mother. Max is great, and if we were to become a family, I'd want some time with just him. But I also think it's good for a kid to have a sibling. So I'd like to have two children. Total."

My sister Dianne and her husband Jim, July 1985. Jim's holding newborn, Max. Di holds their daughter, Megan. It would be seven years before these two babies would become cousins.

Max became cousins with Dianne's kids, Megan and Matt after they'd already been friends since babyhood.

Tom leaned in and kissed me, then lifted the covers taking a playful peek at my naked body. His eyebrows wiggled with Groucho Marx silliness. "How about some breakfast?" he asked. "I know a great place on a horse ranch near here. They raise the chickens, so the eggs are really fresh."

"Sounds good."

"Up and at 'em," he said with a playful swat to my covered behind.

For Tom, this conversation was just that simple, and he wanted to have it out of the way. He was clearing all of the obstacles to forming a relationship with me, protecting his own heart from disappointment in the process. Once this obstacle was cleared, he had no need to belabor the topic and he easily moved on to the idea of breakfast. He had no idea about the winding journey I'd taken to this simple destination of talking honestly and openly with a man about making a family.

Family planning complete, we enjoyed farm-fresh eggs and home-cured bacon for our first breakfast as lovers, and our first morning toward becoming a family.

An Envelope, a Closet, and a Videotape

Standing at the stove in Tom's kitchen, stirring a pan of sizzling mushrooms and onions, I felt his arms reach around my waist from behind. We swayed together. "This house is a lot nicer when you're in it," he whispered into my ear. He nuzzled my neck. Despite the scratchy stubble of his beard I melted into him, relieved to be in such warm company after a disappointing test prep session.

"Hey," he said pinching a mushroom from the pan. "Why don't we go get your clothes from Susan's?" He popped the mushroom into his mouth and huffed while it cooled. "I cleared some drawers for you and moved some of my stuff in the closet to make room."

I turned toward him. My landlord had sold the San Francisco flat I'd been renting just as Tom and I started dating, and since then I'd been looking for a new place. The only semi-habitable place I'd found within my budget was a 350-square-foot studio in San Francisco's Tenderloin district with a great view of the heroin and crack trade being plied at the curb. Discouraged, I was tempted to take it, but wise friends talked me down. I was done with wacky roommate drama and other people's hair in my bathtub drain. Unable to find a suitable place in time, I'd put my furniture in storage, and my friend Susan had invited me to stay with her and her family while I hunted for an apartment. Even in 1991, San Francisco rents didn't make this an easy task.

"Get *all* my clothes from Susan's? That sounds a little like moving in," I said to Tom. "That's sort of a big deal."

His eyebrows climbed toward his hairline and it gave him a sweet, boyish look. "Not so big a deal," he said. "Simpler than what we're doing now. I like the house best when you're here with us."

We'd been together for only a few weeks. Living together officially, rather than in the informal way we had been living, seemed a big step.

"I don't know. I probably can't afford half of this mortgage. But I'd want to contribute, I mean—if we were to— Maybe when I'm licensed. But—"

We hadn't yet talked about money. There'd been no real reason to. Tom is a carpenter who, at that time, worked for UCSF doing facility maintenance and building custom cabinetry for labs and offices. I had no idea at that moment what his salary was, but I imagined that for a single dad, having lost his wife's income, living in the Bay Area, money might be tight. I felt squeamish about not pulling my own weight.

"I'm managing the mortgage. Things are fine as they are for now," he said. "You've been buying a lot of the groceries lately. And doing the cooking. I think that's fair."

My brain was an objection factory. "But I've got to study. I just crapped out on a practice test this morning," I said. "My written exam is in three weeks. And I'll have the orals after that, if I pass—"

"When you pass—"

"It's a hard test. I have to be realistic. One of my friends failed it twice. And he's really smart." Tom didn't yet know the source of my extra fear about taking standardized tests. Knowing the material is one thing, but filling in the answers, in my case, is quite another. Tom smirked and made a *pfffft* sound that dismissed my objection. "We can set up a desk in my office so you can study in there. I can pick up the cooking workload and I promise I'll do whatever you need to let you study."

At that point, Max wandered into the kitchen. "What's a workload?"

Tom pulled away from me and wrapped his arm around Max's neck, wrestling-hold style, and fluffed his hair with his other hand. "You'll help me out and stay quiet in the house so Betsy can study for her big test, right, Skib? Right?"

Max wriggled, a futile attempt to get out of Tom's grip. "Nooooooo," he wailed, laughing. "Only if you let me go!"

Tom released his grip. "Deal?"

"Deal," Max said, smoothing his hair with his small hands. He grinned, revealing the jumbled smile that would prove to be our orthodontic reengineering marathon for the next eight years. His face then scrunched with confusion. "You have a test?" he asked. "But aren't you, you know, too old to be in school?"

Tom snickered up his sleeve.

"Quiet, old man," I said. "You're ten years older than I am. If I'm too old, you're ancient!"

"Yeah, old man," Max said with a laugh and a poke to Tom's midsection. Max grinned up at me. "Ancient. That's a good one. He should probably go sit in a rocking chair or something." He put his hand up and we exchanged high fives. Making Tom the butt of playful jibes had become Max's favorite game, and he and I had forged a silly alliance.

"As a matter of fact," I said to Max, "I'm not too old to study. No one is ever too old to learn. And I have a really big test coming up in a couple of weeks."

Tom explained the nature of my exams to Max and how hard the test would be. "But she'll ace it, right?"

"Riiiiiight," Max agreed. "You helped me ace my spelling test Friday. So you can do it."

Their confidence was instant, if unfounded. Tom and Max had no way of knowing how long I'd struggled with tests, only finding out why in recent years.

It wasn't until graduate school that anyone identified me as having dyslexia. Ironically, I had been asked to be part of a control group for a Ph.D. student who was doing research for her dissertation research. After my initial screening test, she told me I didn't qualify for the control group because I had a mild form of dyslexia. I was stunned. Terms like clockwise and counterclockwise leave me baffled. Same with maps, sewing patterns, and instruction manuals. I often get lost, even in familiar surroundings. I transpose numbers and sometimes write letters, or even whole words backwards. I developed ways to compensate without knowing what I was compensating for. I selected classes heavy on writing rather than tests. In pre-GPS days, I kept a notebook filled with crib sheets of directions, even to places I went often. But as usual, it was the #2 Ticonderoga tests that struck the biggest fear in me. Filling in those damned bubbles on standardized tests had always been my downfall. In preparation for this test I'd hired special coaching from a learning specialist and it had paid off on my first two practice tests. But the one I'd taken earlier that day had been a total flop. I'd left a whole column of empty bubbles on my answer sheet even though I'd thought I'd answered every question. A major setback in my preparations, and a big confidence killer. My progress with overcoming dyslexia sometimes felt like a game of Chutes and Ladders, and earlier that day had been a big slide backward down a chute and back to square one.

But now I had Max and Tom as my champions. Watching them together—their ease, their comfort, the trust Max had for his dad, the encouragement they offered each other—made me hungry for something I'd never before tasted. I wasn't jealous of Max for the safety and trust he had with his father; I was unfamiliar with it. And now I was stepping into this world where support was instant and unconditional. Tom and Max's encouragements meant that whether I passed or failed, these two would always be on my side. I liked the new and delicious flavor of this kind of support.

I couldn't help but wonder if confidence is just that simple; we receive encouragement and the seeds of confidence grow within us. Confidence, hopefulness, and optimism are casualties in families broken by mental illness, addiction, and abuse. Accomplishments go unnoticed. Flaws are exaggerated and failures are grounds for ridicule and shame. When we know that, whether we succeed or struggle, we have the unconditional support of those who love us, we feel we can tolerate the risk of failure—that to fail is not to lose what's most important. When love and approval are conditional, the risk seems too great. By choosing a partner who would also be my champion, I wasn't just making healthy choices for a happy family. I was also choosing a man who would help me find the pieces of family support that I'd never known I was missing.

⟋⟋⟋⟍⟍⟍

Despite all my early cautions about easing Max into the new idea of my becoming part of Tom's life, my transition from a date to a houseguest, then to being his dad's girlfriend, had been smoother than I could have hoped. Part of me thought that we should all sit down and talk through the ramifications of the changes we'd made, check in with Max about how he was doing. But the father and son had established their own rhythm of communication. It was simple. Tom considered Max's needs in every choice he made. Max appeared undaunted by our changes, his trust in Tom implicit, if unspoken. They talked through very little, instead having sort of a Skipper and Gilligan arrangement, Max almost always ready with the aye-aye and Tom always ready with a back pat for his little buddy. I was learning that their loving father–son relationship wasn't missing words; it just didn't require very many of them.

My sister Dianne had married an equally trustworthy guy when she chose Jim to be the father of her children. At his best, our father had been an obstacle to get around, at worst a dangerous menace to survive. But Dianne's children and Max had experienced nothing but safety, support, and adoration from their dads. Though only in elementary school, the three of them exuded a kind of confidence I'd never experienced.

The next day, after Tom suggested I move in, we went to my storage unit and retrieved my desk and my small desktop computer. Tom eyed the rest of the contents. "Hey, that's a nice side table. Want to bring that?"

"Sure," I said. The scalloped antique table had been passed down from a great-aunt.

"Look at this!" Tom said as he pulled the table off of the stack. "It has the exact same claw feet as my coffee table. A perfect match!" He turned the table over. "I knew it. Same maker. I bet it's the same year." He wore a triumphant look on his face. "Even our furniture was meant to be together. Let's take it home and see how it looks."

Home. The word echoed in my ears and reverberated in my bones. I'd lived in houses, dorms, apartments, flats, in half a dozen cities growing up and since going away to college. When I'd moved to San Francisco, it was the first city I'd chosen myself—though, admittedly, Di and Jim had chosen it first and I'd followed them. The Bay Area was the first place where I felt fully comfortable and at ease. But while the Bay Area was my adopted community, Tom and Max were fast becoming my home. *Home.* It was an old word with a brand new meaning.

My modern desk took its place beside Tom's battered roll top in the extra bedroom he used as an office. It became my study cave.

We retrieved the last of my clothing from my friend's

house. "Thanks so much, Susan," I said, embracing her as I took the last box from her storage closet. Tom was already at the curb, configuring my clothes and my few boxes into the back of his Jeep.

"Tom's a great guy." She lowered her voice to a whisper. "And he's clearly nuts for you."

"I'm a little nuts for him, too."

Together Tom and I drove down the Pacific Coast Highway just south of San Francisco toward the small coastal town of Pacifica. Toward home.

That afternoon Tom moved his expansive collection of plaid shirts and worn jeans, rearranging the master closet to accommodate my clothes. His sweet whistling of "I Want To Hold Your Hand" accompanied our task.

As we began to work, without notice, tears threatened and my throat tightened. It hadn't occurred to me until that second that my clothing would now hang where Janet's once did. They'd moved into this house just a year before she died. The image of Tom sorting through all of her clothes, folding them, bagging them up, donating them, made my heart feel thick and heavy in my chest, in contrast to the cheerful trill of his whistling. I wondered if he had help, or if he'd done this task alone. I wondered how it must've felt for him every day since to walk into the huge closet and see the vacancy left behind. Tom and Max's general exuberance and playfulness made it easy to forget, at least for short periods, the blow they'd sustained just a year and a half prior to my arrival on the scene. In moments like these, I felt the full force of what that loss meant.

Tom's whistling continued. I hid my tears.

lee____eel

After another round of studying before supper, this time with a more successful outcome on my practice test, I stepped down the stairs ready to reward myself with a glass of wine. I heard unfamiliar voices and children's laughter from the family room and wondered if Max had someone over to play. But when I rounded the corner I could tell that the conversational noises were from the TV. Max and Tom had proven true to their word and kept the volume low during my study hours.

The sound from the TV was a different pitch and rhythm than the familiar bells and whistles of *Rugrats*, *Inspector Gadget*, or any of the other Nickelodeon cartoons I'd become familiar with in recent weeks. As I entered the family room, I could see Tom and Max seated on the sofa, their backs toward me, Max snuggling under Tom's arm as they watched, his head resting against Tom's chest. On the TV played a scene of a child's birthday party. The cameraman had a shaky hand.

I remained silent, watching the TV from behind them. The grainy footage played. Children, most of them about four or five years old, lined up in front of a cardboard wall painted with an ocean scene. A woman with her back turned to the camera helped kids manage a plastic fishing rod, hanging it over the wall, only to reel it in to find prizes dangling from the end of the fishing line. I heard an off-camera laugh I recognized. It was the hearty laugh of my brother-in-law, Jim, snickering at the antics of the kids. As soon as I heard the laugh, I knew what I was viewing.

It was Max's fourth birthday party. Janet was the woman in front of the cardboard ocean mural helping the kids. My niece Megan and nephew Matthew, just a toddler, were two of the children in line. Max, pudgier and blonder then, scurried around handing out plastic goodie bags. His face wore innocent delight. He was a happy little boy who had not yet sustained the loss that would come one short year later.

Janet's hair was cropped short, almost a crew cut. Her skin was gray. She was impossibly thin, her glasses seeming huge on her slim, angular face, but she smiled and cheered each child's catch. She'd occasionally look toward the camera with an expression that said, "Did you get that?"

Children jumped excitedly as they reeled in their prizes. Jim's laugh was the off-camera soundtrack. Tom, the likely cameraman, wasn't in the scene.

I wondered about the ritual I was eavesdropping upon. Did Tom and Max watch videos together often? Did Max select the one they were watching? Or had Tom? I had no name for the new feeling that oozed through my veins. It wasn't jealousy. It wasn't resentment. I just wondered about my place in the story I was watching. Was I a replacement? A guest? An intruder? My mouth went dry.

With a suddenness that almost made me gasp aloud, the figures in the video disappeared into a snowy field of granulated pixels and the happy sounds of kids at a party became a hissing whirr.

"Okay, Skibber," Tom said softly to Max. He pulled Max tighter to his chest and kissed the top of his head. "Time to go play. I'm going to work outside."

I stepped backward, away from the entryway to the room. It didn't seem right to step into the their private moment, but I couldn't resist peeping around the corner to watch what happened next. Max rose from the sofa and extracted the videotape from the player, returned it to its sleeve, and replaced it in the empty slot on the shelf behind the TV.

Before I could be seen, I snuck back up the stairs and into the office. In another moment the stairs were alive with the scurried bumps of Max's footfalls and soon, from behind his bedroom door, came the unmistakable sound of a giant bucket of Legos being dumped onto the floor. I peeked out the office window to the back yard to see Tom stooped over, pulling weeds from a planter box on the back deck.

That night we all snuggled together on the same sofa, watching Tommy and his brother, Dil Pickles, Chucky and the twins, and the naughty Angelica in a *Rugrats* episode.

"Watch this part." Max had seen every episode multiple times. He couldn't contain himself when something especially funny was about to happen and this time jumped off the couch toward the TV. "Angelica is going to really get it this time."

I squeezed in closer to Tom, comfortable watching a world where everything turns out okay and naughty children get their instant, but gentle, karma in the form of spaghetti bowls turned over on their heads. And little boys get to keep their mommies and daddies forever.

~~~~~

I took my written exams to be a licensed marriage/family therapist three weeks later. The arduous preparation for the orals followed. I had to study for the orals as though I'd already passed the written, though it would be eight to twelve weeks before I had my results. I was a walking knot of anxiety. I'd already invested all that I could into my exam prep courses, extra coaching from the learning specialist, thrice-weekly prep sessions with my study buddy, and I'd clocked so many hours of study on my own that my brain felt like a dirigible full of lead. All of this while working full time, to say nothing of wanting to spend time with Max and with my new love. My salary would rise from barely manageable to almost livable once I was licensed, and I'd have more options to consider as far as jobs. A lot was at stake.

Between studying and work, I began preparations for Max's birthday party. He'd been so excited to find out that my birthday, July 15, was just three days before his. "That's so cool!" he'd said. "You could invite some of your friends to my bowling party if you want."

His generosity made me smile. "Thanks, bud. I'll already have friends there, though. Dianne will be there, and Jim, and Matt, and Megan."

"I keep forgetting Matt and Megan's mom is your sister," he said. "Your friends are already my friends. Sweet."

Sweet, indeed.

As I prepared for his party, I kept recalling the image of Janet helping the kids fish for prizes. I realized that I was stepping into her role, and wanted to do so tenderly. Together Max and I planned a bowling party with the dinosaur theme he'd chosen. He joined me on a trip to the bakery to order the dinosaur cake. We stood at the counter, leafing through the book of laminated pages. Max picked a T-rex with a mouthful of menacing teeth.

"Pretty scary," I said.

"Yeah, cool." He tilted his head from side to side. "I think we should put some flowers on it so it's your birthday cake too," he said. "You really like flowers." My one financial splurge was fresh flowers each week for the dining room and a small vase on my study desk. I viewed flowers as study incentive.

His snaggle-toothed smile was irresistible. "Yeah, I like flowers."

"Then there should be flowers at the bottom. I don't think old Rexie would mind." Max clucked his tongue and nudged me with his hip.

"Maybe the dinosaur stepped on some flowers, but there are still a few pretty ones," I suggested. I was touched by his generous gesture, but I didn't want to girl up his cake too much.

"Cool." His face suddenly wilted with a worry. "Just um—" His face wore worry.

"Sweetheart, you don't have to have flowers if you don't want."

"No, it's just—" He fidgeted and squirmed.

I feared he regretted the offer of sharing our cake. I squatted down to be nearer his eye level. "Honey, we don't have to have flowers if you don't want. It won't hurt my feelings. I promise."

"Just—can we not have any pink flowers? I *reeeeally* hate pink."

I had to suppress my grin. Once again, the situation was far simpler than I'd feared. "How about blue flowers? And most of them smashed by the dinosaur. Maybe just one that he hasn't stomped yet?"

"THAT would be cool."

⌇⌇⌇ ⌇⌇⌇

The next day was July 14. I walked to the mailbox at the end of our driveway and pulled out a stack of mail. The state emblem of the California Board of Behavioral Sciences and return address were unmistakable. The envelope was thin, with a window in it. I'd been warned by fellow grad students that a thin envelope meant you'd failed. Fat envelopes contained instructions for how to obtain your place for your oral exams. Such rumors were wildfire among all of the anxious students in study groups.

Fear was an ocean wave, leaving me a little wobbly. I stood in the driveway, unable to open the envelope in my hands. Before Tom, my fear was simple—not passing the test. Now I had a new kind of nerves. I wanted Tom and Max to be proud of me. I wanted their confidence in me to be warranted.

I snuck quietly into the house and up the stairs wanting to be alone with the envelope. I closed the door behind me in what had become our shared office. I could tolerate the envelope in my hand no longer and set it on the desk in front of me. Then, I couldn't stand sitting next to it. It lay there on the desk and mocked me. *Chicken.* I paced the small room, glancing back at the envelope with each pass I made by the desk.

A knock came at the door and Tom peeked in. "What were you thinking on timing for dinner?" he asked.

I shrugged. I was afraid to speak for fear that my anxiety would get the better of me. That skinny envelope was now radioactive, glowing from the desktop.

"What's a matter?" Tom asked.

I jutted my chin toward the desk.

Tom looked at the envelope, then at me. His face brightened. "Your results?"

I nodded.

"Wow, they came early." His brows pleated. "You haven't opened it?"

I shook my head. "It's a skinny envelope."

"So?"

"Skinny envelopes are bad news."

Tom grinned. "You won't know until you open it."

"I sorta do," I said. Then, despite my resolve, tears came. Of all the feelings I'd anticipated if I failed, being embarrassed in front of Tom wasn't among them.

"Come on," he said, wrapping his arms around me. "Open it up. If you didn't pass, you'll take it again. But open it up. You'll feel better."

I wiped my face and nodded.

With my mouth dry and my face wet with tears, I opened the envelope. The first word of the letter changed everything. *Congratulations . . .*

"See," Tom said, wrapping his arm around me. "Nothing to worry about. You had it all along. All of that worry for nothing!"

I felt muscles relax that I hadn't even noticed were tense. I took a deep breath. I needed Tom to know that I wasn't just being neurotic about the test, that there was ample room for concern on my part. "There was a reason I was especially nervous about the written exam," I confessed. There with Tom in our office, in the home we now shared, I told him about being dyslexic. I told him how visual images get turned around for me, that maps are impossible, and that until grad school I never understood why I inverted numbers and sometimes wrote letters, words, or even whole pages backward. "Filling in bubbles on tests has always been my Kryptonite. No matter how well I know the material, the test form can do me in." I described growing up feeling that I was stupid, of being told by teachers that I needed to focus, that I needed to study harder.

Tom listened and held me while I cried tears of relief. I expected a rash of questions. Telling Tom about this embarrassing flaw of mine had been hard. We'd been, to that point, in a honeymoon state with everything about one another being a new and delightful discovery. I didn't want to seem like a broken thing, like damaged goods. Dyslexia was a minor flaw compared to the shadowy secrets of addiction and abuse in my family. But telling this particular secret felt like the beginning of us being more deeply honest with one another.

Whatever response I expected from Tom about my disclosure didn't happen. He took this information like he did most everything—in stride. He asked nothing. All he said was, "Well, it seems like you did all right anyway. Right?"

"Right," I conceded.

Tom proposed a fancy supper to celebrate my good news. He booked a last-minute sitter for Max, and we shared a long and luxurious meal at the Mountain House, a gorgeous, pricey restaurant in nearby Woodside—a major splurge.

After the waiter had set our plates before us, Tom asked about my upcoming oral exams. "I was most nervous about the written," I confessed. "Though the fail rate for the orals is even higher."

"So your dyslexia shouldn't be a factor in that one, right?"

"Not really. But the fail rate for the orals is over seventy percent, so it's no slam-dunk."

"You'll do great," he said. "I thought people with dyslexia can't read," he said, lifting a forkful of Chilean sea bass to his lips. "You read all the time."

"There are different types and degrees of it. I read well, though slowly." I sipped my wine. "So, how do you feel having a roomie who can't balance a checkbook to save her soul?"

"I'm pretty good with maps and money. I like having a roomie with your other skills." Tom offered a playful twitch of his eyebrows. "I think I can live with someone who can't fill in bubbles on tests."

"So what's the worst I need to know about you?" I asked, sipping my champagne.

Tom took a long time to choose his words. He wiped his lips with his napkin and set down his fork. "I've been told I'm not communicative enough."

I restrained the *duh* lodged behind my lips.

"And when I was younger I drank too much. I was pretty rowdy back then. We all were. But not since Max."

I'd witnessed a bit of that rowdy youth and had heard plenty about it from my sister and Jim over the years. Their shared college experience at Purdue and living together in San Francisco in the '70s had spawned more than a few stories of wilder days for all of them. But the whole group had settled down since marrying and having kids. Still, my father's alcohol abuse had made me cautious. "I'm no prohibitionist, mind you," I said. "But I won't live with a drunk. Been there, done that."

"Me neither." He pointed to my empty champagne

glass. He twitched his eyebrow again, then his somber expression returned. "Getting hammered in my forties isn't like it was in my twenties. The kid still gets up at six and there are bills to pay."

Simple. Straightforward. Practical. Tom.

Tom suddenly seemed so together, his life so simple. Janet's death had been a tragedy, of course, but one that was completely outside of Tom's control. The complications in my family were not naturally occurring events that came from outside, but troubles that came from within the family itself. Bad choices. Crazy behavior. Mental illness. Abuse. Addiction. I was beginning to worry that my family history, and even in some small way the bafflement and confusions that come with dyslexia, were impurities I was adding to his orderly life. My ears got hot.

"It's okay," he said, taking my hand. "Maps and money I can manage. You're good at other stuff. I'm pretty happy you like to cook."

"But you cook."

"I do okay," he said. "But Janet wasn't into food at all, so the cooking fell to me if I wanted anything but canned or frozen food. It's nice to be cooked for."

This was the first time I'd heard anything that even slightly smacked of a complaint about Janet. Dating other men, I'd heard *ad nauseum* about "psycho bitch" exes and court cases for child support and fights about custody. I'd dated the occasional Disneyland dad, big on buying dirt bikes and toys, but not so great at paying child support on time, or taking their kids to the orthodontist. Those dates never evolved into anything. I couldn't admire or trust a negligent dad. What bugged me most were those guys who had a trail of "psycho ex" stories because it always seemed inevitable that, if I'd chosen one of them, I'd eventually be the next psycho in the sequence. But Tom had none of this. Listing this one foible of Janet's, her food oddity, was without venom. It was just a fact about her, simply stated. Theirs was a relationship that ended with her death, but the privacy and respect he'd had for her while she lived continued. He honored her in life. He honored her after her death.

Tom and I talked for a while longer, confessing our flaws to one another, until I grew serious and said, "I'm not joking about the honesty thing. Trust is a deal-breaker for me."

"I've never found much use for lying," he said. "Telling the truth is just an easier way to live. Lying takes too much energy. Too much drama."

"So, it's laziness that keeps you honest?" I said, teasing.

"That and a bad memory," he said with a smile.

Our meal came to an end once we noticed the waiters clearing all of the empty tables around us.

$$\textit{lee ___ eel}$$

That night, after we'd made love, Tom lay beside me in the warmth of what we'd shared together. "That was pretty nice," he said.

I tucked myself more tightly into the crook of his arm, my head on his shoulder.

He cleared his throat, a signal I'd identified that he was about to say something important. "I'm having a really hard time seeing a future without you in it."

My skin contracted. Whether it was panic or excitement, my body knew before I did that something big was up.

"What do you think about getting married?" he asked. He lifted my hand to his lips and kissed my fingertips.

My mind was a ten-screen multiplex with different movies playing all at the same time. I watched the shadows play on the ceiling, giving myself time to take in the question. I'd felt more at peace, at home with Tom in the last four months than I had with Ernie in the nine years of our relationship or the five on-and-off years with Carlos and the small handful of other people I'd dated since my divorce. I'd seen the kind of father Tom was to Max and the kind of husband he'd been to Janet, throughout their marriage, but especially when she was ill. I'd dated guys with more theatrical gestures of romance and more flowery words than Tom, but those verbal showboats had proven to be the craftiest liars.

"What about Max?" I whispered.

Tom gave a little shrug. "You're great with Max."

There was nothing pushy in his statement, nothing that implied he'd chosen me just as a mother for Max. As always, Tom's words never meant more than what he said. "Didn't answer my question," I said.

"Max is a fan of yours."

Tom was so sure about our future together, so unwavering. I loved him, that much I knew. I loved Max too and already felt the natural pull to mother him. But had Janet not died, I also knew that Tom would never have ended their marriage. I'd chosen to end my first marriage. He'd had no choice. That funny feeling I had when I'd eavesdropped on the birthday video was coming into focus. It wasn't exactly jealousy I'd felt, but it was the knowledge that I'd not be in this picture were it not for a tragedy.

I didn't have a psycho-bitch ex to worry about, no broken heart. No betrayal. For me, grief, loss, and powerlessness were the psycho bitches that had preceded my arrival on the scene. I would never face the hassle of exes and shared custody, weekend drop-offs, and hostility between divorced parties. But grief and loss would be ever-present in my marriage, part of my relationship with the boy I was considering taking as my son. Grief and loss . . . those bitches never leave.

We lay there together in the dark and Tom listened as I talked about my worries. Was he ready? Was it too soon after Janet for him to marry again? Would Max feel I'd tried to replace his mom?

Seconds ticked like days as I waited for Tom's responses to my concerns. "Losing Janet was really hard. On both of us," he finally said. "But she'd want me to be happy and for Max to have a mother. I think you and I want the same things. We have the same values. The important things are all there. The rest will work out. And we're pretty good together," he said, kissing my fingertips again. "Don't you think?"

I paused and let that soak in. Tension left my shoulders. The barrage of my worries ebbed like a lowering tide. But one more concern still lingered for me. "What about Max and me?"

"What about you?"

"If we were to get married, I'd be his mother, not just your wife."

"Seems kind of obvious."

I struggled to find the words for what I was thinking. "I'd want to respect Janet as Max's mom," I said. A fist formed in my throat and I thought of Janet as the mom in the birthday video. This was tender territory. "But if you and I get married, I'll be picking up where she left off. I'll be Max's mother for a much longer time, and through his teen years, and beyond. I can't do everything like she would have. I'm just not the same kind of person that she was."

"I wouldn't expect you to be."

"And would you see us, you and me, as co-parents?" I asked. "We'd back each other up."

"I'm guessing that won't often be a problem, but yeah, I suppose so."

"Because I wouldn't just be marrying you. We'd be becoming a family."

"Is that a yes?"

"Was this a proposal? I thought we were just talking."

"Well, there you go thinkin'."

Our exchange of kisses served as an answer to his question. This nonverbal communication was working out pretty well.

ℓ———ℓℓℓ

The next morning, Tom and Max vacated the house, leaving me to my studying. With all that was on my mind from the night before, I'd forgotten for the moment that it was my birthday. I labored to focus on the intricacies of the *Diagnostic and Statistical Manual of Mental Disorders*. I tried to concentrate, but a new slate of movies played in my mental movie multiplex. My mind was a jumble of practicalities and timelines. When would we get married? Would we stay in Tom's house in Pacifica or move somewhere new together? I didn't want to disrupt Max's life too much.

Was I sure? Really sure? I thought of calling Dianne, but found myself hesitant to burst the fragile cocoon of our new promise, feeling that the caterpillar was not yet a butterfly ready to greet the larger world.

I gave up the measly study attempt, instead opting for something practical and physical to quiet my mind. I started a load of laundry, scrubbed both bathrooms until they gleamed, and began dusting the already dust-free furniture downstairs.

When my dusting efforts led me to the top of the oak cabinet in the living room, I was faced with Janet's collection of ceramic Beatrix Potter figurines. They were arranged in little vignettes, as if in various conversations of twos and threes. I held each one in my hand as I dusted around them, then tried to place them in the same arrangement where they'd been. I studied the figures—rabbits and kittens, geese and frogs, some wearing tiny jackets, or bonnets, one pushing a wheelbarrow—and wondered if they were arranged as Janet had left them. Soon I found myself rearranging the figures into new conversations. Bunnies now chatted with kittens. Geese and frogs conspired. I felt like I had as a child, staging scenes, having one figure in one hand, another in the other, and moving one at a time as the conversation ensued.

"Hello there, Peter," I said aloud in a low-pitched voice, moving the figure in my left hand. It seemed to me that the goose wearing a waistcoat would be a baritone.

"Well, hello there," Peter replied, more timidly from my right.

The dialogue was uninspired. But I felt a small kinship with Janet as I animated her characters. We were so very different, Janet and I, but Tom had chosen us both. As

I reflected, it came to me that our differences were more of style than of substance. We enjoyed different activities and had a different kind of energy. She loved cats and romance novels, country décor and stuffed animals. Cats had always freaked me out a little. I like modern art, historical and literary fiction. She was slim and indifferent to food, whereas I am rounder and love culinary adventure. She was organized and exceedingly tidy, and I get lost on the way to the post office and misplace my keys twice a day. But at our cores, Janet and I shared the same values of friendship and family, honesty and hard work. She had been a devoted partner to Tom and a loving mother to Max.

Janet and I shared the same love for Tom but in different moments, and now, as I considered the future, we had our devotion to Max in common as well. Every loving mother wants to protect her children, let them know they're loved, celebrate their milestones, help them through hard times. Every good mother wants to protect her children from pain. I looked at the small ceramic figurines, each one that somehow seemed to be a part of Janet, and my heart ached. I tried to imagine what it was like for her to know that she was gravely ill, to face Max, and to know she would not see him grow up. It all seemed so profoundly unfair. I wondered if she thought that Max might look at that birthday party video one day and remember her. I wondered what a mad rush it might have been for her to make sure his baby photo album was complete before her death and to know that photos and videos would be all he would have to remember her by. I wondered if I could be as strong as she had to be to mother her son while she knew she was dying.

I examined the ceramic figures before me and hoped

I'd be strong enough for the job I'd be assuming. "What do you think?" I asked aloud, animating a frog this time. "Do you think I'll be a good mom?"

"Hard to say," Peter Rabbit replied. I heard Tom's Jeep pulling into the drive and I felt suddenly silly. I tried to arrange the figures as they had been, but before I could complete the task the door opened.

"Happy birthday!" Max shouted as he bounded in the room. His grin was wide and he moved as though he had springs in his shoes, despite his hands being behind his back. "We got you a present!" he announced. "I helped pick. It's a goodie!" Glee danced in his eyes. He looked over his shoulder at Tom who entered the house carrying a bag of groceries.

"Now?" Max asked of him.

"Let me put these in the kitchen first. Don't want the ice cream to melt." Tom gave Max a wink and Max nodded in reply.

Max tried to stand still, but his body appeared carbonated and every bubble caused another jiggle. He twitched and wriggled, shifted from foot to foot and his eyes darted impatiently toward the kitchen.

Tom stepped back into the room.

"Finally," Max sighed. He hung his tongue and panted in exaggerated dog style, his signature gesture of relief. "Now?" he asked, looking up at his dad.

Tom nodded and Max pulled a small package from behind his back. He held it out to me. "You have to open it now," he said. His small hands covered his lips making it look as though he was suppressing a secret smile.

I glanced over at Tom. This was the first gift he'd given me since the Joni Mitchell *Blue* album for Christmas when

I was fifteen. This was the first birthday we'd shared as a couple.

"Wow!" I said, taking the package. "Beautiful wrapping."

"I picked it," Max said with a vigorous nod. "They only had purple or black at the store. They wrapped for free! I thought you'd like the purple."

"And you were right. Thanks."

"Open it. Open it!" Max said, now full-on jumping.

Inside I found a small velvet box. In it sat a ring, a simple solitaire diamond. We'd talked about getting married the night before, but no glimmer of a thought had come to me that I'd be facing a ring in a box as my birthday gift the next day, no less one delivered by a boy just three days shy of his seventh birthday. I'd never been the kind of woman who dreamt of rings and wedding dresses. I'd never bought a *Brides* magazine nor had I been a girl who practiced writing her name with the last names of her boyfriends. I had no fantasy wedding in mind. I felt frozen, surprised by the traditional ring delivered in such a nontraditional way.

"My dad said you're going to marry us!" Max said. By this time his smile was so wide I thought he could split a lip.

I looked over at Tom. He offered a sheepish smile that said, *Yeah, I told him.* I'd assumed we'd talk to Max together, ease him into the idea. I'd been wrong about Max's need to be eased into anything that Tom felt so sure about. Then it hit me. *Us.* Max hadn't said I was going to marry Tom; he'd said I was marrying the two of them. With that small, two-lettered word I felt the last buds of my worries wither before they'd even had a chance to bloom. Calm washed over me. With that two-letter word all of my fears floated away and I was sure of the steps we were taking together.

"Aren't you gonna wear it?" Max asked, gazing at the ring. "It costed a lot of money. It costed—"

"Skib," Tom interrupted. "Not polite to talk about the price of a gift." Tom shrugged at me.

Max shielded his lips with the curve of his hand and spoke in a loud stage whisper. "But it did cost a lot."

I pulled the ring from the box and began to put it on.

"No!" Max said, his hands splayed to stop the action. "He's supposed to put it on you."

Where exactly a small boy got his engagement ring protocol, I wasn't sure, but he called Tom over to where we stood with the wiggling of his index finger.

"The kid's right," Tom said. "What can I say?" Tom slipped the ring onto my finger. "If you want something different—"

Before I could respond, Max began jumping up and down. "We're getting married!" he shouted with each jump.

We're!

Getting!

Married!

The Outlaws

I give the house a last-minute spot check. Karl and Verna will be here any minute. The whole place is sparkling. I know because I sparkled it, fuelled by nervous energy. I didn't sleep last night. I prepared two different desserts, just in case. I've fussed for days about what I'd serve for a simple summer lunch. Tom keeps telling me that Karl and Verna are not "fancy" people, so not to go to too much trouble. He putters in the yard as he always does, his calm pace unaltered by the impending arrival of our visitors. My whole body is a hive full of agitated bumblebees.

Tom and I have been living together for a few months and, with Max, we've settled into our new life together. We just got engaged. Our families are thrilled for us. All of our shared friends, including the ones who knew Janet, have showered us with love and congratulations. I've met Tom's family in Indiana. They're all elated that Tom has found love again and they welcomed me as a newly grafted limb on the family tree. But the relationships I'm about to form today could be big bumps in our otherwise smooth road.

How is one supposed to feel when meeting the parents of your fiancé's deceased wife? I try to imagine how Karl and Verna might feel toward the woman stepping into the home their daughter shared with her husband and their grandson. My clothes occupy the space where hers once hung. I cook in her kitchen, serve food on her dishes. I love her husband. I will mother her son. The bumblebees hum louder inside my skull. My biggest fear, the one that has robbed me of my slumber, is that Janet's parents will resent my arrival on the scene and that this might somehow interfere with their loving relationship with Max.

Tom told me how, while Janet was sick, and then after she died, Karl and Verna often stepped in to help with Max. "I don't know what I'd have done without all of their help." They live across the bay in Vallejo, just an hour away, but often, while Janet was ill, they'd stay in the guest room. They got Max to and from school, helped with meals, took Janet to medical appointments. Since her passing not quite two years ago now, they drive over often to attend Max's school functions and take him for outings and on camping trips. They've been on an extended cross-country trip in their camper since Tom and I began our romance, so it's been more than three months since they've seen Max, when they usually see him several times a month. While they've been gone, Tom, Max, and I have begun to be a family.

I glance around the room one last time. I've made almost no changes to the downstairs of our shared house, but for the scalloped cherry-wood accent table that Tom was so thrilled to find in my storage unit. Janet's stern-looking relatives still peer down from the wall at the dining table from their bubble-glassed frames. Her Beatrix Potter figurines remain atop the oak cabinet. The sofa that Tom told me originally belonged to Karl and Verna still resides in the living room, just as it did when I arrived. The changes of my moving in and our upcoming marriage seemed enough for Max to manage. Not wanting to make him feel as though I was pushing his mother's memories aside, it seemed only right to let changes come organically, over time, when they feel right.

The doorbell rings and Max scrambles down the stairs to the front door while my stomach turns cartwheels. "Grampa!" he sings, throwing his arms around Karl's waist. "Grandma!" Now Verna gets her embrace. They both pretend to be nearly knocked over, but laugh during the exchange. Verna carries an aluminum foil-covered lid of a box that she uses as a tray with two Tupperware serving dishes inside. I have no way of knowing in this moment that her box lid was but one of the many salvaged items that Verna treats as treasures, as were her margarine tubs, rubber bands, and other miscellanies she collected. From Karl's clenched hands dangle half a dozen bulging white plastic grocery bags.

In their seventies, Karl and Verna Lundgren appear to have been sent from Central Casting as "the average American grandparents". Karl is fit and wiry, silver hair on the sides, none on top. Verna is tiny. I'm five-foot-three and I tower over her. Her hair is styled as so many women of her era, in that once-a-week do done at her beauty parlor, and preserved with Aquanet, hairnets, and bobby pins for the week between visits. They both wear glasses, big smiles, and modest, practical clothing that one might buy at J. C. Penney or Sears. The same clothing my mom has always worn.

Karl greets me with a rib-crushing hug, more powerful than his slight, though muscular frame prepared me for. "So you're the new one," he says. Tom has called them and told them about me, about our engagement. Karl's voice is gruff, his words abrupt, but there's no meanness in it. I know in an instant that he is a straight-talker and does not embroider his words.

"I suppose I am," I say, returning his hug.

"Here," Karl says, offering one handful of the white grocery bags to me. "I don't know what all she's got in there." He and Tom shake hands in the fashion that men did in my parents' generation, with vigor and shared pats on the shoulder.

"Hi," I say to Verna. "Nice to finally meet you."

Verna smiles awkwardly and we exchange a stiff embrace. She lights up when she looks at Max, her expression transforming to the picture of joy. She takes one of the remaining bags from Karl and dangles it in front of Max's smiling face. Max rubs his hands together with glee. He's one of Pavlov's well-conditioned dogs, it seems, and the bag serves as a dinner bell. This particular bag is filled with all manner of treats: knock-off Cracker Jacks, chocolate snack cakes, red licorice, and peanut butter cups, all facsimiles of products I recognize, but without a recognizable brand name among them. I'm guessing they've been purchased at a 99-cent store. Another bag contains a giant bunch of grapes, green apples, and baby carrots—all things I've learned are Max's favorites and which are already in our kitchen. Max pulls the imposter Cracker Jacks from the bag, and licks his lips with a slurping sound, followed by an *mmmmmm*. He looks up at me wearing a question on his face.

I glance at Verna. Which one of us is the authority on pre-lunch treats? I wink at her. She nods. Message received. The steps of our new dance are strange and unfamiliar. We make them cautiously. "Go ahead then, Max," she says, taking his chin in her hand. "But just one treat before lunch," she says. "Don't want to spoil your appetite."

"Yea!" Max says, clutching the sugar-filled prize to his chest.

"Ooh, look at you," Verna says to Max. "You've lost all your teeth!"

"Heh," Karl barks, "who knocked your teeth out, kiddo? I hope you got a couple of good slugs in."

He and Max chuckle together with identical staccato laughter. Max's face is shaped like Karl's—angular, with a small boy's version of what will eventually become an aquiline nose. But Karl's fair complexion and blue eyes hint at his Scandinavian lineage, while Max's warm golden skin-tone, brown eyes, and dark hair come from Verna's Portuguese heritage.

They examine the new vacancies in Max's smile, marveling over how much he's grown since they last saw him three months ago. Their obvious love for Max brings a lump to my throat and I cannot imagine any two grandparents have ever loved a child more.

"Max," I whisper, with a twitch of my eyebrows toward his grandparents.

"Oh," Max replies. "Thanks for all of the goodies." Max gives another round of hugs to his delighted grandparents. Verna gives me an approving glance. We've just cleared our first speed bump.

"Come on in," Tom says. "We don't have to spend all day in the doorway."

Verna then unpacks the other bags, showing me folded boy's pants, sweatshirts, jackets, and toys. "You just wouldn't believe what kids leave behind everywhere," Karl comments. "Every morning on our walk, we find this stuff just laying around. And look, there's some of that Nike stuff in there." He pronounces Nike without its second syllable, like bike. "That's some money, but they don't take care of it. People just buy these things and don't take care of 'em. All over the playgrounds and the parks," he continues, waving his hands in gestures of exasperation. "They just throw stuff around. Just wasting good money is all."

He and Verna shake their heads in unison, Verna providing a soft *tsk, tsk, tsk.* The two of them were like so many of their peers that had grown up with little, and had lived through the Great Depression. Little makes them angrier than wastefulness.

"Don't worry," Verna says. "I washed them all up."

"She scrubbed every mark off of 'em," Karl adds.

I wonder for a moment about the kids who returned to the playground to retrieve their belongings, only to find them missing. I imagine the scoldings of angry parents all over Vallejo.

The next hour is full of munching and swapping stories. Our shared focus on Max makes our small talk bigger. Max brings his end-of-the-year first-grade folder down from his room at his grandma's request. "That's good,

Max," Verna says as she peruses the spelling tests and the folded art projects. "I can tell you've been a good boy at school. That makes Grandma so happy."

Karl asks Max about the little league games he missed during their travels and Max tells him about his best play at short stop—throwing a runner out at first to win the game. Karl wears unabashed pride on his face when he says to me, "I might just bust my shirt buttons off. My chest just puffs out when this boy does so good."

Verna has made three different kinds of desserts—that's five between us, plus all of the sweets in the bag—including Max's favorite, chocolate chip cookies. "He doesn't like nuts in them," she informs me, her hand forming a cup around her lips as if it's a secret. The same gesture I've seen so often in Max. Tom and I begin to clear the table, while Verna runs nervous circles around us, insisting on helping. Karl draws Max into his lap, regaling him with a story of a rattlesnake they saw in their campsite in Utah. I have no way of knowing that this will be the first of countless rattlesnake stories I'll hear from him, and that Verna will be a whirling dervish following every holiday meal I serve for years to come. I have the impression that if I left her to her own devices, she'd replace the shelf liners, re-grout the tile, and sew new kitchen curtains.

After the cleanup is done, Max pulls Karl's hand to take him to his room to show him his newest Lego spaceships and gets tips on how to break in his new ball glove.

"We should show Verna the new bedroom set," Tom says to me. He turns to Verna and says, "I think you'll like it."

Tom guides Verna to our room and shows her the antique reproduction oak set we just bought. It's our first shared purchase. "Betsy got us a great deal on this," he says. Verna nods her approval of the bargain. She admires the oak finish as she rubs her palms across the glossy surface of the dresser, her lips pursed all the while. "What do you think?" Tom asks.

"I think this'll be really nice for when you're married."

Tom shoots me a mischievous look and I can see he's repressing a snicker at Verna's not-so-subtle commentary about our living together before being married. I widen my eyes to him in warning, afraid he might be tempted to tease on this topic. I'd rather keep the worms in this particular can.

We meet Karl back in Max's room.

"How about we take a walk together?" I suggest. Tom has told me that Karl and Verna are big walkers and it seems like a little activity may settle everyone's jitters.

"I have to get the rest of my strawberry plants in, but Betsy hasn't seen the wildlife trail yet." Tom looks at me. "You don't mind if I stay back and get my gardening done, do you?"

Though it might be a bit more comfortable with Tom along, I nod my approval.

"You remember that trail, don't you, Karl?"

"Why sure. Saw a bobcat up there last time we hiked it." Karl plants a firm hand on my shoulder and gives a squeeze. "I'll show this girly the trail." Karl's terms are a throwback to another era, and might be less than politically correct today. But they feel affectionate in the best way.

Karl, Verna, Max, and I head to the nearby wildlife preserve, where Karl guides us to the trailhead. He points out landmarks and hills, and cautions me to watch where I step. "Keep an eye out," he warns. His eyes are keen, spotting small bugs and lizards skittering on the trail long before I do. "Rattlers show up all the time on these trails." Max dashes ahead of us, gathering a collection of small white rocks that he intermittently shows to Karl, convinced they're not rocks but petrified dinosaur bones. Each time Max presents one to him, Karl announces, "Nope. That's just a rock. But keep looking." Then he turns to me, and chuckles. "He's somethin', isn't he?"

"Look, Grandma!" Max shouts. "A nickel!"

"Bring it here," she says, "I'll save it for your piggy bank." She turns to me as she tucks the coin into her sweater pocket. "Little acorns make big trees," she tells me. Max runs ahead of us on the trail, in search of other treasures.

Karl and Verna have always enjoyed the outdoors. They tell me that they walk five miles a day and spend much of their time camping. Karl's been a fisherman and a deer hunter his whole life. In short order, I learn that they both came from meager beginnings, that fishing and hunting were part of their subsistence as children. Karl fills every silence while we walk with endless stories about his outdoor adventures. His stories meander and lack the normal crescendos and punch lines that most storytellers employ, so it's difficult to tell when one story ends and another begins. As we walk, one story spills into another.

"So Tom tells us you're Catholic," Verna says to me, apropos of nothing. Her tone has a forced cheerfulness.

This feels like a setup, but I'm not sure what for. "I was raised Catholic," I say. "But I don't really practice any official religion. Kind of like Tom, really."

"Oh." Her expression flickers from cheerful to dour, then back to cheerful again. "We're Lutheran. But we just thought that, well, that maybe you might, you know, if you're Catholic and all, you might want to get Max baptized. We hoped that Tom and Janet would do it at some point, but—well, that didn't happen."

"Hard headed," Karl says. "Our Janet was hard headed. Couldn't talk her into or out of a damned thing." He says this without disdain. Like everything Karl says, it's just a fact to him. He offers a bark of a laugh. "I suppose she got that from me." Karl presses his palms against his chest. "See, they used to call me Swede. And you know what they say? You can always tell a Swede, but you can't tell him much."

I chuckle with Karl at what is clearly an oft-repeated line.

Verna looks into the distance at the mention of Janet's name and pulls a wadded bit of tissue from her sleeve, dabbing her nose with a sniff.

I'm not quite sure what to say. We take a few dozen silent steps together on the trail. Turtledoves coo from the distant trees, offering their melancholy song as accompaniment. I stop and look directly into Verna's brown eyes. "I'm so sorry about Janet. I can't imagine how hard it was on you to lose your daughter. She was a lovely person."

Verna's eyes blink rapidly. "You knew our Janet?"

Our Janet. The phrase makes my heart ache. I start walking again and Karl and Verna match my steps. "I didn't know her well, just casually. We'd see each other at various gatherings at my sister's house. Janet and I hosted Dianne and Jim's baby shower together before Megan was born."

Verna's expression softens. "Oh, we've known Dianne and Jim for a long time. I didn't know she was your sister." I hadn't thought about Karl and Verna already knowing my sister and Jim. Tom's and my connections are an intricate web, so it makes sense. We are all just discovering how the limbs and roots of our family trees are comingled and figuring out the connections.

"They were so good to Janet," Verna adds. "All of their friends—"

Karl pulls a hanky from his pocket and blows his nose with a honk. Shaking his head, his blue eyes glisten. "Terrible thing. All that business. Terrible to—" He waves his hand as if swatting a fly and turns his face away. The wound is still fresh for these two and I wonder if it will always be this way for them. I can't imagine the pain of losing a loved daughter as they have. As we walk, Karl wraps his arm around my shoulder as if he's known me for years. He clears his throat. "We're just so happy you're gonna take care of that boy. We won't be around forever. He's a good one. He is."

"He sure is," I say.

"We only hope—" Verna's words come to a hard halt.

I shield my eyes from the sun and look into her softly lined face. "What? What do you hope?"

Her face shows her labored search for words. Karl charges past her silence. "Oh, she's been worried that maybe you wouldn't want us to see Max any more. I told her not to fuss about it."

I stop in my tracks and step aside so that I can see both of them. Of all the things I feared about meeting Janet's parents, never had the idea surfaced that they might be afraid of losing their relationship with Max because of me. She wasn't resentful that I might replace Janet; she was afraid that I might replace her and Karl. "Mr. and Mrs. Lundgren," I say. "I want you to know, I see you as Max's family. I would never do anything to interfere with that."

My "Out-Laws" Karl and Verna Lundgren, proud grandparents, in the stands for countless ball games. Spring 2006.

Karl's chin crinkles. When he speaks, his voice is missing its prior bravado. "I told her that. Didn't I tell you that?"

I recognize in the relief and fatigue on Verna's face that I was not the only one who'd likely been awake half the night, nervous about this meeting. I'd been afraid they'd disapprove of me or resent me. Their fears are far more important; they are afraid they'll lose Max.

We all share a round of sniffs. Max trots toward us, his pockets bulging with rocks. "I've got a bunch of them, Grandpa. Let's get back to the house. I bet I've got some bones in there."

Karl barks a single syllable laugh. "All right, kiddo. Let's go check them out." He turns to me. "And you, Missy."

I brace myself for some kind of scolding at Karl's gruffness.

He presses his palm to his chest. "I'm Karl. And this one here is Verna. You just call us that. Can you do that?"

Heat rises to my cheeks and tears blur my vision. "I can do that," I say. "Let's see, now. When Tom and I get married in a few months, you guys will be—" I calculate. "Well, you won't technically be my in-laws, I guess."

"I guess not," Karl says. He strokes his chin with the tips of his fingers.

I give Karl a wink. "I suppose I'll have to call you my out-laws, then."

Karl gives another bark of a laugh. "Outlaws! You hear that, woman? We're the outlaws of the family."

Verna wears confusion on her face at the new term.

Karl extends his elbow to me on one side, and his other to Verna. "Ha. Outlaws. I'll be darned." The three of us walk back to the car with Max running circles around us.

Ghosts, Saints, and Green Beans

I t's a silly story that Max invites me to tell, even now that he is well into adulthood. He'll cue me to tell it, usually when we're swapping stories and he has a buddy visiting who has yet to hear the ditty. Max smiles at me in a secret way I'm not sure he's aware of. He most often sends me the cue when I serve Italian-style green beans for supper. He will twitch his eyebrows and say something like, "I bet you never thought I'd be happy you're making green beans." I readily pick up his cue for me to tell The Green Bean Story. Families are like that. Our well-worn stories get new lives when we have new audience members. We cue one another. We dovetail funny details into the teller's tale. *Tell about that crazy trip to the Russian River.* Or, *Remember the time when you were a kid and you ran away from home all the way to the house next door?*

Max laughs at his little boy self when I tell The Green Bean Story, unaware of the story's undertow—the one I experienced at the time—which for me lurks just below its funny, sparkly surface. To me, it was one of a handful of seminal moments when I first felt that I was truly becoming Max's mother and that I'd need to design a motherhood that fit me. It also marked the first moment of my awareness of the presence of a ghost in our family. A mommy ghost.

Janet was a good wife to Tom, a beloved daughter and sister, and a beautiful friend to a close group she'd kept since childhood. She was organized and efficient. She always sent thank-you notes. Her home was spotless and without the little piles of clutter I manage to amass. Her tastes ran toward the country *tchotchkes* popular in the '80s. I have to give her the benefit of the doubt, though, since she didn't get a chance to grow out of that style, but given her personality I rather doubt she would have. She loved cats like only real cat lovers can. She was straightforward and no-nonsense like her own father, Max's beloved Grandpa Karl. Her fashion style was functional rather than for show, much like how she was in every aspect. She was blunt and sometimes socially awkward. Quirky is the word most often used to describe her.

She was also a really good mom who loved her boy.

In one of the rare times Tom grew tearful talking about Janet with me, all he said was, "She was so bummed at the end knowing she wouldn't get to see Max grow up." I can't even type these words without feeling an ache in my heart.

I was fortunate that I knew Janet because it made the task of keeping her memory alive possible, and I was able to include it as a natural part of my role with Max. Helping him know about his mother has been a part of mothering Max that I've been proud to carry as my responsibility. In our tacit division of labor, emotional stuff and preserving memories are on my task list.

When someone dies, it's tempting to make her into a flawless painting and not a real person. It's easy to make a dead person into a saint. The whole picture of who Janet was, the memory of her I promised to uphold, also had to include her flaws, though I don't recall ever once having talked about any flaw of Janet's with Max. I remind Max of his first mother's love for him, of how admired she was. I tell stories of how she and I hosted my sister's baby shower together, of how she sent me a thoughtful card afterward thanking me for my help. It never seemed necessary to talk about her few flaws with him. But one of Janet's foibles arose early in my relationship with Max.

Janet had a strange relationship with food. Her food peculiarities were common knowledge among family and friends. Picky doesn't begin to describe it. At first blush one might just view her food oddities as an extension of her general quirkiness and eschewing of anything fancy and frivolous. But it was more than that. Her food behavior was, at the least, eccentric, and most likely a peculiar sort of eating disorder, though she was physically fit and seemingly healthy until leukemia invaded her body.

If you invited Tom and Janet to dinner at your house back then, Tom would arrive with his hearty appetite and enthusiasm for a wide variety of foods. Janet would arrive with a Ziploc baggie containing the foods she would consume supplemented by the few non-offending items her host might serve. While others enjoyed the meal the hosts prepared, Janet—without a complaint and being neither conspicuous nor secretive about it—would amicably munch her uncooked potatoes and carrots. She was not a vegetarian, nor dedicated to a healthy-eating lifestyle. She liked very few foods and would eat absolutely no others. The other allowable foods included hot dogs, spaghetti, chicken, potato chips, diet Pepsi, a select handful of sweets, and the peanut-butter-and-jelly sandwich she ate every single day of her life for lunch. Janet regarded food as fuel and she ate it only out of necessity, drawing no apparent pleasure from the experience and desiring no variety or adventure.

Over the years since Tom and I married, I've heard stories from Janet's parents and sister about family wars over food when Janet was a kid. Theirs was a family in which conformity and cooperativeness were highly prized and defiance was not tolerated. In most every other way, Janet was a docile daughter, but food was her line in the sand, her area of unbudging willfulness, and nothing they could ever do would get her to cross it. She was so defiant about her stance that all the family could do was either to be in a constant battle with her trying to force her to eat other foods, or just to accept it. They eventually surrendered.

Because of Janet's disinterest and Tom's desire for culinary variety, Tom became, by default, the cook of the family during their marriage. When he and I started sharing a home, he gleefully accepted my role as primary cook. Experimenting with new restaurants is one of our favorite ways to spend time together, much to the chagrin of both our bank account and my waistline.

It was during my first weeks as family cook that The Green Bean Story occurred. We'd been living together, the three of us, for about four months. Tom and I were engaged. Max had just turned seven. It was a regular week-night meal, nothing fancy. I made hamburgers and oven fries, an easy kid pleaser. I also made steamed green beans, the way my Italian family makes them, *al dente*, drizzled with a little olive oil and lightly dusted with garlic salt and toasted pine nuts. Every kid in my family loves green beans this way. As I dished up the plates to bring to the table, Max stood guard at my shoulder. "Tomato?" I asked.

"Nope."

"Ketchup?"

"Yup. Lots and lots of ketchup, please."

"Got it," I said, squeezing a veritable lake of ketchup onto his plate. The bottle emitted the customary ketchup squeeze-bottle sound beloved by every boy I've ever known and Max burst into a giggle.

"The ketchup gassed," he said, snickering.

I tried to be cool, but it was giggle-worthy. "Mustard?"

"Nope."

"Probably not onion, huh?"

Max pinched his nose and shook his head like a dog shaking off water.

Then, without asking, I piled a small helping of the crisp green beans on his plate.

"Nope!" he pronounced with an increase in volume that surprised me.

In the split seconds that followed, my mind ran through all of the options. Should I indulge this preference? I wanted him to have a nutritious meal, complete with green vegeta-bles. I didn't want a war, but I also wanted to encourage him to try new foods. Deferring to Tom on every matter would begin to diminish my emerging role as co-parent, but we hadn't talked through rules, or discipline, or parental authority. Frankly, Max didn't require many of these.

Janet's food rituals popped into my mind. I didn't particularly want to encourage such a limited diet. Standing there, serving tongs in hand, I felt a cold shudder, a *ghostly* presence that threatened to discourage my stance. I fought back, against whom, I wasn't sure. *Come on. It's just a bean, not a war with Janet. For godssake!*

"How about you try just one?" I said, in my most pleasing possible voice.

His face registered the shock of my first-ever opposition to his first-ever rejection of my instruction. Until this moment, Max and I had experienced no conflicts. He was an amiable, cooperative little guy and I wasn't prone to exerting my will unnecessarily. When I'd asked him to pick up toys, help with a chore, or take his bath, each task was executed immediately and with good cheer. In his little boy way, I think Max was still tentative about having any conflict with me, too. But green beans were a bridge too far.

Tom tended the grill outside, so it was just Max and me there in the kitchen. Max, me, and the green beans.

I removed two of the three beans from his plate. "It's important to try everything, kiddo. Just one bean. If you like it, you can have more." I decided to use peer pressure, invoking his soon-to-be-cousins' names as my allies. "Matt and Megan *love* these." I tried to put a positive spin on it, though I could hear my own heartbeat as I watched Max hang his head over his plate as he carried it to the table.

It's one damned green bean! I told myself. *Stop worrying about one damned bean.* But then, for the first time in my new life as a mother, the doubt of comparison entered my thoughts. *Janet wouldn't make him eat that bean.*

This wasn't just a conflict with Max. This was me being different than his first mother. This was my first potential "mean stepmother" moment, and I didn't want to be a mean stepmother. I also didn't want to compete with Janet. There'd be no winner in such a contest. But I knew that I couldn't let a seven-year-old set every rule, and that small moments become markers for later patterns. I needed to be the grown-up. It would be wrong to default to the "ask your dad" method.

Memories of Janet and her baggie of raw potatoes flashed. I didn't then know all the details, but I knew her relationship with food was far from ideal. She'd been enviably thin, but her food peculiarities had always been troubling to me, even though we'd never been close enough that I'd comment or inquire about them. No, I could not, *would* not mimic this particular aspect of who she was. She'd left countless wonderful mothering examples behind, but this was one pattern I couldn't follow.

We sat at the table together. Max ate his burger. He dragged each oven-baked fry through ketchup, forming swirling patterns on his plate. His two missing front teeth offered a vivid view of the mastication process inside as he chomped away with his molars. Tom and I ate and shared news of the day while Max wiggled in his chair and completed his meal. Each of my sideways glances revealed what I already knew; the green bean remained untouched. This was our OK Corral, and that bean was Max's holstered six-shooter.

After most of the food disappeared from his plate, Max looked up at Tom. "All done!" he announced. One tail of the single bean peeked from beneath a remnant of burger bun that had been casually placed atop it.

"Okay," Tom said. "You can play in the yard for a while before bath time." He was unaware of my prior green bean proclamation.

My burger churned in my belly. Not only was I being called to exert my new authority, I had to veto Tom's announcement to do it. In the good cop/bad cop role assignment, I didn't like the casting. Again, the rapid-fire recriminations came. *Just let it go. It's a bean, for Chrissake.* A single sweat bead ran lazily down my spine toward my waistband and I breathed deeply to slow the racing of my heart. In that instant, I was transported from the new family table I shared to my own childhood dinner table, with an unyielding, violent father who'd insisted my siblings and I eat liver every Thursday and fish every Friday. I loathed both at the time. We were required to clean our plates of whatever quantities of whatever foods had been deposited there, without option, without regard to our opinions or hunger levels. I'd vowed I'd never subject a child to such abuse at my table, would never make them sit for hours in front of a cold plate of liver.

Perhaps the presence I felt wasn't Janet's ghost at all, but the ghost of my own history with an abusive parent. And here was Max, sitting in agony in front of a single green bean just as I had sat for so many nights with foods I couldn't bear. My stomach waged war in me as I recalled my dad, his face red with drink and fury, insisting I eat the fried rabbit leg I'd been served, despite my silent horror at eating an animal I'd held only weeks after its birth, and whose mother's fur I'd petted that very afternoon. I didn't want to be *that* parent, that unyielding Great Santini of a parent like the one I'd known.

In the seconds that ensued, I devised my good mothering yardstick. My parenting style would be this: Be loving. Be clear. Be fair. Be consistent. Be reasonable. Be kind. I quickly assessed my stance and found a tiny corner of solid ground.

"Ahem," I coughed. I cast my eyes toward the offending spear on Max's plate. "Not quite done yet, bud. Remember, just one green bean. I won't make you eat piles of foods you hate, but you need to at least try everything." I glanced at Tom for rebuke or approval. Happily oblivious, he took a generous bite of his burger. No help. No interference. This would not be the first time, nor the last, that Tom would be unaware of the nuances of my exchanges with Max.

Max looked at his dad, convinced, I guessed, that Tom would veto my veto, but Tom's oblivion was genuine and non-discriminating.

Max slunk back into his chair. His cheeks sagged, drawn down by the weight of his dramatically extended bottom lip. His eyelids drooped. His shoulders slumped. He actually panted. The chipper, energetic boy who'd laughed at the ketchup fart before dinner had transformed right before my eyes into an aging basset hound.

And there he sat.

As we cleared the dishes, Max sat. As Tom loaded the dishwasher, Max sat. During our multiple trips back and forth from dining room kitchen, Max remained unmoving, the glossy green bean broadcasting its uneaten-ness.

"But I don't like these," Max finally whined, mostly to Tom, but while I was nearby.

"Come on, Skib," Tom soothed. "It's good to try stuff. Just one and it's over."

Tom's unsolicited backup stopped the churning in my belly. We'd had no conversation and no precedent for it, but without notice we'd become a parenting partnership. Though Max's suffering brought me no joy, Tom's support elated me beyond words. Tom was Max's dad. This was my first step in becoming Tom's partner and Max's mother. Above all else, I wanted for Tom and me to be united in a way my own parents never were.

Tom and I worked together in the kitchen, finishing the cleanup. "Is it okay?" I asked. "This making him eat the bean thing?"

Tom shrugged. "He'll get it done." Tom raised his voice enough for Max to hear from the dining room. "Come on, Skib. Finish up. We want to put your plate in the dishwasher."

Now the clock was ticking. I peeked into the dining room. Max was a deflated balloon, slumped in his chair, his eyes fixed on the dreaded bean. He was in agony. I was in agony. Tom whistled in the kitchen. How I've envied his oblivion over the years.

As I returned the last of the condiments to the fridge, Max bounded into the kitchen. "All done!" he announced. The balloon was buoyant again, not only full of air, but helium, his feet barely touching the ground as he skipped through the room. A quick survey of his plate revealed not so much as a single speck of green.

"Wow. Great job," I said. "Did you like it?"

"Yeah, it was really, really good." He scraped the remaining crumbs into the trash and set his plate on its edge in the dishwasher.

Triumph, silent as a butterfly, fluttered in my heart. My first mommy moment as disciplinarian, and I'd passed the test. It had worked. I'd established my parental precedent for limit-setting, and Max had responded. This was a fine beginning.

Max bounded out to the back yard with two Hot Wheels cars in his small hands.

A few moments later I went to use the downstairs powder room off the front hall. Beside the toilet, in the open waste paper can, I spotted it—the bean. In all of its green glory, the intact bean glared up at me, altered not by a single nibble. I know it had no eyes, but it glared up at me, mocking me.

Shit. Shit. Shit.

For Max, the story ends here. It's a sweet, funny story about a little boy getting caught in an act of inept deceit. I never retell the part of the story where Tom and I sat down with him and told him about how important it is to tell the truth. He likely doesn't recall our parental wisdom nuggets about trust and honesty, about the need to try foods that you think you won't like. He's never mentioned our lesson about honoring instructions we give him, how we only ask him to do things that are for his health and safety and because we love him.

Max just laughs at the silliness of a little boy and a green bean. He comically rues the fact that he wasn't crafty enough at least to have hidden the bean better than sitting it atop the used tissues in the bathroom trash can, but that's the part of the story I like best—that he was so innocent and lacked skills of deceit. It overjoys me that, decades later, he still lacks such skills.

Though she was his mother for barely five years, Janet's early touches on Max left fingerprints on the man he has become. I recognize her indelible prints. Janet not only passed onto him half of his DNA, but a thousand intangible suggestions that would become traits, that would become qualities, that would become who he is. I recognize Max's first mother in his quirky food preferences—though he has a much wider palate than his mother's—and his tolerance for eating the same foods day after day. Food is just fuel to him, the way it was for her. I see Janet in his utter disregard for whether someone else agrees with him and his steadfast dedication to being who he is. He laughs just as she did, with a particular way that he bobs his head with each chuckle. His lean body is the masculine version of hers. His relationship to fashion, like food, remains one of function more than form, though the woman in his life is placing her own influences on his style choices.

While Janet was a loving mother to Max, and a woman I've come to appreciate more as each year passes, she was neither saint nor recriminating ghost. She was flawed. She had her own family challenges. The recriminations I feel have nothing to do with being haunted by Janet's ghost, or even by any rational fear that she would disapprove of my choices. Over time I've learned that these are the doubts that plague every mother, regardless of how her child came to her. The mothering of my older child was begun by another, one whose values I share but who was so different from me. I love to cook and to eat and to celebrate around a table. I enjoy a clean house, but sometimes have untidy piles of papers in my office. I love Beatrix Potter stories, but not enough to commemorate the characters in my home's décor. I love big, sweet dogs. I don't much like cats.

Our relationship as mothers, Janet's and mine, is not a competition. It's a relay race, and we run it for the same shared outcome. Her leg of the race ended sooner than planned. I picked up where she was forced to leave off. My leg of the race has been decades long, but we both earned the victory of a son well raised.

Janet left big shoes to fill, but I've also learned it was not just my job to fill them, but to walk around in them too, to make them my own, seek my own path, find my own stride. I like to think she'd be happy with the mothering I completed in her absence. I wish she could know how grateful I am for the mothering she started.

Who Will This Be to Me?

A few months before Tom and I were to be married, Max wandered into the dining room of the house we shared. I was sorting through a box of old photographs. Max tossed a bright orange Nerf ball, said nothing, and didn't look at me. His focus was completely on the ball. Though he was barely seven, I could already recognize the quick reflexes and fast hands of the athlete he would become. He threw the ball straight up and caught it. Soon he began to twirl around after each toss, catching the spongy ball behind his back. Then, he bounced the ball off the wall over the table, then off the ceiling.

"Hi, bud," I said. "Nice moves."

No reply. Wall. Ceiling. Twirl. Wall.

"Whatcha doin'?" he finally asked.

"Just trying to organize some of my pictures."

In my months of living with Tom and Max, I'd learned to let Max come close on his own. If I crowded him or moved too quickly he'd skitter away, his tolerance for closeness dissipating like so much water vapor. If I was patient, we'd often end up playing, laughing, and recently even snuggling on the couch with a book or a TV show.

"Who's that?" he asked, peeking around my shoulder.

"My mom when she was young."

"What's she sitting on?"

"A paper moon. They used to have them at fairs and carnivals. People liked to pose for pictures on them."

"That's dumb. It doesn't even look like a real moon."

"After the wedding, I suppose she'll be your Grandma Sylvia."

"Cool." Wall. Ceiling. Wall. Wall. Twirl.

He caught the ball and, then sidled up beside me, leaning his warm body against my arm. He pressed a dirt-smudged finger on another photo. "Who will that be to me?" he asked.

"He was my grandfather, the one who died a few months ago."

Max shrugged and resumed his ball tossing, this time switching hands. Right. Left. Right. "I already got a grandfather," he said, not unkindly.

"Lots of kids have two grandpas. I guess my grandfather would have been your great-grandfather."

"Hmm. Too bad he had to die. I coulda used one of those."

As I continued my sorting and stacking, I felt a pinch in my chest. Death is a barbed topic, but particularly with a child who lost his mother only two years before. I shuffled quickly past the pictures of dead relatives.

The Nerf ball stilled again and Max propped his elbows on my desk, resting his chin on the heels of his upturned palms. "What about them?" he asked, pointing to a picture of my sister and her family. He'd known them his whole life, just as he had known me, played with my niece and nephew regularly—Megan just a year older, Matt two years younger than Max—attended birthday parties and family dinners. But I could see that he was beginning to grasp the change that we were about to undergo.

"Di and Jim will be your aunt and uncle. Megan and Matt will be your cousins."

"Sweet," he said, looking into my face for the first time since he'd entered the room. His eyes were chocolate pools, his thick dark hair a sleek, shiny coat that made me want to run my fingers over it. "I don't have any boy cousins. And how about him?"

"My brother, John. He'll be your uncle." I was especially happy to share my younger brother with Max. John loved kids and, being much like a giant kid himself, had a knack for being silly with them.

We sorted stacks of aunts and uncles, cousins and friends.

"Wow, you have a lot of people," Max sighed.

"I suppose I do."

He began to finger through the stacks, messing up what I'd already sorted. My original task no longer mattered. As we neared the bottom of the stack, a honey-thick warmth began to fill me. Perhaps my family was to be the unexpected dowry I'd bring to this little boy who had lost so much. "Whoa," he exclaimed, laughing at my third-grade picture, the one where my hair had been expanded to new dimensions by an especially humid Indiana day.

At moments like those, Max was just a little boy, buoyant with energy, easy with a laugh. He played Legos and watched *Teenage Mutant Ninja Turtles* and tossed balls. At other times, when he was still or thought no one was looking, it seemed that the earth's pull was just a little stronger where he stood, tugging the corners of his mouth downward, making his eyes appear years older than the number of his birthdays would imply.

Just as I was about to put the last of the pictures in the box, Max pressed his finger once more to a face. "And who will *this* be to me?"

Beneath his finger I could see the edges of my own face. I was suddenly flooded with a heart-swell for which I had no name. This child of the man I loved was becoming my son. We'd have family Christmas cards and school art stuck with magnets to the fridge. I'd make goodie bags at birthday parties, snap pictures at graduations. All these things, I'd never allowed myself to want, thinking that perhaps my own history had left me too wounded to allow myself children of my own. I was becoming a mother, but without the benefit of a growing belly or a baby shower to prepare me. I should know the answer to his simple question. I should know how to say just the right, wise, magical thing. But I didn't. So I offered the therapists' cop-out question.

"Well, what do you think?"

Max shrugged. Then he looked away and I knew it was my job to field this one. Jumbled words bobbed to the surface of my mind, like those triangle-shaped answers floating in the blue waters in a Magic 8-Ball.

Finally the image rose to the surface. "I'll be your second mom," I said.

"Oh."

"I'm sorry that your first mom died. I liked her a lot."

Silence floated between us, then Max leaned against me, his chin still in his palms.

"What should I call you?" he asked, not looking at me. I'd known him his whole life and he'd called me Betsy all that time.

My heart pounded against the cage of my ribs, my stomach turned over. *Mama,* I wanted to cry. *I'll be your mama and you'll be my son.* I resisted. "You can call me Mom, or Mama. You can also call me Betsy, if you'd rather. Whatever feels okay for you."

He stood there a minute, and I waited, thinking I'd get a pronouncement of my new title.

"What's for dinner?" he asked, picking up his ball.

"Burgers."

"Sweet," he said, tossing the ball as he walked out of the room.

⟶⟵

At our wedding, a few months later, Tom and I said our vows to one another. Then Max was invited to stand beside us. I then made vows to Max. I promised to step into the shoes his mother had been forced to leave behind and to be the best mother I could be. I promised to help him remember her.

After the wedding, for the next days, Max tried on a new title for me. "Can we go bowling?" he'd ask, and he'd follow the question by mouthing the word *Mom*. The word was silent. It seemed he was trying it on, seeing how it felt in his mouth. "Whatcha doin, *Mom*?" "Can I watch TV now, *Mom*?"

My hopes floated like a pink helium balloon. Then,

like a thousand hornets, guilt attacked the balloon, piercing it until it lost its air and sank. It felt wrong to take such pleasure in seeing his little plumb lips form that singular syllable. After all, this new son of mine was an inheritance I'd not have if he and Tom hadn't sustained such an enormous loss. I felt small . . . and smaller still when old habits resumed and Betsy was once again my only title. I tucked this shameful disappointment away, telling no one.

⌇⌇

Weeks later as I drove him home from school, Max pulled a baggie full of Cheez-Its from his Ninja Turtle lunch box. He munched away, licking each finger of its orange dust. With his focus deep inside the near-empty snack bag, he suddenly said, "I notice I don't call you Mom."

Oof. Who threw that rock at my chest? Dead hit. I breathed to calm my voice. "I noticed that."

One last cracker, then four fingers to lick. "When I say 'Betsy,' I mean 'Mom.'"

I swallowed past the dry rock that formed in my throat. "Thanks," I said. "That's nice to know."

He looked out the window. "Moms die, you know. I think it's maybe safer if you're just Betsy."

We could have a long talk about magical thinking and death, and how nothing he could say or not say could cause me to die, or could have caused his mother to die. But this just didn't seem like the time for all of that.

I willed tears away, not wanting to overwhelm him. He had enough to carry. "Thanks, bud. I appreciate you telling me."

Those big chocolate eyes found mine. I waited.

"Hey, Betsy?"

"Yeah," I said, delighted with the new sound of my old name.

"What's for dinner?"

My mom, Sylvia Graziani House. Taken at a fair in 1943.

Tom's parents, Elsie and Clarence Fasbinder. How I wish I'd gotten to meet them.

By Any Other Name

Like lots of modern women, my name has undergone some remodeling in my adult life. I've often wondered what this particular aspect of "maleness" is like, knowing that you'll likely never be asked to consider changing your name. It's a jealousy of the tiniest variety, in the category of wishing it was as easy for women as it is for guys to pee outside without getting our shoes wet. I wonder now, in the advent of marriage equality, if men who marry one another and choose to form families might now undergo the same "should-I, shouldn't-I" questions about their surnames that women of my generation, and back in time, have wrestled with.

My name didn't undergo the single transition of my last name changing from maiden to married. My name underwent a complete renovation—a series of them really—front to back. My name's final makeover is part of my inherited family's love story.

I was born Betty Marie House; an inauspicious name to be sure. I was never called Betty by my family, nor by close friends. The only place I was called Betty was at school where my official name was registered. I was too shy to tell teachers that though Betty was the name on my birth certificate, my "real" name was Betsy, and that's what I strongly preferred to be called. My mother once hinted that she wanted my legal name to be Betsy, the name she called her younger sister, but that my grandma wanted to honor her own sister, Betty (not exactly a beloved favorite aunt in our family). Ma even once implied that Grandma "forced" her to name me Betty, though I can't imagine how that might have happened.

From kindergarten and all the way through high school, whenever a teacher called me Betty, it felt as though they were speaking to someone else. Aside from the Betsy Wetsy doll which arrived on the scene when I was small, and the occasional car or cow that shared this name with me, I liked having the name Betsy. Betty always felt like somebody else's ill-fitting clothes. Betty seemed like the unsexy, plain-Jane sidekick to all of the much more interesting Veronicas of the world.

When I left home for college, I took it as my chance to finally be myself—Betsy. I enrolled with this name and introduced myself as such. Few people who've met me after the age of seventeen even know that Betty is my given name. Name transformation number one.

House, as is traditional, was the last name I inherited from my father's family. It was some mutt version of English, Irish, and maybe some German, but ethnicity was never fully talked about. Having this particular noun for a last name had its challenges as well: outhouse, shit house, whorehouse, cathouse, doghouse. None were any too flattering. My surname had been the subject of more than a few schoolyard taunts.

When I married at nineteen, I was thrilled to shuck House as my last name and was oh-so-eager to adopt Osborne as my new one. I wasn't thinking politically. I wasn't even thinking of the playground taunts. My father, who passed away when I was thirteen, was a difficult and dangerous man, and an abusive father. He died at forty-eight, which sounds shocking to most people, but given his three-pack-a-day smoking habit and the frequency with which he emptied a gin bottle, it's miraculous he lived that long. My mere thirteen years of exposure to him were quite enough, thank you. I had absolutely zero attachment to his name and an understandable revulsion for its connection to him. By this time, both my sisters had shucked their last names in favor of their husbands'. I was eager to step into my new family and readily took their surname. Betsy Marie Osborne I became. Renovation number two.

Like so many decisions made in one's late teens, getting married proved to have been an impulsive choice, and one that I did not want for the rest of my life. Whenever I've entertained the idea of getting a tattoo, I remember that even decisions I once thought were permanent later became regrets. I remained tattooless until the age of fifty-six, when I figured I trusted myself well enough to do something so permanent. At twenty-six I was divorced. I then once again bore a name that felt as though it was not truly mine.

I didn't want to go back to House. I couldn't keep Osborne. What to do?

About that time, my cousin Mark passed away quite suddenly, at the age of seventeen. Mark was my mom's brother's only son. What was thought to be flu turned out to be a virulent form of cancer and sweet, funny Mark was shockingly gone in a matter of weeks. After his passing, I sat with my maternal grandfather at his table. Grandpa Graziani was a sweet, sentimental man, his voice kissed with the soft accent of his Italian birthplace. He tearfully mentioned that Mark was his only name-bearing grandchild. Grandpa's other son had only daughters and his daughter's children, including my brothers, bore their father's names.

My grandfather was a man I'd admired for his decency and kindness. He was a man of modest means, but of simple needs, and because of that he lived in a constant state of gratitude. He was adored by all of his children, so very unlike my own father. That's when it came to me. I would change my last name to my grandfather's name, my mother's maiden name: Graziani. I officially changed my name to Betsy Marie Graziani. Gone was the Betty. Gone was the House. Gone was the Osborne. Name renovation number three.

I *finally* had a name that felt like it was my own. It was clothing fashioned of soft, cozy flannel and it fit me perfectly.

I owned this name. I cherished this name. I liked being Betsy Graziani. I liked that the *Italianness* that I loved as part of my family's culture was finally apparent despite my ethnically deceptive red hair and freckles. I liked its musicality and the alliterative repetition of the unlikely "ts" sound in both names. *Be-TSEE Gra-TSEE-ani*. When I told him that I was changing my name in honor of the good man that he'd been to his children and grandchildren and of how important he was to me, my grandpa brought his handkerchief to his eyes. "I guess I got a grandchild with my name again," he said. His tears and simple words were worth all of the name change hassles that the DMV, Social Security, and I.R.S. offices required. Another aspect of the name-change process most men are spared.

I declared aloud, as well as deep in my soul, that no matter what happened, I had my rest-of-my-life name. With all the wisdom and foresight endowed to a twenty-six-year-old, I said to all who then knew me that I wasn't sure I ever intended to marry again, but that if by some preposterous series of events I did, I absolutely would NOT change my name.

Fast-forward seven years.

The week before the event, Tom and Max and I prepared for our wedding and all of the guests and festivities. Max, then seven, referred to it as "our wedding." "Who's coming to *our wedding*?" he'd ask. "Can we have pasta at *our wedding*?"

We all started calling it "our wedding," though I'm not sure either Tom or Max noticed the specialness of this particular pronoun. That little "our" made my heart sing. It validated the "we-ness" of our new family structure. I was not just marrying Tom, we were becoming a family, and Max's inclusive pronoun was validation of the rightness of the choice and his acceptance of my stepping into my new role as his second mother. I said nothing about the "our" pronoun, for fear that this gossamer little pleasure might disappear if I made a big deal out of it. Instead, I tasted it every time it was uttered like a secret treat enjoyed in private.

Just a few days before *our* wedding, Max stood on a footstool as I marked his new pants for hemming. "Stand still, bud," I mumbled, my lips holding a row of straight pins. "I'm trying to get this straight and I don't want to poke you."

"Are we almost done?" he asked. A seven-year-old boy has limited tolerance for the necessary tasks of tailoring wedding garments.

"Almost."

Max splayed the fingers of both hands outward and stilled his jiggling feet. "Hey look," he said, holding out one of his small, outspread hands. "Looks just like a starfish. Huh?"

I looked up at his face and removed the last of the pins from my mouth. "Sure does, kiddo. All done here. You can get down, but be careful. Your pant hems are full of pins. I suppose it's better than ants in your pants." He gave a one-syllable laugh to humor me.

Max took careful steps down to the floor. "No pokes," he announced.

"Careful when you take them off. Do you need help?"

"Got it." He took stiff-legged steps toward the stairs, his fanned hands still stiff in their starfish shape. "Hey." He turned to me, his face lit with a new idea. "I just thought of something. In four more days you'll be Betsy Fasbinder. That's kinda funny."

I gathered up the sewing supplies and stood. "Actually, honey, not all women change their names when they get married. I'll still be Betsy Graziani."

Max's shoulders sank. His body and face went slack, his buoyancy gone. The starfishes wilted back into regular little boy hands. "So, we're not going to be a *real* family?"

he asked. His voice was low and his stare penetrating, await-
ing my response.

Tom and I had already talked about my name. He
had no objection, not that I'd really left room for any, to
my retaining my name. Still wedded to my proclamation,
I hadn't so much as entertained the thought of taking on
yet another name. As if to reiterate my prior proclamation,
I'd let Tom know that he'd be marrying Betsy Graziani and
that Betsy Graziani I'd remain.

But there, at the bottom of the stairs, was a face and a
question I could not ignore. In Max's mind, to be a family
we needed to share a name. His first mother had taken Fasbinder as her name. She'd been family. *Real* family. In his
boy's mind, having a shared name meant being a *real* family. For me to be his mother, we needed to share a name.

"We'll talk about it later, okay bud?" I said, stalling for
time and trying to fight back tears. I plastered on a fake smile.
"Look out for the porcupines in your pant legs, will you?"

His smile resumed. "Porcupines. Ha!" He ascended
the stairs.

As his small feet disappeared up the stairwell, I lost
my battle against my tears. "My name," I whispered with
more hiss than intended. "It's *my* name." I felt like a child
who wanted to bang her high chair tray in protest. *Mine.*
Mine. Mine.

Anger, or some bastard cousin of anger, bubbled in
my gut. I wasn't angry at Max. How could I be? I couldn't
be angry with Tom. He wasn't even part of the discussion and he'd been supportive about whatever choice I'd
wanted to make about my name. But anger, hot and ugly,
boiled just the same.

I'd made all of the big, hard decisions. I'd chosen to marry, to become a mother, to step into the empty place of loss that my man and my boy had incurred. I saw none of this as heroic, mind you. I was not rescuing these two after the unfairness of losing their wife and mother to that rat-bastard leukemia. I never saw one little morsel of rescue in what I was doing when I answered yes to Tom's proposal. I loved him. I loved them both. I was joining the two of them, as much for my own gain as for theirs.

But now I was facing a choice I didn't think I had to make. I resented feeling that I was being selfish to want to keep the name I'd designed and embraced as my own. But then, I saw Max's face, his starfish hands, his deflated shoulders. I heard his question, *So we're not going to be a real family?*

In that moment, at the bottom of the stairs, with the weight of the sewing basket dangling from my fingers, despite every personal intention, political notion, and emotional connection I'd ever had about my name, my resolve evaporated. Utterly. Shakespeare's words bubbled to the surface of my mind. *A rose by any other name.* The only person to whom my name mattered more than it did to me was Max. And Max, and his bonding with me, mattered more to me than even my own name.

I'd been thinking of everything I'd be adding to my life by becoming Max's mother, but I'd not yet considered what I'd be giving up.

I considered a hyphenated name. But Graziani-Fasbinder is not exactly a last name that rolls off the tongue. Such a hyphenated albatross would be more than I could subject any future kids to endure. Besides, then our family

would still be bifurcated by the slice of our different surnames of the plain and hyphenated varieties. No, it was
clear; I'd be Betsy Fasbinder. In one last attempt to soothe
my inner high chair–banger, I elected to retain Graziani
as my middle name. Marie, my given middle, had always
seemed like a placeholder anyway. Ah, well, another one
bites the dust.

None of the three names I'd bear thereafter were orig-
inal-issue. On February 15, 1992, my name underwent the
latest of its renovations at *our* wedding. I am wiser now, well
past the mossy side of my fifties, so I'm not foolish enough
to say I'll never change it again, but it seems pretty unlikely.

I am a rose. A rose with the cumbersome, clunky,
unlikely name of Betsy Graziani Fasbinder.

My namesakes. My grandfather, Samuel Antonio Graziani and my
mom, Sylvia Graziani House. I just love how adoringly Ma looks at
her father in this photograph. Taken sometime in the late '70s.

Vows

The day before our wedding, and ten months after our first date, was Valentine's Day, 1992, the first Valentine's Day Tom and I shared as a couple. The day was bright and beautiful, with only a small tang of chill in the air. It was one of those surprising winter days that makes you feel as though it will never be cold or rainy again. California had suffered a four-year drought, but my mind wasn't on the diminished snowpack or the fact that flushing our toilets had become a luxury afforded only at the most necessary of times.

We'd planned a simple wedding and had lucked out in the lottery that allows couples to put their names in for the wedding venue in San Francisco's Stern Grove. Both beautiful and economical, the cozy room in the Victorian Stern Grove Clubhouse was just what I'd hoped for, intimate with a sense of history. A friend would be officiating the services with the tone of family, love, and friendship we wanted. Loved ones had begun to arrive. Another friend, a professional baker, was making our cake. My sixteen-year-old niece, Michelle, would be deejay for the reception, with a small boom box at the back of the room. Clothing was pressed and hanging in garment bags waiting for the next day's ceremony. I felt an uncharacteristic serenity about it all.

ℓℓℓ⸺ℓℓℓ

The morning of our wedding, California's four-year drought came to a theatrical end. It didn't just rain, it poured. Spoiled by the dry winter, we'd somehow assumed the day would be clear and our guests would be able to hang out on the wide wrap-around porch of the Stern Grove Clubhouse where our ceremony would be held. But between the deluge and the raging winds, even the porch was no shelter and everyone huddled indoors for the ceremony and the following reception.

Dianne and Jim stood beside Tom and me as best man and matron of honor. My sister, who'd known Tom for over twenty years at that time, would become his sister. Jim, Tom's college roommate, would become his brother. Their children, Max's cousins. It was clear to me on that day, as it would be for years and years to come, that I didn't just marry Tom, and Tom didn't just marry me. Like Max said, it was *our* wedding, all of ours.

Our wedding was happy and stress-free. Even being surrounded by friends and family members, I was aware of another presence in the hall. Every time my eye caught Max darting around the room, I was aware that he existed, not because of my union with Tom, but because of Janet and Tom's union. He was born into their shared home, with their shared vision of how they'd raise him. I'd thought of her so many times in those first months of my relationship with Tom and Max, and on the day of *our* wedding I felt this awareness even more acutely. But it was not sadness that came with my awareness of her; it was my deep gratitude, and the gravity of the responsibility I was taking on in continuing to mother Max when Janet no longer could.

Tom and I said our simple vows to one another first. When our friend announced us as married and we exchanged our kiss, the crowd cheered and clapped in the most fun and raucous explosion of joy that it felt as though my heart doubled in size. Tom's cheeks were pink, his smile broad.

I knew, though, having thought of Janet so often as we'd prepared for the day, that our wedding required another layer of vows. These would be vows I'd make to Max. We brought Max up to the front of the room with us and I made my own vows to him, ending with two simple promises: "I will continue the tasks of mothering that your first mother began so well. And I will encourage and preserve the memory of her. From this day forward, I will be parent to you and whole-heartedly call you my son."

I knew that Max was too young to understand the gravity of my vows to him, but that didn't matter. It was my promise to make. It was also my promise to keep. And while I said these vows to Max, I was also saying them to Janet, as a promise to love the boy I'd inherited from her and to preserve her memory for him.

❧

Our wedding and the reception following was packed with our friends and family and scads of children. The rain and wind thrashed around outside, but the candlelit room was a haven filled with joy.

It turned out to be as big a party for Max as for us. Unable to go outside, the kids made the large room into a playground, removing their shoes and sliding on the wood floors. Max orchestrated contests according to age level, with treats from the buffet table as prizes. We'd made a separate kids' buffet table with child-friendly food and drinks and the kids foraged to their delight.

Many of the friends and loved ones at our wedding had been at Tom and Janet's wedding. They had also attended Janet's funeral and had known her throughout her struggle with leukemia. These good friends had been there for Tom after he'd lost Janet, and they now celebrated the two of us finding one another. Whatever the weather outside, I'd never felt warmer or safer than I did on our wedding day, nor had I ever felt more sure that I was making the right choice.

Di and Jim standing right beside us, the day friends became family.

Our wedding, February 2, 1992. Max looks on for our kiss, and seems relieved when it's over.

Sex Ed and Reality Checks

One Friday morning in May of 1992, just a few months after Tom and I were married, I stood at the counter making Max's lunch. I'd stepped easily into this morning routine, and often picked Max up from school to spare him the dreaded "after-school program." The sheer mommy-ness of my new tasks delighted me.

As I spread peanut butter onto soft wheat bread, Max sidled up beside me. He bumped my hip with his shoulder. "Ready for school?"

"Yup."

"Teeth brushed?"

"Yup." He spread his lips, revealing the new scaffolding of metal and wire, only a start to the orthodontic architecture to come.

"Nice work," I said. "Tricky to get all the crumbs out of the barbed wire, huh?"

He nodded. "Barbed wire. Good one." He began to fidget.

"Something up?"

"Could you put, um, less peanut butter and more jelly?"

"Little dry, huh?"

"Yup." Relief smoothed his face. He was still learning how to approach me on matters of such grave importance. Emboldened, he queried further. "Oh, and can I have a candy bar in my lunch today?"

"Sorry, we don't have any candy bars." I zipped the Ziploc bag of Cheez-Its.

"Yeah, we do," he sang as he made a pudgy-fingered count of the crackers. Sixteen was his preferred quantity. If I put more, the exact difference would return home in his Ninja Turtle lunch box, uneaten. Fewer, and I'd receive a good-natured request for the next day's adjustment.

I squinted, trying to think of any candy bars he might be thinking about. "Honey, we don't have any candy bars."

He tilted his head to one side and looked up at me with a limp-cheeked, slack-jawed expression of exasperation. "Your *special, secret* ones." His eyes widened to emphasize the words *special* and *secret*.

I shrugged, knowing I had no such secret stash— though I wouldn't be above it—and returned my attention to packing the lunch box. "Besides—" I was about to launch into an explanation of how caramel or nuts wouldn't work because of his new braces, but when I turned Max was gone.

I gathered my keys and the lunchbox and headed toward the door. As I arrived, Max leapt down the last three stairs, landing inches in front of me. Hands behind his back, he delivered a heavy-metal grin. "See, the *special, secret* candy bars."

There before me, his chocolate-colored gaze locked into mine, was my brand new seven-year-old son, holding in his upturned palm a plastic-wrapped tampon. The unopened wrapper was shiny white, bespeckled with tiny pink flowers.

What to say. What to say. Tom and I hadn't talked about where Max was in the sex ed department. I was a latecomer to this motherhood process and somehow my new position lacked both job description and instruction manual. *Damn that Tom for leaving early.* Janet had died when Max was barely five; surely she wouldn't have covered these particular facts of life. I quickly resolved to K-I-S-S, Keep it Simple, Sweetie, and answer only what was asked. I drew a deep breath. "That's not a candy bar."

His brow crumpled. "What is it?"

Damn. "It's a tampon."

"What's a tampon?"

Double damn! "It's something women use when they get their periods."

"What's a period?"

Christ, I cannot catch a break here. And now I can barely remember the flow, no pun intended, of words that escaped my lips. "Once a month . . . If there's no baby . . . tampons are kind of like a Band-Aid you wear inside and . . ."

As I spoke, Max's face wilted, until finally he wore an expression so full of revulsion I had no name for it. When I finally stopped chattering, he lifted his still upturned palm a little higher and dropped his eyes to the floor like someone making a sacrificial offering to a menacing god. "I don't think I want it in my lunch."

I accepted the offending item and we made a silent ride to school. He stared out his window, now and then sneaking a glance at me as though he'd just discovered I was actually an alien creature inhabiting human form.

ree____eel

That evening when Tom got home, I grilled him on Max's sex ed status. Tom's shoulders rose to his ears. When I told him of our morning exchange he cackled up his sleeve. "Better you than me, baby!" he said as he opened the fridge and pulled out a beer.

Half of me wanted to pelt Tom with the bottle cap he'd left on the counter. Then a warm molasses feeling came over me. That morning had been one of my first motherly milestones. The awkwardness of the exchange, my hesitancy about what to say, all of it was exactly what I'd have experienced if Max had been born to me. Just two days before my first Mothers' Day and it was official. I really was Max's mom.

ree____eel

I don't know exactly what I was expecting on the morning of that first Mothers' Day, but it didn't happen. I stalled the appropriate amount of so-are-we-going-to-a-special-brunch time, but when Tom got a cereal bowl down for Max, I figured *that* wasn't happening. As the *Inspector Gadget* theme song trilled from the TV, it became clear that though I had marked this day as my first Mothers' Day, it had escaped Tom's and Max's awareness. How could I say anything? After all, what if there was some sweet little card waiting for me, yet undelivered?

By early afternoon, I felt a full froth of resentment. When my sister Di called and said, "Happy First Mother's Day! How did you guys celebrate?" I said only, "Oh, pretty low-key. We had breakfast at home." It's the only half-lie I ever remember telling her.

The day wore on. Tom worked in the yard. Max batted whiffle balls up the slope of our backyard hill and waited for them to roll back, only to repeat the procedure three hundred more times. The adaptive play of an only child.

In my stomach broiled a vile cocktail of disappointment and sadness. The clock's hands ached around with sluggish insensitivity, keeping the day from ending.

I poked my head out the back door. "I'm taking a shower," I called to Tom.

He leaned his elbow on the handle of his shovel and smiled. "Let me know when you're done, baby. I'm next."

In the shower, I let myself cry raw, self-indulgent tears. I let myself mutter angry mini-speeches I knew I'd never deliver. When I'd exorcised the worst of my bitter little demons, I got out of the shower and wrapped my long hair into a white towel turban. My puffy face mocked me from the steamy mirror.

Robe- and turban-clad, I descended the stairs. Max sat at a TV table, a bowl of baby carrots before him, Nickelodeon on the screen.

"Hey, bud, would you tell Papa I'm out of the show—"

Max turned to me, but before I could finish my sentence he leapt from his chair, toppling the table, sending carrots like small torpedoes across the floor, the bowl tumbling with a clang. Like the surprise of dry lightning in summer, the room was split in two by his scream. It was the shriek of an otherwise silent animal—a deer or a rabbit—caught in a trap. Max's mouth was a gaping maw stretching his baby face into a contorted mask.

I sprang toward him. "What!? What!?"

His screams were a siren with a deafening rise and fall that reverberated through my skull. He flailed as I tried to hold him. What agony caused this happy, easy boy to scream so? A burst appendix? An aneurism?

With a bang, Tom flung open the sliding glass door to the family room, his faced washed of all familiarity, wearing only garden dirt and panic.

"Take it off!" Max screamed. Finally, words. He was a human again, if not one I recognized. "Take it off. TAKE IT OFF!"

I puzzled about the "it" in his newly found words. Tom grabbed Max around the shoulders. "Make her take it off!" Max screamed and he started to sob, fat tears escaping his eyes.

When my eyes caught Max's, I could see that he looked at my towel-wrapped head. "This?" I asked.

He nodded through his sobs. His small body convulsing as he gasped for air.

Tom looked at me and shook his head. I unwrapped the towel and let the long wet strands of hair fall to my shoulders. As each damp tendril fell, Max's face relaxed, his breath becoming rhythmic gasps. Tom held him in desperate containment, wearing utter confusion on his face.

And then it clicked.

From the time when he was three and his mother got sick, until she died when Max was five, Janet had been in one or another stage of losing or re-growing hair robbed from her by chemotherapy and radiation. She'd worn a collection of turbanlike hats, some knit, some felt, and one white. I'd seen her wearing it when I'd bumped into her once at Safeway. Unwittingly, I had embodied a dormant image that Max had tucked into the recesses of his memory. I'd marched right into his grief, his trauma, his most profound loss.

I felt so small and petty for my earlier self-pity, for my wanting of the lacy cards and burnt pancakes that husbands and children delivered on Mothers' Day in movies and Hallmark commercials. This wasn't just my first Mother's Day, a little play to be acted out. It was a day rife with barbed memories and painful loss for the boy and the man whom I'd only gained through inheritance. I was not just the maker of PB&J and the deliverer of tidbits of facts-of-life education. I was the understudy, a replacement for the star for whom the role had been written. Shame tightened with a straight-jacket grip around me. A "real" mother would have thought about how hard this day might be for this boy.

llee——uel

That night, the three of us snuggled together on the couch, watching "Animal Planet," no one talking. As if it was the silky edge of a well-loved blanket, Max rubbed strands of my long hair with his fingertips as we watched TV. Eventually, he fell asleep there, his fingers woven into my hair, his small body's weight a comfort against mine. I stroked his powdery cheek. I followed Tom as he carried the Raggedy Andy boy up to his room and together we tucked him into bed.

When finally the two of us found our way to our bed, we both fell into it, exhaustion making our limbs limp and eyelids thick. Tom wrapped his body around mine spoon style, and I listened as his breathing slowed.

"You're a good mommy," he whispered.

It was the very best Mother's Day present I could have gotten.

Mirror Image

I stand outside of the boys' fitting room at Mervyn's Department Store, waiting for Max to come out. His pajamas are all too small and the hems of all of his pants have recently risen inches above his ankles. High waters, he calls them. We called them flood pants when I was a kid.

Max steps out into the store, walking stiff-legged and holding his shirt up to look into the three-way mirror and examine the fit.

"What do you think?" I ask.

"Yup," Max announces. "Just right and not too scratchy."

Like his father, Max has a complete intolerance for any item of clothing that pinches or scratches. I keep my seam ripper handy for removing tags from shirts for the both of them.

We find the same sweats in blue, black, gray, and red to add to our pile of T-shirts, pj's, and socks.

"How about sweat shirts?"

"Nope. Got plenty of those."

"How about undies?"

"Nope." He looks up at me with a sheepish smile. For the last few months, I've bought items and brought them home for him, but this is our first time shopping for his clothes together. He's had a major growth spurt since the wedding and needs nearly everything. But the subject of undies between us is new, and perhaps embarrassing, territory.

I'll check the size on his Underoos when we get home and I'll buy a couple of packages in the next size up. He still likes the Teenage Mutant Ninja Turtles ones the best. But I'll check that again before buying. He's already growing and changing so fast it's hard to keep up.

We stand together at the register while the clerk rings up our purchase.

"What do you say we get pizza tonight?"

"Yessssss," he replies with a pump of his fist. "Pepperoni and black olive, please."

"Got it." It's the same order every time.

The clerk, a woman about my age, smiles. She folds the clothes and tucks them into a bag, handing me the receipt. As if Max is not standing there, she speaks to me. "Your little boy looks just like you," she says.

I return her smile and look down at Max. He's grinning up at me. He and I are in on a secret and he's delighting in it. Max has stick-straight, dark hair, dark brown eyes, olive skin, and angular features. I am porcelain fair, freckled, and curvy with curly auburn hair and light green eyes. Objectively speaking, we bear zero physical resemblance to one another.

Max twitches his eyebrows at me as if to silently say, *Hear that? She thinks we look alike.*

I know that any resemblance that this clerk recognized was of her own making, but I walk out of the store happier than when I entered.

Pledge Drive

Max and I are in the car, on the way to yet another orthodontist appointment. Max is nine. KGO radio, from nearby San Francisco, plays the ad for the Cure-a-thon I've heard for years. Their perennial pledge drive.

"What are they talking about?" Max asks from the back seat.

"It's a fundraising walk they're doing. People walk a lot of miles and they get people to pledge so they can raise money for research to find a cure for leukemia." I pause, not sure if Max remembers this detail. "Leukemia is what your mom had, sweetheart."

There is a long silence from the back seat while the ad plays on.

"That sucks," Max grumbles.

I'm confused. Max is by nature kind and generous. Maybe he just didn't understand. "It's a nice thing to help search for a cure. Don't you think? And they need money to do it. Research will help a lot of people."

"Yeah, but if they find a cure now, it's too late for my mom."

Goldfish

"I'm naming them Mike and Natasha," Max says as he gazes into the new fishbowl. He won two free goldfish at the elementary school carnival, tossing ping-pong balls into tiny bowls. His free fish just cost us fifty bucks worth of supplies at the pet store. Bowl. Food. Fishnet. Blue gravel. Underwater scuba guy. That carnival booth ought to come with a warning label.

"Mike and Natasha? Where'd you get those names?" Tom asks.

"Just look at them," Max explains. "What else would you call them?"

Tom shakes his head. "Can't argue with that, I suppose." His face is so tender that I fall in love with him a little more right that minute.

We get Mike and Natasha settled on the nightstand in Max's room. I give him all of the cautions about overfeeding. "Just once a day," I say. "Too much and it'll make them sick."

"We don't want that, do we, Mikey? We don't want you and Natasha sick," Max says in a soothing baby-talk voice, petting the side of the bowl.

"And we'll have to clean the bowl now and then so it stays clear and clean."

"Okay," Max replies. "I promise to take good care of these guys." He's mesmerized looking into the bowl, watching the matched pair of golden jewels navigating their new sea.

After supper and bath, Max scampers downstairs in his jammies. Long johns with little spacemen on them. "Hey, come look at Mike and Natasha! They've learned a new trick!"

"Trick?" I ask.

"Mike can swim upside down and Natasha swims in circles."

Tom shoots me a quick, worried glance. We ascend the stairs to find Mike floating belly-up and Natasha swimming spastic circles at mid-bowl level. Max's face is painted of pure joy, showing us the new "tricks" his pets have learned.

"Did you feed them again, Skibber?" Tom asks. The gentleness in his voice makes me want to weep.

Max wags his finger. "Nope," he says, his exuberance undaunted. "Only once a day. I remember." I wonder if I wagged my finger when I told him not to overfeed.

Tom and I have an entire conversation in glances. I notice a soap bubble clinging to the glass at the water's surface. "Um, honey. Did you put anything in the water?" I ask. I'm trying to make my voice as light as whipped cream, but I feel the brick weight of it in my throat.

"I washed the bowl super good. You said we had to keep it clean."

Tom and I engage in another round of silent conversation. Tom kneels down next to Max and looks into the bowl. His voice is wrapped in cotton batting. "Skibber. I'm sorry, but I think Mike has died."

Every muscle in Max's face changes from taut to slack. The corners of his mouth wilt. With kindness and gentleness in a quantity I've underestimated, Tom pulls out the details from Max. He'd used the net to put the fish into a water glass while he washed the bowl with Mr. Bubble bubble bath to get it *extra clean*. Then he returned Mike and Natasha to their new bowl. "Let's get Natasha out of there," Tom whispers. "If we give her clean water, she might be okay."

Together we complete the transactions of one fish to a water glass, the other to a small box with a nest of tissue. I scrub the bowl, the gravel, and the scuba guy for the second time in the same day, triple rinsing the Mr. Bubble from the mix, and reassemble the watery world just as it was. I introduce Natasha to her new single life, letting her slip from the small net into the water, hoping against all hope that her sideways swimming rights itself. We take the small box with Mike inside, and bury it in the back yard. Max makes a headstone of white rocks, then plucks a sunny yellow dandelion and places it on top. Then he slinks back into his room.

Max stares into the bowl watching Natasha, his eyes dewy. We wait. After a few hours, the little jewel stops her staggered swimming and floats to the surface.

"I killed them," Max says between tears.

It feels as though my heart is a throbbing bruise. I wish I'd never mentioned the need to keep the bowl clean. My too-tidy boy doesn't need such admonishments.

"I killed Mike and Natasha," Max repeated.

Tom wipes a tear from the corner of his eye. "Aw, honey. You were trying to do a really good thing. You just didn't know. It wasn't your fault. I'm sorry about your fish. But it's all fixed now. Now you understand better. We'll get two more fishes and they'll really like the blue rocks and the scuba guy."

Max covers his face with his hands. "I never want any more fish," he says. "Never ever."

"You might feel differently after a while," I say.

"Never," Max says. The muscles in his jaws tighten.

Fifty bucks worth of fish supplies are placed in the basement, waiting for this boy to change his mind. Waiting for his grief to pass. But this is a boy of his word. This is a boy who knows he can tolerate no more losses.

Five years later we sell the whole kit for three dollars at a garage sale to another kid who's just won goldfish at the school carnival.

Family Portraits

I study the collection of framed photos on the scalloped side table in the living room of our new house. It's the first home that the three of us chose together and we've just moved in. Most of the boxes are unpacked. I framed the photo of my mom sitting on a paper moon. I've always loved that picture.

My grandpa in a sepia portrait, looking dapper and dignified.

Tom's parents, in a wood frame that Tom made himself. In the photo, his mom stands on a box. She was so tiny, she was still a head shorter than Tom's dad. I wish I'd had the chance to meet them, but they were both long passed by the time Tom and I got together.

A photograph of Janet, forever preserved in her youth, holding toddler Max on her hip.

Verna and Karl, Janet's mom and dad, on their wedding day.

A family picture of the three of us: Tom, Max, and me, Tom's arm around my waist, Max leaning against me. Looking at that picture gives me an unnamable kind of joy.

A small picture of Tom at about twenty-five in a heart-shaped frame, bearded, with an embroidered shirt. It's how he looked when I first met him. Another small photo, this one of me at about six with pale, wild hair, big eyes, lips tucked in. Looking at photos of me as a child might lead a person to think I'd been raised in a dark closet, allowed out only seconds before the photo was snapped.

Max sidles up next to me. "Whoa," he laughs, pointing at my picture, covering his snicker with his other hand. Max always laughs at pictures of me as a kid.

"Go ahead, laugh," I chide. "Someday you'll be grown up looking at pictures of your silly self. Then we'll see who's laughing, buster." I poke Max in the ribs and he squirms.

Max cannot contain himself. "But your hair! Did you stick your finger in electricity or something?"

We laugh together.

A new question forms on Max's face as he continues to study the arrangement of photographs. "You don't have any pictures of your dad."

Oof. I didn't anticipate this question, though it seems odd that I wouldn't have. I've never talked to Max about my dad. It's not an easy subject. It strikes me, quite oddly for the first time, that I am like Max in that I lost a parent at a young age. I've never connected this similarity before and, in this moment, I know why. My losing my father was nothing at all like Max's loss of his loving mother. Loss, it seems, comes in different hues.

"No," I say. "I haven't put any pictures of my dad out."

His voice is light and musical. "How come?"

The air in the room has thickened. "This might be hard for you to understand because you have a really good daddy, but my dad wasn't a very nice man. I don't really like having pictures of him around. I've got some in a box, but I just look at those now and then. Not every day, like these. The rest of these pictures make me feel really happy."

The question on my boy's face does not go away. "He's dead, right?"

"Yeah, he died when I was thirteen."

"And he was *really* mean?"

"He was."

"Were you sad when he died?"

My pulse pounds behind my eyes. I want to tell the truth, but Max is eight and his life has been untouched by the kind of cruelty I knew when I was his age. How do I tell him this truth, my truth?

"Part of me was sad," I answer. This is technically true. I can't say to my small boy that by the time I was thirteen I'd wished my father "gone" a thousand times, though I didn't ever explicitly wish for him to die. His death at age forty-eight, just five years older than Tom is now, was sudden and shocking. For a long time I thought—magical thinking being what it is—that I had somehow killed him with my wishes. I tried to feel guilty about this, but couldn't. I consider the commitment I've made to myself never to lie to my son, so I decide I must tell him the other part of my truth, too. "But part of me was glad my family and I didn't have to be around someone so mean anymore. I feel sad saying that, but it's the truth."

Without a beat of hesitation, Max looks up at me. His face is a boy's face, but the expression in his eyes seems ageless and ancient. "I'm not sad if mean people die." There's no unkindness in his voice. Only an innocent's black-and-white notion of justice. "Your mom is super nice, though."

"She is."

"I'm glad you have a nice mom."

"Me, too." And I am. I count myself rich and fortunate for this.

Max picks up the picture of the three of us, the one I like so much and the picture of his mom holding his toddler self. "I have a really nice dad and two super nice moms."

My happiness cannot be measured. I kiss the top of his head. "Thanks, bud."

Our first family portrait. 1992.

Small Comforts

I f I close my eyes, I see my mother in her hospital bed. After more than fifty years of smoking—at last count four packs a day—her lung tissue is so fragile and thin that it could not withstand the air pressure of the oxygen that tubes pumped into her during surgery. And now those tubes cannot be removed without risking her life. Her flimsy lungs are like wet tissue paper and cannot contain the forced air, so that air leaks through them and seeps from her lungs into her chest, then inflating her entire body. Unconscious and writhing, her body inflates. My slim, slight mother becomes a Macy's Thanksgiving Day Parade balloon, near double her size. Her face, her hands, her breasts, her lips, her feet all expand to monstrous, unearthly proportions, an overfilled inner tube ready to pop. Her fingers and toes are swollen sausages. Her lips would be comical if they didn't look so painful. It looks as though she might float above the bed at any moment.

Once we learn that her only living fate is a perpetual state of what we see now, my siblings and I make the agonizing choice to allow her struggle to end, to untether her from the tubes and wires that simultaneously sustain her and torture her. We will not hasten her passing, nor will we interfere with it. We stand around her, each touching her. Dianne and I hold onto one another. John can barely make eye contact with any of us. Our oldest sister, Jan, a nurse, monitors the monitors. Our oldest brother, Rich, has crossed the country several times during Ma's illness. He's back in Atlanta tending to his family at this moment and I'm glad he's spared of this because I know it would tear him up. The geographical distance in our broken family gives him a special brand of pain right now. Once the tube is pulled from Ma's throat, together we watch her body deflate, her balloon-taut skin wither to the natural crepe of a seventy-two-year-old woman who has smoked for nearly sixty years. For the next hours I recognize my mother again. I'm able to say hello again to a mother I recognize as my own, only to say good-bye to her one last time. Then the monitors stop beeping and the screen's green-lined mountain ranges that show her heartbeat and respiration that we've all been watching for hours go flat. She never regains consciousness.

It is the epitome of mixed emotions, this ending. It is the end of her suffering. It is also the end of my having a mother.

With Dianne as my companion, I drive back to Marin County after six days in California's Central San Joaquin

Valley. The days before are a blur. My siblings and I have closed out my mother's accounts, paid her bills, sold her mobile home and her car. One evening we spent sorting through photographs, my older siblings filling in some of the blanks for me about relatives who died before I was born, identifying mystery faces in photos I've seen for years. We laughed at our young selves. Unceremoniously, Rich tore up a group of photographs from the fifties of a woman wearing a black-and-white pleated skirt. I've always wondered who that was in the picture. "We don't need to keep those," Rich announced as he ripped them. My older siblings exchanged a look that tells me these were photos of a woman my dad had an affair with long before I was born. I push down the urge to fish for details. It's not the time. I just wonder why my mom kept the photos all these years. We've donated all that wasn't treasured or junk. Most of what she had was junk, so we hired a hauling crew to take it away. After it was all done Rich flew back home to Atlanta. Ma's body is likely being cremated at the very moment that I haul my suitcase across the threshold of my home after dropping Dianne off at her house.

I'm unspeakably tired, so tired that it feels as though my veins are filled with lead.

I press the button to listen to messages on our answering machine. *Sending love. So sorry to hear about your mom. Let me know if you need anything.* Loving friends. Kind messages. I cannot listen to them all right now and don't know why I pushed the button at all. The dining room table boasts a vase of white roses and yellow snapdragons and a card that I'll read later is suspended on a plastic stake amongst the blooms. It's two o'clock. Tom is still at work and Max still at school. After so many days of talking and making decisions, packing up rusty, banged-up cookie sheets and chipped knick-knacks, signing documents, I'm happy to be alone for a few moments. But every time I close my eyes I see that macabre Macy's Thanksgiving Day Parade balloon that was my mother's body during her last hours in this world. I wish I could take back those moments of her misery.

My siblings and I are now the highest limbs on our living family tree: no parents, no grandparents left above us. I feel as if I'm in a house with no roof, nothing above me to protect me from the elements.

I try to nap, to chase away the sleeplessness of the last days, but sleep won't come. I turn on the TV just to distract myself. Oprah has gotten slim but her hair is gigantic. So is the hair of all of her female guests. Big hair. Big shoulder pads. Big earrings. When did everything get so big? Local news follows. It's always the same. Murders. Car accidents. Political scandals. The TV noise is a distracting swarm of gnats. My head pounds. I curl up on my bed, pull the ugly brown afghan I took from my mom's house—the one she crocheted—around me. It smells of cigarette smoke, which pulls barking sobs from my belly through my throat and out into the room.

I must have slept because when I next open my eyes, the light is different in the room. Shadows play on the walls and I hear the front door bang closed downstairs. There can be no secrets in this old house; every noise can be heard from everywhere. I hear Tom's heavy footsteps on the stairs, followed by Max's lighter ones.

Tom sits next to me on the edge of the bed. He strokes

my cheek with his fingers. Kisses my forehead. Asks me if I'd like him to bring me anything. The thought of food makes my stomach turn over, but a glass of wine sounds like heaven, so Tom leaves to fetch me one. His touch is comforting, his voice reassuring. His kindness is a balm, but I don't know how to tell him about the parade balloon that was my mother and the beeping monitors and how long it took for them to go silent.

The door creaks. Every joint and hinge and floorboard in this house has something to say.

Like a cat, Max takes silent steps into the room until he is standing beside me. He is ten, still just little boy enough that it makes my heart leap when I see him. He is still young. He has a long time on this earth. He is my son and he knew my mother. She was his grandma for three years. I only hope he will remember her as he grows. If Tom and I have other babies, they'll have never known my mother or my grandfather and I find this fact impossible. How can people so important to me never have a chance to meet one another? I grieve for Max, that he had such a short time with her. I wanted my children to have her as a grandma for all of their growing-up years, the way that I had my grandma and grandpa. I grieve for my future child and pray to a god I'm not sure I believe in that I can be a strong branch in the tree above my children. As I think of this, my ribs contract and threaten to crush my beating heart.

I can feel Max standing over me before I even open my eyes. His warm brown eyes find mine and he rests his small hand on my shoulder. "I'm really sorry your mom died. It's okay if you need to cry," he says with wisdom and compassion that no boy of ten should possess. But

Max always surprises me in these moments. This is a boy who knows, long before he should have, how hard it is to lose your mother. His words are the kindest words that anybody has ever said to me.

Footprints and Angels

If I can trust my math, Tom and I conceived within hours of our decision to start trying to have a baby, validating my lifelong feeling that I'd get pregnant the very first time I had unprotected sex. When, only a few weeks later, I had to force the driver to stop the commuter bus on my way into work so that I could puke over the railing of the Golden Gate Bridge, I already had a strong suspicion that I was pregnant. On the way into work in San Francisco's financial district that day, I bought an EPT pregnancy test at Walgreens and got my confirmation in the ladies' room at work.

It's an odd place to discover life-changing news, the bathroom at work. I worked for Wells Fargo at the time, offering counseling assistance to employees and their families. As usual, the day provided enough distraction to keep me focused, with four different bank robberies and an employee in a domestic violence crisis to respond to, so I could resist the urge to call Tom. I wanted to tell him in person.

My job at Wells Fargo was to assess, over the phone, all kinds of mental health needs and the need for trauma counseling or on-site trauma debriefing after robberies and critical incidents in branches all over the country. Most people don't go to work expecting to be the victim of a felony, but it happens in bank branches a lot more often than most people know. One of the tellers, who'd been robbed at gunpoint that day, was eight months pregnant. When I first started working at Wells Fargo, I was shocked to learn that bank robbers often select pregnant or elderly tellers as the target for robberies because they anticipate no resistance. Fewer robberies involve male tellers. I listened to the pregnant teller on the phone, who was sharing how it was her last day before maternity leave. She was having her first baby. She talked of how she hadn't been afraid for herself, but that she was terrified the robber would hurt her unborn child. "It's the first time I've really felt the maternal instinct kick in for real," she said. I thought about that pink line on my pregnancy test and about how I'd only just learned of this tiny collection of cells, but that I'd already begun to love what Tom and I had created out of our love for one another.

After seeing several friends suffer through infertility, I was grateful not to have that struggle. I told Tom about the baby that evening, after we'd tucked Max into bed. He lay beside me, resting his head on my shoulder, rubbing my belly. "Hello, little baby," he said. "You picked a really good mommy."

Happy, salty tears ran down my face.

"I know you're already pregnant, " Tom said, between kisses. "But maybe we could just practice trying for a while more. Make sure we get it right."

I didn't mind the extra practice at all.

‹‹‹———›››

My mom had died just a few weeks before Tom and I decided to try to get pregnant—or at least stopped trying *not* to get pregnant. Everybody grieves differently. Profound losses are often clarifying, giving a new sense of scale for measuring what's important. The trivial distractions of daily life become unimportant. Loss reminds us how little time we have, clarifies how we want to spend it, and puts a neon light on what we should no longer waste time worrying about. I've made some of the biggest decisions of my life in times of grief.

After Ma died, I no longer cared about our budget, about how the house needed a new foundation, about how we'd get the money for it. It never seems like a perfect time to have a baby, never the right time to lower your income and increase your expenses. But the hole that my mother's death left in my heart ached to be filled. After weeks in hospital rooms, I longed for some good news. A baby, loved and wanted, adored even before its conception, was just the right bit of miraculous good news that our whole family needed. I'd been Max's mom for nearly three years and adored every second of it. I wanted him to have a sibling. With my mom gone, I was aware that siblings would be the family we'd have when our parents leave this earth. I had mine. I wanted Max to have his.

A couple of weeks after I found out I was pregnant,

my extended family gathered at my house for dinner just days before my brother John's wedding.

"I have a little eensy, weensy bit of bad news," I told them. "Looks like I won't get to enjoy any of that fabulous champagne you guys bought for your reception."

Everyone looked at Tom and me with puzzled looks. Tom beamed. John got it first. "Really?" he said, looking at me. His face glowed with joy. Ma's death just weeks before his wedding had added an extra heap of grief on him. This was the first big smile I'd seen on his face since Ma died.

I couldn't help but grin as it dawned on each of my family members what was happening. Jim started laughing and patting Tom's shoulder with congratulations. Dianne got tears in her eyes and jumped out of her seat to hug me. Max, Megan, and Matt remained puzzled.

"Betsy can't drink any wine because she's going to have a baby," Tom said, clarifying it for the kids. "That means you'll be a brother in about seven months, Skibber."

"And I'll be a cousin again," Megan sang. She was eleven and promised babysitting services.

"Me, too," Matt echoed.

Our niece, Michelle, now sixteen, applauded, her face the picture of delight. I knew she'd be a beautiful cousin-auntie.

Max's mouth flew open and he jumped out of his seat. "Yesssss!" he said with a pump of his fist.

"You'll have a baby brother or sister for Christmas," I said. "Maybe even Christmas Day."

"Brother," Max announced. It was not a question. He nodded and fist-bumped his cousins. "I'm gonna have a brother." He pranced and marched around the room.

"Could be either a brother or a sister," I said. "We don't know yet."

"Nope. It's a brother."

Tom shrugged. No sense talking about it now. We had time to get him used to the idea of a sister if I was carrying a girl.

In the coming weeks I felt as though my body was about fifty percent miracle and fifty percent hostile takeover. Smells became assaults. I couldn't tolerate the olfactory invasion of the detergent aisle in the grocery store, scented candles, or the smell of gasoline at a filling station. Nausea was not just in the morning, but all day. I could eat only the simplest of foods: toast, ramen, oyster crackers. I couldn't tolerate preparing meals that included meat; the odor and texture of raw chicken sent me running to the nearest bathroom with my hand over my mouth. I'd never been able to sleep on planes or on car trips, but suddenly I was falling asleep on the bus coming home from work. I'd sleep through my stop and have to call Tom from Fairfax, the next town over, to come pick me up at the end of the bus line. It felt as if I'd been shot with an elephant tranquilizer!

Despite my hormonal hurricane and constant barfing, I grew splendidly happy. I was already a happy mother with Max as my boy. Adding a baby to the family, giving Max a sibling, seemed just the right bow to tie onto our perfect package. I gathered clothing and toys from local garage sales. Our upscale neighbors had bigger budgets and bought designer baby stuff that we couldn't afford, so their garage sale cast-offs felt like a luxury. The stack of tiny onesies and adorable rompers from Baby Dior grew right along with my belly.

Tom joined me for the first several appointments with my OB/GYN. Sylvia Flores had been a friend before she was my doctor. Her son played on the same soccer team as Max. We were in trusted hands and it comforted me that the woman who would deliver our baby shared my mother's first name. It gave me the feeling that a little piece of my mom was with me through the pregnancy. We listened to the oceanic noises of the first ultrasound at about the twelve-week mark and watched the tiny phantom image floating on the screen.

"Not much of a looker yet," Tom said as Sylvia pointed out the head and the site of future eyes.

"He'll get cuter," Sylvia said with a laugh.

"Is that *he* in the specific?" I asked. We'd decided to find out the gender as soon as possible so we'd have plenty of time to get Max used to the idea of a sister, if necessary. I didn't want the day the baby was born to be a disappointment for him.

"Hard to say this early. But sometimes, if the little ones pose just right—" Sylvia said. "Let's see if he shows us his secrets." She moved the stylus across my gel-covered abdomen.

Tom held my hand as we studied the screen, which looked to me more like outer space than the inside of my body. We watched as the little alien life form stretched and turned, floating among the white-pixel Milky Way.

"There, we have it." Sylvia pressed the button on the machine, snapping another photograph. "Yep, definitely a penis," she announced.

Tom squeezed my hand. He hadn't said so, but I'd known he preferred to have another boy.

When Max got home from school, we told him he would be getting the brother he'd wanted. He jumped out of his chair and stood, karate-man style, and made multiple Ninja-move chops, saying "Yess! Yess! Yessssss!" after each chop.

"But what if it had been a girl?" I asked.

"It isn't," Max said. "It's a boy. I knew it was a boy."

I was clearly the cootie-bearing gender to this ten-year-year old. I would soon be outnumbered three to one in our house.

A few weeks later, I went alone to Sylvia's office on my way into work. Tom was saving his days off so he'd have maximum paternity leave time, and the check-up was routine. As usual, Sylvia greeted me with a hug and warm inquiry about how I was feeling.

"Emotionally, great," I said. "Minus the fact that an American Express commercial made me cry the other day."

Sylvia laughed. "Hormones. Does it every time. How about physically?"

I shared my litany of discomforts and tales of my constant and increasingly inconvenient vomiting. I'd actually thrown up into a trashcan at work, unable to make it to the restroom down the hall. "But I assume this is just par for the course," I said. "I'm not complaining."

"Those are the usual symptoms, though you did get them early and pretty intensely. Let's take a look at the little guy," she said.

I hadn't known we'd be doing another in-office ultrasound. I'd already been marking each developmental milestone. I'd been reading the maternity bible of the 1990s, *What to Expect When You're Expecting*. And at each stage of the baby's development we'd found a food to compare the baby's size to so that Max could understand. The baby had been a peanut and a lima bean, a grape and a jumbo olive. We were a couple of weeks away from entering the stone-fruit period.

Sylvia applied the cold gel onto my belly. "Does anyone ever get used to that feeling?" I asked.

"No," she said with a wink. "It's just the beginning of all of the strange things you'll be going through and that you'll never get used to."

Sylvia passed the stylus over my abdomen and looked up at the screen. "Hmm." A crease formed between her brows. She turned up the volume on the machine and the sloshing sounds of the underwater world grew louder. "Hmm," she repeated.

I felt my face grow hot. "Anything to worry about?"

Sylvia turned her face toward me. She wore a broad smile. "I'm pretty sure we have two babies in there. I'm hearing two fetal heartbeats. But one seems to be fainter."

My ears rang as I heard the power of my blood flowing past my ear canals.

"Twins?"

Sylvia nodded. "Let's look closer." She moved the magic wand on my belly again, scooping it around from side to side. As I watched my two tiny inhabitants, I felt like one of those boy cartoon characters when he sees a pretty girl cartoon character walk by, with his eyes popping out of their sockets. The only thing missing was the *Ahh-ooo-gah* blast and steam blowing from my ears. Sylvia pointed out two heads, two spines, four legs, four arms. I stared in disbelief. "This would explain how quickly you had pregnancy symptoms. With double the baby, the hormones come on pretty rapidly."

"But I've had two sonograms before this. How come we didn't see two?"

"It's tricky to see them at first. One guy was hiding behind the other, I suppose, and the heartbeat is really faint at that stage. And the second baby is a lot smaller. It was easier for him to hide out." She started pressing a button that snapped pictures and labeled Baby A and Baby B. My heart galloped, terror and excitement indistinguishable from one another.

"And are they both boys?"

Sylvia squinted as she studied the screen. "It appears that the two babies share one amnion but they have two chorions." She must've registered the confusion on my face. "That means one large outer egg sac holds them both, but they're each in their own separate inner egg sac. That means that they're necessarily identical, and both boys. They don't share a single chorion. That would mean risk for conjoined twins, which, thankfully, isn't a concern. These two little fishes each seem to be swimming in their own private ponds."

She explained that everything looked just fine, but that twin pregnancies could be harder and have more complications, so I'd need to be monitored more frequently, and might need to start maternity leave sooner than I'd anticipated because twins often arrive before full term. "Our goal here is to keep those little guys in there cooking just as long as possible," she said. "You're not very tall, so they don't have a lot of room. You're going to look very pregnant, very soon." As she explained the details, it felt as though my heart had climbed into my throat. I hadn't been afraid of pregnancy to this point, but with twins and all of the added risks, now I was terrified.

The news was exciting, and scary, and I couldn't help getting nervous about telling Tom about how our financial concerns just got doubled. I vividly recalled the first time we'd talked about having children and how clear Tom had been. *Max is enough for me*, he'd said. He'd talked of his willingness to have another child, but had been crystal clear that, given his age and income level, he felt he only had resources for one more child. I knew Tom well enough to know that he'd love and care for whatever children, in whatever quantity, we brought into the world. Still, I already felt so overwhelmed that I dreaded facing his being worried on top of it. I went straight to work from my appointment and waited the day out. Anticipating my conversation with Tom made the day feel like a month.

At home, before supper, Tom and I sat together on the wicker love seat on the front porch of our craftsman fixer-upper. It was a cool April day and the trumpet vines on our front gate were doing a spectacular job of showing off their new spring garments. My palms started sweating. He talked about how we needed to get the palm trees in the front yard trimmed and that, because they were so tall, it would cost about twelve hundred dollars. Then he started talking about other fixes he thought we should take care of before the baby arrived.

"That heater grate in the hallway isn't safe and the old furnace isn't efficient," he said. "We're going to need a new furnace eventually, but I'm not sure that's the priority right now." He talked about the peeling linoleum in the kitchen and the wobbly railings on the back deck. I tried to listen, but all I could think about was how to tell him about the twins.

"I got some news from Sylvia today," I said, my voice cracking mid-sentence.

He turned to me and took my hand. "I forgot you had an appointment today. Is everything okay? Are you okay?"

I realized my tone was making our situation sound more ominous than it was. While I was thinking about a complicated pregnancy and financial issues, what registered on Tom's face was fear. Tom was a man who had lost his wife. He'd suffered terrible news from doctors. He'd spent days and weeks in hospital rooms. He'd faced having to tell his son that his mother had died.

"No, I'm fine," I said. I kissed him as extra assurance. "It's just that the sonogram—" Words dried up like autumn leaves in my throat, leaving me parched.

"What?" he said. His body, so relaxed just a moment ago, was now taut.

"It's just, we saw two babies in the sonogram today."

A breeze filled the silence that hung between us, offering the scent of lavender as comfort.

"Two?" he said. His face smoothed in every direction. "Twins? We're gong to have twins?"

I nodded, and started to cry.

"Why are you crying?" he asked. "Is everything okay? Are you okay? Are they all right?"

I wiped my tears. "They're fine. I'm fine. It's just, I know you wanted only one baby, and I'll probably have to leave work earlier and for longer. And financially—"

Tom pulled me toward him and wrapped his arms around my shoulder. "Give me a second here to soak this in," he said. He rocked me and I felt myself calm. "Well, maybe the palm trees and the heater can wait for a while."

I laughed. "That's your reaction?"

He shrugged. "I don't know. It's just that's where my head was. I'm adjusting." He kissed me sweetly. "Twins? Really?"

"I was kind of afraid you'd be mad."

He shook his head. "Mad at who? It's not like you did this on purpose." He grinned. "Or by yourself. Seems like we both did this."

"I suppose we did. And you're okay with it?"

He pulled me back toward him and we leaned back together. The lavender breeze sent another dose of comfort. "Let's treat this like really good news, huh? We'll figure everything out."

In the following minutes, and days, and weeks, and years, I'd learn again and again not to be afraid of Tom's reactions to any news I had to share with him. I'd come to understand that my fears had nothing to do with him, but that they'd sprung from the roots of my own history with a bombastic dad who exploded and blamed my mom for every mishap or unanticipated event. He'd rage if the hot water heater needed to be replaced, as if my mom had caused it. He'd scream at John if he got the hiccups, telling him to shut up. He'd go ape if one of us spilled something or broke a dish, or forgot to close a kitchen drawer. It would take me a long time, but eventually I would learn that with Tom as my partner, I didn't need to fear his rage. There was nothing I ever needed to fear with Tom.

After the initial shock of it wore off, Tom and I started to feel excited about having identical twins, the first either of us knew about in our extended families. Verna, a twin herself, was especially thrilled. "I finally get my twins," she said. The difference between the impending arrival of two babies instead of one didn't just double, but multiplied. My girth multiplied as well. At five months I was already in full waddle mode. I couldn't imagine lasting nine months. But that became my goal. All the statistics led us to believe that the babies would likely arrive weeks before their Christmas holiday due date, so we began readying our home. Soon gifts began to arrive, in double scoops, two of everything.

Like all of the rooms in our old fixer-upper, the future nursery was a hazard of cracked plaster, antiquated wiring, and sticking windows, all of which Tom would be fixing during evenings and weekends.

Over the next weeks, we had to get a bigger car, one that could accommodate two car seats and that also had room for Max in the back seat. The twins' room was undergoing a transformation, and every day seemed to involve another delivery.

"Wow, babies sure do need a lot of stuff," Max commented as he carried in another UPS package from the front porch.

"They sure do." I was feeling a little bowled over by it all, too. I felt a twinge of worry. A baby was already a stage hog, but having twins as younger siblings was the ultimate in being upstaged. "Hey, bud. You know you'll always be my first kiddo, right?"

Max's face broke into a grin. "I know," he said. "Hey,

look at this!" he said, opening a box containing two baby baseball gloves and two identical pinstriped jammy sets. "Maybe we should have six more boys. Then we could have a whole team!"

My worry disappeared as easily as that. Max was just as excited as Tom and I were, and showed not one molecule of jealousy.

"Baby A is right on par," Sylvia said as she showed me the newer, higher-resolution sonograms. She'd sent me to an imaging center to get more detailed analysis of the twins' development.

Tom sat beside me in Sylvia's office, his eyes glued to the images before us.

"But Baby B is just not growing at the same rate. "

Sylvia went on to explain that in addition to sharing a single outer amniotic sac, the babies were also sharing a placenta. "This isn't uncommon with identical twins," she explained. Not uncommon, but definitely an issue. Sharing a placenta meant that the babies shared a single circulatory system. "Baby A's heart is bigger and pumps harder. So his chorion—the inside egg sac—is getting bigger than his brother's. He is getting more nutrients, more blood, more amniotic fluid."

She suggested amniotic reduction. The same kind of needle that they use to draw amniotic fluid for an amniocentesis is used, but they actually reduce the amount of fluid in one baby's egg sac to encourage the other baby's growth. She explained the physics of it all and that we might need to do this multiple times over the next weeks.

"But it won't hurt Baby A, will it?" Tom asked. I loved that he was already protective of both of the babies.

Sylvia explained that this procedure was no more dangerous than the amniocentesis I'd already undergone. I could see the relief on Tom's face, but I felt none of it. I recalled all of the disclosures and warnings for our routine amniocentesis weeks earlier. We'd calculated the risk and taken it like so many expectant parents do. I silently braced myself against the fear of rolling those dice multiple times, increasing the odds of problems due to the amniocentesis itself. But Sylvia thought this was the best strategy for the health of both babies and I trusted her implicitly. We did the procedure the following day.

As I approached the beginning of my sixth month, on Sylvia's advice, I decided to reduce my stress and go on maternity leave early. Though I'd wanted to work as long as possible, I had to admit that I was relieved. My work was stressful. Getting to and from work on the bus was an ordeal. By the end of each workday, my feet looked like over-risen bread dough and I couldn't wait to take off my shoes. My Wells Fargo colleagues gave me a beautiful shower on my last day of work. I couldn't wait to get home, where I could wear sweats and flip-flops and never put on another pair of maternity panty hose again.

That night, Tom and I cuddled on the couch watching a rerun of the Tom Hanks movie *Big*. It was just the right amount of sweet and silly to capture my attention and keep it. Tom rubbed my protruding belly as we watched and the babies moved in response to his touch. "I'm glad you're off work," he said. "Time to just stay home and let the babies grow."

"I know, but my salary—"

"Shhh," Tom said. "Doesn't matter. We'll figure it all out. Right now you have only one thing to worry about."

And worry I did. I've always had overactive worry glands. With the sudden absence of work and commuting, I had more time to obsess. While Tom was at work and Max at school the next day, I went to the library. I pored over books about pregnancy, twins, birth anomalies, premature babies. We did two more amniotic reductions in the first week I was off work, trying to get Baby B to grow, but there'd been only a small amount of change. My new goal became carrying both babies to eight months. I figured that by that point, they'd be little, but they'd be strong enough to be okay.

Whenever Tom and Max were home, or we were out with family or friends, I did my best to wear my cheeriest, most optimistic face. We talked of baby names and return-to-work plans. But when I was alone during the day, my worry kicked into overdrive. The constant morning sickness I'd felt in early weeks had not abated as the books promised, but had worsened. I felt simultaneously huge and malnourished, hungry all the time, but unable to eat without being ill. My sciatic nerve was pinched and electric pain shot down my right hip and down my thigh whenever I walked for more than a few steps.

One night at the very end of my sixth month, Tom and I lay in bed together. The babies wiggled and kicked and turned. "Look at this!" I said to Tom. I lifted my pajama top and we watched as my belly moved, with one side going flat while the other went wide. I'd felt the babies move for weeks, but this was a whole new level. I felt elbows, knees, and heads poking around and it seemed that they were both doing somersaults.

"Calm down, boys," Tom said sweetly. "Stop rough-housing. Time for bed." Tom set his reading glasses atop my belly and we laughed watching the glasses tip and turn as each baby claimed his own in utero territory.

"This is really weird," I said.

"I think we've got circus acrobats in there," Tom said. He rested his palm against my belly and rubbed. Soon the movement settled to quieter flutters instead of the Cirque du Soleil auditions. After a while, the movement quieted and we all went to sleep.

⌇⌇⌇

Dianne and a dear friend of mine, Linda, were co-hosting a baby shower and decided to move it up to October third from our original November date. We had no idea if I'd be put onto bed rest at any moment. The morning before the shower day, I woke up feeling great. I was hungry. My sciatica pain was all but gone. The heartburn that had felt like active lava flow had cooled. I did errands and got more done in one swoop than I had for weeks. I drove to the imaging center for another set of sonogram assessments for how things were going. Tom always came to the amnio reductions, but I had to do so many of these sonogram checks that he didn't come to every one of them. We were still trying to preserve his paid days off, saving them for when the babies came home, thinking that's when I'd really need him nearby.

The young imaging technologist, one I'd not met before, helped me up onto the table. Adrianna was adorable in her pink scrubs and her jeweled hair barrettes. She was probably in her early twenties, but appeared like a young teen to me. Though I was only thirty-five, I felt huge and ancient by comparison. I knew the drill. I'd drunk a copious amount of water before arriving. I lay on the table, trying simultaneously to hold still and fighting the urge to pee. She gelled up my belly, as usual.

"How long have you worked here?" I asked.

"You're my very first solo scan," she said. Her smile was bright. "I just got my certification three weeks ago. I've only assisted before."

"That's so great. Congratulations."

I crossed my legs. "Sorry," I said. "Not peeing is the hardest part of this." The images are clearer if the patient's bladder is full, so I'd learned the abusive routine the first few times around.

"Oh," Adrianna said. "I'll do my best to hurry. I know it must be uncomfortable." Uncomfortable didn't begin to describe it.

She dimmed the room lights and squirted gel from a bottle that sat in a warming tray. She moved the wand across my belly as we continued to chat about her training and her next goals. She planned on going to med school in hopes of being an OB/GYN and this job would give her good experience and a better chance of getting into a good school. We chatted breezily about Sylvia and what a great doctor she is, about Max and how much he was looking forward to having two baby brothers.

After a moment, Adrianna stopped speaking. In the

silence, I felt my heart start to race. The young tech stood up, set the stylus down, and made a sudden turn for the door. "I'll be right back," she said, her voice filled with artificial cheer. She didn't look into my eyes. Instantly, what had been a raging urge to use the bathroom disappeared under the pounding of my heart.

Soon a man in a white lab coat entered the room. He introduced himself as Doctor Somebody, but the sirens in my head drowned out his name. "Hi, Mrs. Fasbinder," he said.

"Betsy," I said. I became utterly still. In the fight, flight, or freeze scenario, I've always been one to freeze. I get still and time slows down. I appear cool during a crisis and the impact hits me after.

"It seems the babies are a little camera shy today. Adrianna asked for my help." His was the voice of authority. I glanced over at Adrianna whose sole focus was the shiny tile floor. *She just doesn't know the procedures yet,* I reassured myself. I felt badly for her. It must've been hard to ask for help on her first solo run.

After multiple passes with the stylus, the doctor looked into my face and tugged the paper gown over my belly. "I'm so sorry, but I'm afraid the babies no longer have heartbeats. It seems that they have expired."

Expired? Milk expires. Babies don't *expire.* My breath caught in my throat. I looked over at Adrianna. Her young face had aged twenty years in twenty seconds. I coughed to keep myself from choking. "Both of them?"

"I'm afraid so."

"But I was feeling so good today. I was—" I stopped. Calm became a veil over me. With my eyes closed, because I couldn't tolerate the expressions on the faces of the doctor and Adrianna, and for fear that I might break apart, I asked, "How?"

I kept my eyes closed while the doctor explained that while we didn't have an exact cause, the probability was that the larger boy's heart had grown so much bigger and stronger than the smaller that the pressure of its pumping caused a cardiac arrest in the smaller baby. This was what we were trying to prevent with the amniotic fluid reductions. Then, with the smaller deceased, and the two sharing a circulatory system, the larger baby's heart wasn't strong enough to sustain. I recalled the acrobatics of the night before. Had that been my babies' last struggle for life while Tom and I had made jokes about them joining the circus?

I took this all in like the dry, barbed information that it was, though I didn't fully absorb any of it at the time. I was simply gathering and storing the details for later. All that registered in the next moments was a list of headlines. *Nothing you could've done. No concern about future pregnancies. I should wait at least two months before trying to get pregnant again. Twin pregnancies are higher risk.*

Suddenly I had to use the bathroom with an urgency I could not resist. Dr. Somebody helped me to my feet. As I stood I caught a glimpse of Adrianna in the shadows of the darkened room. "Please. Can you wait for me here while I use the bathroom?" I said.

She nodded.

After emptying my bladder I sat in the bathroom, rubbing my belly. I tried to remember if I'd felt the babies move that day. I couldn't. All I could think of was how good I'd felt, how much energy I had, how hungry I'd been. I could still make out the shapes of their bodies with my fingers through the wall of my own flesh. I poked. I prodded. Certainly they were just sleeping. Surely if I moved them, woke them up, the flickering lights of their heartbeats would return on the monitors. But even as I did this, I knew that it was futile. I became a zombie, moving but not alive. A weird thought hit me. Am I still pregnant if I have babies in me but they're not alive? I shook the morbid thought away.

I got dressed and stepped back into the hallway where Adrianna stood waiting for me. I knew she was an adult, but she suddenly looked like a little girl to me. I was her first patient on her first solo scan. This grief was a thousand-ply, each layer of it peeling off one at a time. I reached out and wrapped my arms around her and we cried together. I was a mother who'd just lost her babies. But Adrianna was somebody's baby, too. And her mom was not here. I wanted my mom like I'd never wanted her before. I was sure Adrianna felt the same. It tore at my heart to see her standing there looking so broken.

"I'm so sorry," she said. "I'm just so very sorry."

I pulled away from her and held her at arm's length. "This is a very bad day," I said. "For both of us. But this isn't your fault. You're going to have lots of happy moments in that room. I want you to know that." I heard my words and I meant them, but it was as if someone else was saying them. "Just promise me you won't quit. And you'll still go to med school."

She nodded.

"Promise?"

"I do," she sniffed. "Did you drive here today?"

I nodded.

"You shouldn't drive home. Would you like me to call someone for you?"

The siren in my head hummed louder. *Tom.* No, I couldn't let him get that call from someone he didn't even know. Suddenly the image of Max holding those little baseball gloves flashed in my mind. *Oh, God, how will we tell Max?* I pushed that thought away and moved into the next series of tasks.

Adrianna ushered me to a small side room and handed me the phone. In words I can't now recall, I told Tom about the babies. He said something kind, though I'd be a liar if I told you that I remember what it was. He had to ask a friend to drive him home from San Francisco because he'd taken the bus to work. He'd be there in less than an hour.

≈≈≈

Sylvia met us at Marin General hospital. She explained the details to Tom, the ones I'd already heard. She talked about how sorry she was and how nothing we did or didn't do could have caused this. I looked out the window, watching the first rain of the season dripping down the windowpane like overdue tears. It had been so sunny that very morning. Tom and Sylvia were a gray fog behind me as they talked. But her final sentence brought me back to the room.

"We'll administer Pitocin to stimulate labor, but it could be as long as three days before the babies deliver because at six months along your body doesn't really want to go into labor yet."

The thought of staying in the state of limbo for three days was a siren of an altogether more horrifying pitch; it deafened me, drowning out all the reason that's usually within my grasp. In anticipation of delivering two lifeless infants I'd steeled myself, but I'd been assuming it would be hours, not days. The thought of waiting through two or three more days of it was intolerable. "No," I said. "I'm going to deliver them tonight."

Sylvia shot a glance at Tom, then rested her hand gently on mine. "Honey, I hope that's true, but it might take longer than— "

"It'll be tonight," I whispered. The muscles in my jaw tightened so hard I thought I'd break my molars.

Tom and Sylvia had another unspoken conversation. I felt like a willful child making an unreasonable demand, but I couldn't stop. I was frozen, in a state of limbo, but I knew I couldn't maintain it for long without falling apart. I had to complete this gruesome task, and I needed to do it before my numbness wore off or I might not be able to do it without breaking.

Sylvia apologized that she'd not be there that evening, but that I'd likely not go into labor until morning at the earliest.

"It's okay," I said, my jaw still so tight I could barely speak. "I don't want you to deliver these babies. I want to save you for my happier birth."

Sylvia lifted her glasses and wiped a tear away. "I'll be here early in the morning. You rest now." I knew she was sure I wouldn't deliver until the next day, but she was also kind enough not to insist. She and Tom exchanged a whispered conversation at the door. I knew they were being rational and I was not. But it didn't matter.

Five hours later, at about 8 pm, the dream god Morpheus dulled my senses enough to deliver my baby boys, both still and silent as a winter midnight. Another male doctor, whose name I never learned, attended as my body did what women's bodies have known to do since the beginning of humankind. Morphine and grief formed a cocktail and transformed me from participant to observer in what my body was going through. I was in the nosebleed section in a stadium of a far-away event. Numb. Cold. Distant. In the periphery of my awareness, nurses attended the needs of the two babies I'd just delivered. In my stupor, I had only a vague awareness of the medical goings-on. Tom stayed at the head of the bed with me and afterward crawled into the small hospital bed beside me, wrapping his body around me spoon-style. Tom shed salty tears as the rain continued to fall.

Hours later, Tom left to get a glass of water and a nurse came into my room. "Hi. I'm Susan," she said. "I'll be taking care of you tonight." She checked monitors and changed the thick, blood-soaked pad I wore.

"I'm sorry," I said, feeling embarrassed by the mess of it all.

"It's okay. Blood is part of my job," she said. She patted me on the hip, an act of sisterly reassurance.

Once she was finished with her tasks, Susan stood at my bedside. "I'd like to talk to you now that you're alone," she said. Her voice was calm and solid. "I think it's a good idea for you to have a chance to talk. To get your questions answered without having to worry about protecting someone else."

Morpheus was waking from his dream state.

"What you've gone through today is terrible. I'm so

sorry. I'm not a doctor. But I can try to answer questions if you have any."

My lips felt thick and my tongue sluggish. The room smelled like a vitamin bottle. "What do I call this?" I asked. "Is it a miscarriage? A stillbirth?" Though it would change nothing, I needed the right word to describe it all.

Susan shook her head. Her hair was in a messy knot on top of her head, but a few stray fuzzy bits had escaped, giving her the look of wearing a halo in the dimly lit room. "What you've gone through is called fetal demise," she said. "It's a perfectly awful phrase."

It was. But then, it was a perfectly awful experience, so the words oddly pleased me.

Susan echoed some of what Sylvia and Dr. Somebody had explained earlier. She assured me that the babies had been examined and that there was no indication of any abnormalities or congenital problems. This meant that what had happened to them had no bearing on future pregnancies. The whole thing was a result of a shared circulatory system gone awry. She paused. The rain outside counted the seconds for us. "Lots of mothers find it comforting to see their babies, hold them, in such circumstances. Some like to take a photograph or have little footprints made. It can be strange to go home with nothing to remember them by. Some women regret this afterward. If you'd like, I can prepare them for you and let you see them. It's totally up to you."

I felt like a timid child. "Do you think it's a good idea?" I asked. "Seeing the babies?"

"It's up to each person, of course. But generally I think it's a good thing to do." Her words were so sure, so confident. In that moment I knew I had to see my babies. They'd been white pixels on a screen for months. I needed to see their faces, to smell their skin.

"Yes," I said. "I want to see them."

"Often dads don't want to see. That's okay too. Each of you should make your own decision."

When Tom came back, Susan told him about the option she'd offered, and that I'd decided to see the babies. "You don't have to," I said. "It's okay. But it's something I think I need to do. I just wanted to let you choose for yourself, too."

Tom stood in the darkened room, his skin blue in the dim light, the rain on the windows casting shadows that appeared as tears running down his face. "I want to stay with you, baby."

In a few moments Susan came in carrying two small, blanketed bundles. She offered them first to Tom. "I think my wife needs to hold them," he said. Susan handed the near-weightless bundles to me, neither weighing a full two pounds. I held the bundles, my mind trying to make sense of what I saw. Tom gazed out the window. The babies lay side-by-side on my lap. I opened the top parts of the blankets to see that they wore T-shirts smaller than doll clothes and little knit caps the size of shot glasses. One baby, the larger, looked like so many newborns I'd seen in my life, but was about the size of a newborn Labrador puppy. The other baby was smaller still, and perfectly formed, but his skin was dark and purple like a bruise. I released their small hands from the blankets and spread their tiny fingers. I saw that Tom looked away when I did this. "They're warm and soft," I said. My fear had been that they'd be cold and stiff.

"I let them rest under the baby warming lamp," Susan said. "It's nicer that way." It was an act of such immeasurable kindness I could hardly take it in.

I looked up at Tom. It was impossible to tell his tears from the reflected raindrops. Even the walls behind him wept. He wiped tears from his cheeks with the heels of his hands. Susan whispered to him, "Would you like to hold them?" she asked.

He shook his head and looked at me. "It's fine, baby. It's fine," I said. He turned away and pulled his hanky from his pocket and blew his nose. I kissed each of my tiny baby boys twice each on their heads. Once for hello. Once for goodbye. At my cue, Susan took them away.

After she'd left, Tom climbed back into bed with me. After an hour or so, exhaustion and morphine overtook me. "Why don't you go home, honey," I whispered.

"I'll stay."

"There's no sense in both of us getting terrible sleep. And Max needs you. He doesn't know what's going on yet." Tom had called Dianne to pick Max up from school. He was happily playing with his cousins, oblivious to what we'd just gone through.

Tom kissed my bare shoulder. His gentleness brought silent tears to my swollen eyes. After a debate in whispers, I convinced him to go to Dianne and Jim's, pick up Max, and take him home.

Of all of the pain and sorrow and sadness of that day, the worst of it was the feeling that I'd subjected Tom and Max to another round of grief. It felt so unfair. They'd already suffered through hospitals and sympathy cards. They'd already endured the cruelest loss. I wanted to shelter them from this, but it was beyond my power, as so many of the most important things are.

After Tom left, Susan came back into my room. She'd checked my IV and instructed me how to use the call button, then she stood beside me silently, looking out the window. The rain had stopped, but the glass cast a dappled pattern of shadowy droplets over her. Everyone was bathed in tears that night.

"How did you know I should hold them?" I asked her.

"Because that's what I needed. I've always been grateful to the nurse that offered me the opportunity to hold my daughter for the only time."

We sat together silently, holding hands, Susan and I. We were now sisters in an invisible sorority of women who lose babies before they're born. I silently hoped that every woman new to this horrible circumstance would be ushered into the group with the kindness Susan had offered to me.

The next day as I gathered up my things to go home, I found an envelope on my bedside table. It must have arrived while I slept. Inside the envelope were two cards, each bearing a pair of footprints, each one no bigger than a piece of candy corn and a small piece of blue paper that simply said, *Love, Susan.*

When Tom brought me home from the hospital, the house was void of all things baby. Tom had used part of the few hours he'd had at home to neatly box every onesie, every Baby Dior garage-sale treasure, and all of the gifts people had sent and had moved them all to the basement where they'd be safe, but out of sight for me, for him, for Max. I didn't know whether he'd done this just to spare me facing those items when I got home, or as an expression of his own grief. It didn't matter. When I thought of my quiet husband, alone, packing up the boxes of baby clothes, I recalled my feelings when I'd first moved my clothing into the master closet in his Pacifica home.

I thought of how he'd likely faced the task of boxing up Janet's clothing in the same way. Alone. An act of grief. An act of duty. An act of generosity.

In the coming weeks I'd come to think of my two babies as angels, though I hadn't believed in actual angels since my days in catechism as a child. But they became this to me nonetheless. Pure. Innocent. Untouched by this world. Yes, I'd think of them as angels.

Nearly three months later, after the blackest grief had transformed from feeling like a gaping wound to an aching bruise, I returned to work. I took the ferry from Larkspur to San Francisco's Embarcadero, wanting a slower, gentler ride than the bus would offer. The water of San Francisco Bay wore sequins that day, glittering in the morning light, offering me the cheeriest of all possible commutes. I sat in my window seat, trying to count the glittering reflections off the water's surface, pretending each one was one of the things I should count in my inventory of all that I was grateful for. The forty minutes allowed me to tally my beautiful, sweet husband, my adorable son, my family members and friends who'd been so exceedingly kind. I counted our in-progress home, the place that could contain the sorrow along with so many joys we'd already had there. I counted my able, healthy body that had gotten me through the ordeal and had done its level best to act as a life-giving vessel. My belly still felt soft to my touch, a deflated balloon after a party that never happened. But as my mind drifted to this sorrow, I refocused on the sparkles on the surface of the water.

I closed my eyes, welcoming the warm sunlight on my closed lids and meditated. Sorrow still hovered just below the glittering surface of my life, just as the ocean's shining surface hid its depths. But the sequined surface was a beauty to behold.

This loss, like every one I'd ever had, was clarifying. It let me know which friends brought comfort. It revealed which ones avoided the discomfort of not knowing what to say and others whose inability to tolerate the pain of such a heartbreak made it hard for them to be around me. Mostly, I experienced generosity and love in measures I'd never known was so nearby.

It felt odd to return to work, to the place where, when I'd last been there, I'd been showered with the fond wishes and generous gifts of colleagues and friends. Now I returned with no stories of sleepless nights or nursing newborns. When I got off the ferry, I wasn't yet ready to go into the office, so I decided to walk the longer way, down Market Street. Each doorway harbored one or another rag-clad person, huddled, trying to grasp the last moments of peace before they'd be roused and shooed to find another place from where they'd be roused and shooed again.

At Market and Montgomery I saw an old woman selling trinkets. I smelled her before I even got close enough to see the features of her face. Despite her foul odor, I felt compelled to examine her wares. It was junk: scratched

LPs and broken cassette tapes in a digital music age, tattered clothing, dirty Hello Kitty purses, single shoes without their mates. But sitting on her blanket, next to the rest
of the broken and worthless items, sat two small figures,
barely visible, wrapped in a wad of paper napkins.

The old woman looked up at me. She made me think
of Strega Nona, the character in the storybook I'd read to
Di's kids so many times when they were small. Her head was
wrapped in a dingy, sage-green rag. Her dress was black,
ragged, and threadbare. Her eyes hooded. Her nails, long,
yellow, and curved like talons. Her lips moved, though she
said nothing, and I wondered if she was talking to someone
only she could see. I stopped and stood across from her.

The old woman looked up at me from her seat on
a milk crate set on the sidewalk. She said nothing, nor
did I. For a moment I felt suspended there, as if time had
stopped. She looked left, then right. Without saying anything, she picked up the two figures in both hands, keeping them swathed in the blue paper napkin. She held them
out to me and, saying nothing, I took them in my hands.
I unwrapped the napkins and discovered inside two small
angels cut of white stone, identical but one ever-so-slightly
smaller than the other.

I looked back at the woman whose lips still moved,
with no words coming out. She looked at me and nodded.
Saying nothing, I reached into my purse and pulled out two
twenty-dollar bills, all that I had with me. I held the money
out to the woman and she nodded her head. Our eyes met.
I returned her nod and the old woman pressed her palm to
her chest, silently saying thank you. She reached into one
of the many bags she had arranged beside her and pulled

out a clean white handkerchief. She handed it to me and indicated with a small circle motion with her gnarled fingers that I should wrap the angels with the cloth.

While I did this, the woman must have caught a glimpse of something or gotten spooked, because she scurried to gather her things, jam them into her shopping cart, and scoot on her way.

Those angels sit on a shelf in my living room today. I see them often, and when I do I think of my two babies, of Susan the kind nurse, of the baby footprints that I tucked away into my journal. I think of the glittering water on the bay that day, of each shining light and its reminder of all that I have to be grateful for.

A week later, on my way into work, I threw up in the bathroom of the ferry. That night I told Tom that I'd bought another pregnancy test at Walgreens and that we'd have a new baby by Halloween.

Rebel Without a Clue

"You need to get a cell phone!" This is my greeting when I walk in the door. "I paged you three times," Tom says.

"Well, hello to you, too," I say, plopping my briefcase and purse on the table. "Gee, honey, how was your day?" Sarcasm drips off of my words. All I'm thinking about is going to the bathroom and then taking off my shoes. "This baby is dancing on my bladder, would you please chill?"

Tom's voice has a razor's edge. "I paged you and you didn't call me back. And you're late."

"I didn't realize I had a curfew," I snapped. "I'm twenty minutes later than I said I'd be home. Traffic on the bridge sucked. I saw the pages, but what did you want me to do? Get off the freeway to call you, then get back in traffic? By the time I did all that, I'd be home."

"That's why you need a damn phone!" Tom's face is red.

"Could you back it up a bit," I say. My words are sharp and impatient. I'm a notoriously on-time, or early, person. I resent the third degree. "Can't you just assume if I'm late that traffic sucks?"

It's 1995. Cell phones are a new phenomenon for most of us, and I loathe the idea of having one. I'm six months pregnant. My commuter bus ride into work in San Francisco has become intolerable. The fumes nauseate me. The jostling of the bus is just too much. I feel sick at the end of every ride. So I've begun driving to work. I no longer care about the ridiculous parking fees in the city and the Golden Gate Bridge tolls. "I don't want a cell phone," I say. "Nobody needs to be accessible 24/7. I'm on the phone all freakin' day at work. I don't want to be on the phone in the car."

This is not Round One of this argument. We can recite our positions word-for-word, just from the sheer repetition of them over the last three months. I'm cranky and weary of this reprisal. I wear a pager during the evening/weekend crisis on-call shifts that I cover and I already resent that intrusion, the damned thing blasting me awake and demanding that I call into the answering service. The thought of a cell phone screeching in my ear all day makes me want to scream. But Tom's heard these arguments already.

I believe reason is on my side. "I called when I left the office. I have no control over traffic. I'm always on time unless there's traffic that's beyond my control. I really don't think I need a time budget from you and I sure as hell don't need another boss—or a *dad*." I watch Tom recoil with that last word. Given my history with my dad, I've just hit below the belt. "Now, I can finish this fight with you, but it means pissing on the floor. Your choice."

Tom turns and disappears out the back door, headed to his wood shop in the basement. While I use the bathroom, I hear pounding through the floorboards. This is our worst kind of fight. One or two drive-by word-bombs, then we retreat to our separate corners. I read. Tom hammers. Admittedly, I'm the more skilled word-bomber—not a skill I'm proud of. Tom's best weapon is silence, something he shouldn't be proud of either. Conflict avoidance is my go-to strategy, but irritability has gotten the better of me. Bombs away.

We spend a chilly suppertime over takeout burritos. Max wriggles in his chair. "I don't like this. It has onions in it," he whines.

"It doesn't have onions," Tom snaps. "I told them no onions."

"It has onions. And tomatoes," Max mumbles, poking the burrito with his fork. His face droops and his words are barely audible. "Tomatoes are gross."

"Stop fiddling with that!" Tom barks. Max jumps. Tom seldom raises his voice like this. "Eat it or throw it away."

Max chooses the latter, gets up and silently scrapes his burrito into the trash. Tom and I spend the evening in a silence competition. Nobody wins.

———

The next day on my commute home, traffic is a snarled mess even before I get to the Golden Gate. Today this bridge is not an iconic landmark; it's a prison cell and there's no escape. Cars crawl from the bridge down Waldo Grade like a snake that is in no hurry to get anywhere. It's been a rugged day. I didn't sleep well for all of the fuming I did, waiting for Tom to apologize. All I can think about is getting home, taking off the maternity pantyhose that feel like an abdominal straight-jacket, and slipping into a hot bath with a cup of chamomile tea. I turn on the radio. Traffic is stalled all the way through San Rafael. "Shit!" I say aloud. I change the station to classical music. "Okay, baby," I say to the son I'm carrying. "We can't do anything, so let's just relax." I rub my belly while Mozart transports us to a more beautiful place. Then the pager blares.

I glance at it to see that it is our home number, followed by a 411. This is our family code. The 411 add-on just means "need information" or "call when you can". No crisis. 511 is not a crisis, but a little more insistent. Every number between 411 and 911 indicates a higher level of urgency. We've never used anything higher than a 511.

Ten minutes later, after Debussy has invited my baby and me into his celebration of the seasons, the pager goes off again. This time our home number is followed by a 611. Traffic is all but stopped. There's no exit nearby. Nothing to do but turn up the music. Ten minutes later, the pager blasts again with another 611.

"Your daddy could learn some patience," I say. I feel a kick down low in my abdomen. I take this as agreement. It's nice to have an on-board ally. Just as I near the exit toward home, traffic miraculously speeds up. *Finally*! I can jump off here, find a payphone and call Tom, or just charge on home. If I get lucky, I can be home in ten minutes. Surely that would be better, I reason. I take the exit and get onto Sir Francis Drake Boulevard. The slow snake has found another road to crawl. Tom pages again. Another 611. Does he think I'm not seeing these? *Jeesh*!

I finally pull up in front of our house. My feet are swollen and the sciatic nerves along my right side are sending electrical waves down my thigh. I'm locked and loaded, ready to fire my anger grenades at Tom for adding another layer of stress to my already rotten commute.

Before I even get to the steps, Tom comes roaring out the front door. As soon as I see his face, all of my muscles go slack. He is not angry, not controlling, not trying to boss me around. This is a man who is terrified. This is a man who loves me, who cares about my safety, cares about our baby's safety.

It all hits me as soon as I see his face. I have never been more wrong or more pig-headed in an argument. I'm six months pregnant. Just nine months ago, Tom and I looked into the faces of the two babies we'd just lost. Tom has endured the death of a wife. In that instant, I know that he's been suffering every moment that I've been resenting him. I can only imagine the horrible images he's been conjuring. I'm suddenly ashamed and sorry and furious at myself. It could have been prevented if I hadn't been stubborn and willful and ridiculous. I have been a rebellious child.

It's always easy to be sensitive to the fact that Max has lost his mother. I think about it every day. But I've ignored the fact that Max was not the only one who suffered this loss. Tom's quiet nature sometimes gets misunderstood as calm and easy-going. But he gets anxious and worried. He does not have to rely on imagination to know what it's like to lose someone you love. He knows.

"I'm sorry, baby," I say. "I'm so sorry I worried you. I'm such an idiot." I hold out my arms and Tom descends the stairs. We stand in our front yard holding one another while tears spill down our cheeks. "I'm sorry," I say again. "I'm so, so sorry." I'll say it a thousand more times if I need to. Tom's body melts into mine.

The next morning we both get our first cell phones.

Late Adoption

The restaurant banquet hall is packed with nearly a hundred people, most of them over seventy. At the side of the room stands a row of walkers, idle without their elderly humans who sit nearby at draped tables. Canes lean against chairs. A room full of people, many wearing hearing aids, makes for a loud roar. Tom and I, along with Janet's sister Karen, stand at the back. I'm hugely pregnant, past the point of being comfortable either sitting or standing, so I've changed positions half a dozen times. Karl and Verna sit at the head table, a spray of flowers in front of them and a banner behind them that reads *Happy 50th Anniversary*.

The day has been full of food and laughter, and the swapping of old stories among friends. Karl and Verna are fully in their element, surrounded by people they've known for decades: members of their church, their camping and hunting buddies, people from all sides of their large extended families. I've seen some of these folks at gatherings in the last four years since Tom and I were married, but many of them are new to me. I'm greeted with the same question by each new acquaintance. "You're Tom's new wife, aren't you?" And when I say yes, they speak to me in whispered tones about how sad it was to lose Janet. "Oh, I thought it would just kill Karl and Verna," one distant cousin says to me. "So sad."

I serve as Janet's humble placeholder in this crowd. By all natural rights it should be she and her sister Karen cohosting this gathering for their parents. When elderly person after elderly person tells me how profound Janet's loss was, it doesn't feel unkind. Just so very sad. I echo their sadness and tell them that I can see how loved Janet was by everyone in this room and how she passed that love on to Max. Many guests tell me of their happiness that Tom has remarried. They're full of congratulations and well-wishes for our baby to come. Grief and joy are side-by-side in this room, as they are throughout my marriage with Tom and my motherhood of Max.

"This is all so great. Your parents look so happy," I say to Karen. "You outdid yourself."

Karen thanks me for my help, though my contribution was small. With Janet gone, Karen has become the one who looks out for her parents. We've grown fond of one another. She and her girls, Simone and Alison, often join us for holiday celebrations—another branch of our complex and beautiful family tree. Karen and the children are a few more of my bonus "outlaws"—not technically in-laws, but not merely friends. Many years later Karen will write me a Mothers' Day card. In it she'll say how glad she is that I decided to join her family instead of having my head examined first—her inside joke about the workings of her own family—but how happy she is to have a second sister. I've always thought of her as a bonus sister, too. It's a card I'll treasure forever. I occasionally gather tidbits from her about Janet so that I can supplement my limited knowledge of Janet and preserve the details for Max. Karen never expected to become an only child at thirty, of course. She was cleared to be a bone-marrow donor for her sister, but Janet's condition worsened too rapidly when the short remission in her leukemia battle came to an unexpected end. There was no time for such heroic efforts.

Suddenly, the noisy conversation in the banquet room is broken by the ding-ding-ding of a spoon against a glass, and Karl rises to his feet. Verna sits beside him, so small that the table almost hides her. Max, Simone, and Alison, ages eleven, eight, and five, have been summoned by Karl and they stand beside their grandparents at the head table. Simone and Alison are dressed in Sunday best. In honor of Verna's request, Max wears a small clip-on bow tie that causes him to tug at his collar every few minutes, unaccustomed as he is to Sunday clothes in our nonreligious household.

Karl clears his throat and begins by thanking everyone for coming. He thanks Karen and me for arranging the event, and then spends a good long time boasting unabashedly about his three grandchildren. The three children squirm beside him, polite, but not quite able to stand still for the entire length of one of Karl's longwinded talks. He tells a meandering story about meeting Verna and how they built their house after the war with scrap lumber and pipe he salvaged from dumpsters. He gives one of his left-handed compliments about Verna, about how she became skilled at pulling nails from salvaged boards to use for that first house they shared in Martinez, California. They had no money for nails, and building materials were scarce after the war, even for those with money. "Oh, she bent the hell out of all of the first nails she pulled out and they weren't worth a damn," Karl says. Verna chuckles. "But she got better at it and we got that house built." He looks down at her. "Didn't we, woman?" Verna smiles her reply.

As usual, Karl's speech is a long and winding road and includes one requisite story about a rattlesnake. Just when I think he is wrapping up, he stops and looks back at Tom and me, holding his outstretched hand toward us. "And lots of you have met our newest daughter here today." My heart thrums as everyone turns to look back at us. "Tom here got remarried a couple of years back." He puts his hand on Verna's shoulder. "My wife and me are awful happy to have that girl as part of the family. And as you can see, Tom and Betsy are going to have a baby in just a little while, another little boy. She's not just fat."

Everyone laughs. As usual, Karl's been funny when he had no intention of being so. From anyone else, such a phrase could feel insulting to a woman in advanced pregnancy, but I've grown used to Karl's playful barbs and unintentional verbal clumsiness. He is blunt and gruff, but has also always been kind to me. "Oh, heck," he says. "Oh well. I didn't mean it *that* way." The group laughs again and Karl quiets the room with another ding of his spoon against his water glass. "Tom's parents are both gone. Betsy's dad died when she was young and she lost her mom last year," Karl continues. He clears his throat again. "So I guess this new baby won't have any grandparents at all.

And that's just not right." His words are spoken in staccato and he keeps clearing his throat between phrases. He pauses for a long time before his last sentence. "So Verna and me, well, we decided that we'll just need to be Grandma and Grandpa to this little guy, too."

The room erupts with an *awww* followed by applause. Tom squeezes my hand and I smile at Karl, then blow him a kiss.

He swipes his hand at me as if to erase any sentiments mushier than he intended, then pulls his hanky from his pocket and draws it across his nose. "We miss our Janet every day," he says, his voice cracking. He draws a deep breath and his voice comes back with its usual bravado. "We couldn't be more proud of Karen. And now we have two daughters again," Karl says. He raises his glass, his head shaking, and it's clear he's struggling to find his next words. Someone in the room shouts, "To family!"

"That's it then," Karl says. "To family."

My throat aches, and the son I carry gives a series of rapid kicks. "To family," I say with the chorus, raising my water glass. Tom pulls me close. Karen leans toward me. I'm filled with gratitude for my unexpected adoption so late in my life, and more grateful still that both of our sons will call these people family.

First Romance

"I need to tell you something, but don't get mad at me," Max says.

It's his first week of seventh grade. My pregnancy is advanced enough that I'm feeling like Jabba the Hutt sitting on the sofa. "What, honey? You can tell me. I won't get mad." I envision a broken dish or lost homework, or some other high crime of an innocent childhood.

"I sort of have a girlfriend," he says. His cheeks turn pink and he searches the ceiling with his eyes.

I let six heartbeats pound before I reply. This is a tender moment and I don't want to say the wrong thing. I wish I could take a photograph of the look of first love on my son's face. There'll never be another moment as pure and innocent as this one. "Why would that make me mad for you to have a girlfriend?"

"I don't know," he says. He moves an invisible object with the toe of his sneaker and studies it. Now the carpet gets all of his attention.

"I'm not mad, sweetheart. Come sit down." I pat the couch beside me. Getting up requires too much effort in my current state. "Tell me about her. Your girlfriend. What's her name?"

"Natalie." His lips twitch into a flicker of a smile when he says her name.

"Natalie, huh?" I resist a thousand simultaneous urges to wrap my arms around him. I want to smother him with kisses and tell him what a delight it is to watch him grow up, what a privilege it is to be his mom. I want to tell him about love and being kind to girls, being respectful. But this boy needs no such lessons. "How did you meet her?"

"School."

Dumb question. "What's she like?"

"She's nice."

Elaboration is not Max's strong suit. "What does this mean, being boyfriend/girlfriend?" I need to assess what the current social mores are for dating in the world of eleven-year-olds, to make sure it's all as innocent as it seems.

"I walk her to her classes and stuff."

And stuff. Adolescence has just poked its first little tendril of a vine up through the surface of our boy's childhood, the harbinger of blooms to come. I'm finding this to be simultaneously sweet and scary. Max has spoiled us, being such an easy kid. Will adolescence and girls change all of that? "That's sweet of you to walk her to class. What else goes into being her boyfriend?"

"I carry her backpack for her. It's really heavy." He looks so proud of himself. I feel proud in return. Tom is both a gentleman and a feminist. It's a tender balance I've always admired in him and it pleases me to see it in Max.

"That's very gallant of you."

"Gallant?"

"Gentlemanly."

"Oh. Right."

I want to ask if he holds her hand or kisses her, but I know this will embarrass him. I don't want him to go underground with matters of the heart. If I wait, he comes to me. Eventually. "Is that all?" I ask.

"Pretty much."

Weeks pass with occasional mentions of Natalie. Max still plays sports, comes home straight afterward. There's no "dating" of any kind, no movies, no visiting each other's houses. I occasionally check in to see if the boyfriend/girlfriend exchanges stay at the same level of innocence. They do. He gave her his Lance Armstrong Live Strong bracelet. She made him cookies once. Tom pumps me for updates now and then. I'm a better snoop than he is, but he's just as nosy as I am. Our defacto division of labor is that I do all of the interpersonal recon and Tom fixes things around the house that get broken.

Just before Halloween, Max comes through the front door after school. His backpack falls to the ground with a thud. He enters the kitchen where I'm chopping carrots for supper.

"Hey, bud!" I poise my chopping knife above the board for his customary snitching of the carrots I've just peeled and chopped, but his fingers do not approach my cutting board. The air has grown thick. I feel its weight. "How was your day?" I ask.

"Bad."

I set my knife on the board and turn to him. He is a boy version of a rag doll, limp and lifeless.

"What happened?

"Natalie broke up with me today."

His heartbreak is real. I know because I feel my own heart crack right down the middle. "Oh, honey." I reach out and wrap my arms around him. "What did she say?"

"She said things just weren't working out."

I've never seen this girl, Natalie. She's eleven. And I hate her. I hate her for hurting my boy. I hate her for breaking his heart and for using a line that should come out of the mouth of a thirty-year-old, not a girl in seventh grade. I tell myself that she's just a child, like my child. That it's wrong to hate her. I don't even believe in hating anybody. But I can't help it.

I try to comfort him, but he's beyond that. "I'm going to go get my homework done," he says. I watch the curve of his back as he walks away. After he leaves I cry a little for my sweet boy's first romantic heartbreak.

When Tom gets home, I brief him on the day's events. When Max comes downstairs for supper, Tom rests his hand on Max's small shoulder and squeezes. It's a manly gesture, an exchange between dudes. "Sorry about Natalie, Skibber," he says. "It'll be okay, though. You'll see. You're going to have lots of girlfriends."

Max's head jerks with a start. His mouth is a perfect O, wearing the expression of someone who's just been slapped. His face is a snapshot of horror for a split second before he bursts into a sob. "I don't want to feel this way a *bunch* of times!" Fat tears squeeze out of the corners of his eyes. He wipes them away with the heels of his hands.

He isn't hungry. Asks to be excused. When we look in on him after supper, his light is off and he is sound asleep, still wearing his school clothes. Tom gently takes off Max's shoes and covers him with his blanket.

Through middle school and high school, Max will not date. He is cautious by nature, but this is much more than that. I come to believe the residue of loss, for Max, is that he protects himself. He rarely takes risks. He guards his heart. It sometimes worries me that he will protect his heart too well, keeping love away. And though his first heartbreak with Natalie was of the puppy-love variety, it was enough for this cautious boy to cause him to recoil. I worry that he will build his protection too thick for love to find its way in again.

But then I recall Tom calling Dianne before asking me out for our first date. Some of this was Tom's sense of obligation to his longtime friends. But I also believe he had another motive; he was protecting his heart, testing the waters to see if my answer would likely be a "yes." I recalled that first date where he asked me about my first marriage, and then, on the first night we'd spend together, his asking about my desire for having children. He was clearing the way, finding out any obstacles before investing too much. Tom too was averse to risk. It seems that both of my guys are cautious.

All I want is for Max to be happy. All I want is for him to find someone who will welcome the special kind of love he has to offer and to love him in return. I discover in mothering Max that, irrespective of how I became his mother, my hopes for him are like every other mother's hopes for their child; I want him to find someone who will love him as deeply and wholly as I do. I believe that Max will eventually risk his heart again, but only once, and likely to the woman he ends up spending his life with. This is a theory I never share with Max.

I'm pleased, years later, when eventually my theory proves true when he finds a love who is just right for him.

Max with his love, Andrea Chao on his 30th birthday. July 2014.

Blood

With our second pregnancy, Tom and I held off telling everyone about the baby. We particularly waited to tell Max. He'd been so sad when he learned we'd lost the twins. We couldn't bear the idea of putting him through such a loss again. But the real truth was, I was scared to tell anybody. Grief and joy and fear were intertwined in those first months, a braid of emotions where one strand became indistinguishable from the others. As soon as I'd feel joy about the baby to come, fear would knot itself around my heart, and with it grief tightened its grip. I could barely manage the tangle of it for myself. Despite the enormous kindness we'd received after the loss of the twins, managing other people's fear and sorrow on our behalf felt like more than I could stand.

Most people feel comfortable telling loved ones about pregnancies after that imaginary line is crossed and the danger zone of the first trimester has been cleared. Once they enter the relative safety of the second trimester, expectant parents relax a little. They share their news, and embrace the feeling that everything is going to be fine. We had no such safety zone in mind. We'd crossed into the second trimester and had tiptoed into the third when we'd lost the twins.

So Tom and I held it close for the first few months, watched the pages of the calendar turn. We told only Dianne and Jim, asking them to keep our news private, and even them we didn't tell until after the first check-ups showed all healthy signs, and that I carried only one baby. As crushing as it was to lose the whole idea of having twin babies, I was relieved when sonograms showed only a single passenger in my womb, and happier still that the inhabitant was another boy.

～～～

One day when I was about thirteen weeks pregnant, I reached for my daily indulgence of half-and-half for my tea and realized I'd forgotten to buy some in the recent grocery run. Rather than a trip to the supermarket, I decided to go to a convenience market near our house. This was a store I rarely entered, and had likely not gone to in well over two years.

The store was operated by a family of Middle Eastern ethnicity. Indian? Pakistani? Iranian? I'd never known, and had gone in there so infrequently that we'd never made a significant connection beyond polite exchanges during our rare transactions. I knew none of their names and had seen none of the family members anywhere but in the store. Behind the counter on the day I bought cream was a woman whom I assumed was the wife of a man who often worked there. She had her two small children behind the counter with her. They'd transitioned from toddlers to little boys since my last stop in the store. Her children both had the same dark, ancient-looking eyes.

The store clerk rang up my purchase and I turned to exit the store. She reached out and rested her hand on my forearm. It stopped me where I stood.

When I turned to see the dark-haired woman, her eyes were closed, her hand still resting on my arm, but without a grip. Still, I felt unable to move, stilled by her touch. She tilted her face upward, her eyes still closed. Her fingers were long and graceful, her skin golden and glowing. "He's just fine, this baby," she said, her eyes still closed. "Perfect. Healthy."

I looked down. *Am I showing already?* My glance confirmed that my body had not yet revealed my secret. Only five people on the planet knew that I was pregnant, Tom and me, Di and Jim, and Sylvia Flores. I was only a couple of months along, so not obviously pregnant. I drew a shallow breath. The woman opened her eyes and looked straight into mine. "Not like the other two babies," she said holding up one hand and forming her fingers into a V, indicating the number two.

I bit my lip and resisted the urge to pull my arm away from her. When I returned her gaze, I could see only kindness in her eyes. This woman didn't know me. She didn't know my name, my circumstances. I hadn't laid eyes on her since just after we'd moved into the house in San Anselmo, before I was even pregnant the first time.

She blinked several times, her fingers still forming their V. "This one's heart is strong," she said. "His brothers cleared a path for him. This one, he has the hearts of two in one being." She then brought her two fingers together, keeping her hand raised. "He will be very loving, with two hearts. He will be healthy. Very strong. You can be calm now."

I suddenly felt as though I'd traveled through Alice's looking glass, straight into an episode of *The Twilight Zone*. I've never consulted a psychic or an astrologer, never had my aura read or bought crystals for what ailed me. I'm a natural skeptic when it comes to "readings" and such and tend to think that most "psychics" are either well-meaning, super-observant, intuitive people or straight-up charlatans. Then this woman, whose name I didn't know, who had nothing to gain by telling me such things, and no likely way of knowing about either of my pregnancies, touched my hand.

My skin tingled in response to both her touch, and her words. My inner skeptic told me that this was just a woman of great intuition and lucky guesses. Even with my skepticism, and on the other side, my deep desire that she was right, this felt like something more than the mere lucky guessing and vague statements offered by con artists and misguided hopefuls. All I knew was that after that initial tingling passed, I felt a sense of calm that I'd not yet felt in this pregnancy.

I looked into the woman's eyes, so dark that pupil and iris were indistinguishable, giving her an ancient look. Under her eyes she wore shadows as though her skin had been smudged with ash. I put my hand over hers and felt its warmth. "Thank you," I said. "It's kind of you to say such things."

"Truth is not kindness," she said with a soft rolling of her r's. "Is just truth."

I didn't know if this lovely woman was psychic, a medium, or channeling something I didn't understand. I don't know what I believe about such things. All I knew was that after my encounter with her, I no longer felt the need to hide our happy news.

≈

As the second trimester passed and the third approached, excitement outshouted the other feelings. The baby moved from lima bean to jumbo olive, olive to apricot, apricot to peach, and as he did, my spirit began to soar again. I asked Tom to bring up the boxes of baby things up from the basement. I unpacked the tidily folded stacks of second-hand designer baby wear and placed them into the drawers of the furniture that had once been in Max's nursery, along with some of the new items that loved ones had sent. When we had doubles of clothing, toys, and baby gear that had been bought for twins, I placed them in a separate box that we later donated to a local women's shelter. Perhaps another woman would have twin boys and be grateful for them. As I taped up the box, my little inhabitant rolled over.

"It's okay, little one," I said, rubbing my belly. "You're going to be just fine. It's all smooth sailing from here." It felt a little as though I was whistling past the graveyard, putting on more confidence than I felt, but it also felt like words I needed to hear, even if they did come from my own lips.

We decided to name the baby Samuel Joseph. My mother's father, the one whose surname I adopted as my own, was Samuel Antonio Graziani. His elder brother, Joseph, and he had been separated when Joe had emigrated to the U.S. from Italy at the turn of the century. He worked as a tailor in the U.S., sending money to his family in Italy, bringing over to the U.S. one sibling at a time, until finally, my grandfather, the youngest, and his widowed mother were brought over. By then Joe and his wife lived in Palm Springs sewing garments for Ava Gardner, Frank Sinatra, and others, with my grandfather and his mother getting only as far as an Italian/Polish suburb of Chicago, where he'd live for more than fifty years before my mom brought him and Grandma to California. It would be more than seventy years before geographic distance and limited funds would allow the two brothers to see each other again, when my grandfather was 85 and almost completely blind and his brother, Joe, was 95. I'd watched as the two brothers embraced. They held one another and wept, then would part for a moment, have a few moments of conversation of interwoven Italian and English until one or the other brother's eyes would fill with tears. Then they'd embrace again. This happened for the entire two days of their reunion. It would be the only time my grandfather would see his brother before Joseph passed away only a few months later. By the time our second son was born they'd both passed, and it felt right to unite their names forever by naming our baby after the two dear, tenderhearted men. Samuel Joseph.

Sam was due to be born on October 28th, 1995. In a move that would indicate our second son's future insistence on doing things his own way, October passed without any indication that he felt like arriving any time soon. I'd been pregnant for six months before losing the twins, had a three-month hiatus, and then got pregnant with Sam. At this point, it felt as if I'd been pregnant for a decade.

Tom took time off work after mid-October, thinking that the baby would be born within a couple of weeks. While I sat waiting, coughing, scratching, and fretting, he and Max built a beautiful shingled garden shed. It seemed to me that he needed to do something, anything to feel productive and likely to avoid stepping into the landmine of my mercurial moods.

One morning we went to the grocery store together. "My god," I sighed, walking up the front stairs. I panted. Perspiration rolled down my face and neck. Tom carried the groceries. All I could think about was sitting down, lifting my feet, and cooling the furnace inside of me that had caused sweat to run down my spine. I was sick of maternity underwear and swollen feet, heartburn, and being unable to tie my own shoes. Worst of all, I'd developed a nasty, persistent cough that kept me from sleeping. It was so raspy and hacking that I sounded like a harbor seal, and when I got on a coughing jag in public everyone stared, seemingly afraid that I was going to keel over right there. (Months later, after Sam was born, we'd discover that what I had was whooping cough.) "If this baby doesn't get born soon, I'm going to need a wheelbarrow to carry my belly in. Will he *never* arrive?"

"He's only ten days late," Tom said. It was a completely rational statement, but I was not exactly rational.

"What do you mean ONLY ten days! Carry a bowling ball in your belly for ten days and just see how ONLY it feels." I was so uncomfortable, so irritable that what I wanted was a good fight, permission to yell at someone. When I looked over at Tom, I could see he was hiding his snickering.

I stopped on the porch, breathless from the climb. "What?" I asked. It wasn't a real question. I was just gathering my arsenal for the explosion I was trying to launch. No matter what the man had said, it would have been the spark to detonate my emotional dynamite. I felt my face flush in the surprising heat of an unexpected Indian summer. Tom continued to laugh.

He set the groceries on the porch and fished his keys from his pocket.

"What!" My voice was such a shriek that it startled me. Tom's laughter was cold water on my hot mood, and I started to laugh with him. "Oh, my god, I've become a sitcom stereotype. I'm officially a crazy pregnant lady."

"I didn't buy pickles and ice cream," Tom said. "Should I go back to the store?"

I gave him a slap on the shoulder. "No, but if you say the words 'only ten days' one more time, I recommend sleeping with one eye open."

The next two days I felt more like a piece of flabby architecture than a person. Moving was a chore. My shoes no longer fit. I couldn't stand anything rubbing on my over-extended belly, on which a hot rash had developed, so painful that the only options were garments that resembled a cross between a muumuu and a circus tent. I couldn't breathe. I couldn't sleep. All I could do was wait . . . and cough.

leee̶e̶e̶l

On the morning of the twelfth day past my due date, I sat at the kitchen table with a cup of tea and a book, hoping for enough distraction to let me stop looking up at the clock. Max sauntered into the room.

"You look sad," he said.

I closed my book. "I'm not sad, bud. I'm just tired of waiting for this baby to be born."

Max grabbed a juice box from the fridge and sat across from me. "When Sam is born, will he have your blood in him?" he asked.

He'd been learning about genetics in his school science class. "If you mean my genes, then yes."

He pulled the bended straw from the side of the box and punctured the foil seal with it. "And will he have my dad's blood in him?"

"He will."

He took a long, gurgling sip of his apple juice. "And I have my dad's blood?"

I felt like a witness, being boxed in by a vigilant attorney's interrogation. Max had been thinking about this long and hard. "Yeah. You have your dad's blood and your first mom's blood. And their genes."

"And I don't have any of your blood or your genes, right?"

My throat got tight. "No. You're my son, but not from my body. You have the blood and the genes of your first mom and your dad."

I ached to tell him that blood wasn't the only important thing. That love was what bound us as family. That this baby wouldn't be more my son because he grew inside of me than Max, because Max was my son, too. But it seemed that Max needed to ask the questions he needed to ask, so I quelled my urge to reassure him.

"So this baby, Sam. He'll have your blood. And my dad's blood. And my dad and I have some of the same blood. Right?"

I thought about it. The logic was sound. I wondered what he was fishing for. "Right," I said.

"So Sam will be part of all of us, right? He has some blood from all three of us."

I stopped and looked into Max's face. He was still a boy, just eleven years old, but sometimes he seemed like a much older person. Sometimes he connected dots that nobody else would think of connecting. "Yeah," I said. "Sam has all of our blood in him. He's part me, part your dad." Max's eyebrows climbed as he waited for the next phrase. "And he's part you, too."

Max slurped the last sip from his juice box, extending the gurgling as long as possible, and smashed it flat. "So when Sam comes, we'll be a whole family. All of us. All of us will share blood."

The expression on his face was one of such relief that I knew without another word that he'd been thinking about this, perhaps worrying about, it for a long time.

"Yeah," I said, past the lump that had formed in my throat. "We will all be a family. We are all bound together by blood."

"Cool," Max said. He lobbed his empty juice box in a high arc, landing it perfectly into the kitchen trashcan. He raised both arms in a victory pose. "Yes! Just call me Air Jordan!"

With that he bounded out of the kitchen and down the back stairs. Soon I heard the sound of his basketball bouncing on the back deck, then I heard Tom's laughter and playful taunting as he and Max shot a few hoops. It was the happiest sound I could remember hearing for a very long time.

"Man. Maybe if we send in a cap and gown and some car keys, the kid will think it's finally time to come on out of there," I complained to Dianne. "And this cough is unbearable." My coughing had gotten so bad that if I moved quickly, laughed, or sang, or ate anything spicy or sweet, or sneezed, or talked too loudly, it started a coughing fit that ended up with me either throwing up or wetting myself . . . or both. Just another of the pregnancy delights nobody tells you about.

Di fully understood that every day past your due date feels like a year. Both Matt and Megan had been well past their anticipated arrival times. "I know it feels like it'll never happen, but Sam will be here soon."

Di's calm reassurance settled my nerves.

Sylvia Flores had taken every precaution with me during the second pregnancy. She'd invited me to call her any time, to stop in for extra sonograms to assure myself that the baby was fine. Everything was fine. The baby was fine. I was fine. Everything was normal but for my barking cough. But I still carried the worry and the loss and the fear. Whenever I went for more than a few hours without feeling the baby move, I'd poke and prod at my belly, getting him to stir.

"I'm afraid I'm going to give the kid a sleeping disorder," I said to Dianne. "Every time he sleeps, I poke him and wake the poor little guy up."

"That's okay," Di said. "He'll pay you back plenty by waking you up for the next year."

Halloween had come and gone. Indian Summer had

departed and the chill of autumn met us each morning. I saw Sylvia every week and she'd said that if the baby wasn't born by November 10, we'd need to induce labor.

At four in the morning on November 10, I awoke with contractions. It seemed that when threatened with eviction, Sam decided he'd arrive on his own. Just three hours later, Sylvia helped Tom and me welcome our second son into the world. Healthy, if a little bit scrawny. Despite his past-due arrival, my constant cough and frequent vomiting had prevented him from getting that last layer of baby fat before birth. With just a couple of hours from first contraction until birth, Sam arrived wearing a startled look as if he was shocked to be in the world. He was silent, eyes wide open with the whites showing all around.

Tom held him first and the two locked into a shared gaze. Finally, Tom looked over to me, smiling. "It's a little like Jack Nicholson in *The Shining*," he said.

These weren't the words a mom expects to hear from the father of her new baby, but I had to admit that it was true. Sam looked positively freaked. We laughed together and delighted in every squeak and squirm. His feet and hands were huge in proportion to his skinny body, making him seem like a puppy with big paws that he'd eventually grow into. Mixed in with my delight for our new baby was a double dose of relief that he had arrived to us healthy.

Watching Tom holding Sam, I was flooded with a thousand feelings at once. Dominant among those feelings were gratitude and relief. The year prior had been filled with so much sadness, first losing my mother, then losing our twins. Now in those first few moments, with just Tom, Sam, and me together, relief was a waterfall dousing me with its pure, refreshing joy. I also had another relief, one I'd not anticipated.

The minute I became Max's mother, I felt utter devotion to him. Despite our lack of shared biology, he was my son and had grown to be more so every day. Despite this, a tiny nagging feeling had niggled at me, a feeling I hadn't allowed myself to voice aloud. One day while I was pregnant with Sam, a colleague had said something that entered my psyche and stuck in my thoughts like a burr. He meant no harm by it, and wasn't even aware that it had bothered me. It was just one of those weird, sometimes thoughtless, things that people say to you when you're pregnant. Over lunch at work one day, he's said, "I bet you're getting so excited to have a child of your own."

Of my own. The words had wormed their way into my thoughts, not because I felt them to be true—I regarded Max as every bit "my own" son—but because a tiny part of me feared that I might feel differently toward a child that was biologically mine than I did for my adopted son.

The second I held Sam in my arms I adored him, as every loving mother does. I was flooded with love and relief and gratitude, touched by the miracle of it all. Within seconds of holding him, another feeling overtook. *I can't wait to share this with Max.*

I had two sons, plain and simple. The fear that I'd favor one over the other, that I'd love one differently or more because he'd come to me through my body, disappeared. I had two sons, and I couldn't wait for them to meet.

ﾟ

Di brought Max to the hospital to meet his brother.

"You want to hold him, Skibber?" Tom said to Max. Tom held Sam, swaddled in a blanket.

Max's eyes were wide. I didn't know if it was excitement or terror. "I don't want to drop him," Max said.

Tom reassured him. "Why don't you just sit down there and I'll put him in your arms."

Max looked at me, his face stiff, his eyes bugging out. "It's okay," I said. "I trust you."

He nodded and sat in the chair at my bedside. Tom moved the small, wriggling bundle into Max's arms. I feared that Max might be nervous when Sam moved, but he sat stone-still and looked into the face of his new brother. "Hi, little guy," Max said, his voice raised into a soft falsetto. "I'm your brother."

There was no mention of blood or DNA. No mention of steps or half-siblings. In that moment we were just family, united by bonds greater than just biology can provide.

In that moment I knew that I had given to each of my sons the best gift he'd ever had. I'd given them both a brother.

This joyful birth, watching Max adore his new brother, laughing with Tom about our newborn's wild expression— like a thousand other joys we would experience in our shared lives—were joys none of us could have experienced had we not suffered losses before them. Had Janet not been taken so young, Tom and I would never have been together. I'd not be Max's mother. Had we not lost our twins, we would never have gone on to create Sam. Grief and love were the stones from which the foundation of our lives was built, and both were equally necessary. It is the weaving of the two—sweetness and sorrow—that makes our lives together strong and stable. Love and loss are what make us the family that we are.

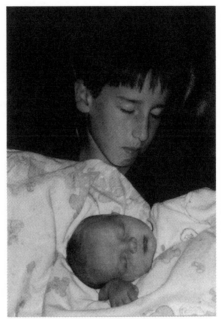

Max holding 24-hour-old brother, Sam.
November 11, 1995

Fighting with Eeyore

"Hey, Max. Time to get going!" I shouted up the stairs. It was one of *those* mornings. I felt frayed and my work-day hadn't even begun. "We're leaving in ten minutes," I yelled.

This was the third time I'd called up the stairs, only to be told in Max's flat, unemotional tone, "In a minute."

Sam banged his sippy-cup against the tray of his high chair and the sound hit my ears like a hammer pounding tin. I scooped the last of the pureed sweet potatoes from his Winnie the Pooh bowl and brought the spoon to his mouth. He rejected it with a rapid shake of his head and his lips pressed firmly together, opting instead to finger paint his food across the palate of his tray.

"All done!" I announced, and started wiping down the tray, then the hands, then the face, then the ears, then the hair. How could one small serving of sweet potatoes become such a disaster?

"Cookie!" Sam said. *Cookie* was Sam's first word. By this time, at not quite two, he had learned many more, although *cookie* remained his most frequently used word.

"It's not time for cookies, silly boy. It's time to go to Robin's house," I said, pulling him from his high chair.

"Bobbin!" Sam said, and his face lit up, all memories of cookies erased. I was so grateful to find a loving, in-home daycare provider around the corner from my therapy practice. But on this particular morning, my gratitude gave way to frenzy. Between Sam's high-chair tray version of a Jackson Pollock and Max's heel-dragging, I was cutting it close for my first client of the day. I turned my voice back toward the stairs. "Max! We pull out in five minutes. With or without you!" With Sam on my hip, I rushed to the sink and grabbed a corner of a dishtowel to blot away a bright orange blob of sweet potato from the cuff of my blouse. Sam squirmed.

"Help, Mama," Sam said.

"Here," I said handing him a clean towel. "Wipe here." I directed Sam's efforts to his own orange-splattered overalls. Useless. Not enough time to change either of us. I rolled the cuff of my blouse and hoped my clients wouldn't notice the stain.

"Max!" I shouted. As soon as I spoke, I turned and saw Max standing behind us at the sink. The boy could have been a Native American tribal scout for how silent his movements had become in his teens. "Shit! You scared me." I panted to catch my breath. "Sorry about the bad word. Are you ready to go?"

"Yeah," Max grunted. Though his voice had yet to transform into the baritone it would eventually become, my older son's little-boy voice was nowhere to be heard. He was in that in-between stage: no longer boy, not yet man. All of his peers sounded the same. When the group of his guy pals talked and laughed together, it sounded like a raucous fight between a flock of geese and a group of honking clarinets.

Almost as soon as his voice started to change, Max's former chatterbox style disappeared and his utterances became monosyllabic, often lacking consonants altogether, and his sentences always ended with a descending pitch. *Ugh. Yeah. Er. Uh-uh.* At some point I started calling him Eeyore. It fit.

We loaded into the car. I had just enough time to drop Max off at his high school, Sam at his daycare, and get to my first client in time. If all went perfectly and I hit nothing but green lights, I might even get to stop for a cup of tea to bring into work.

Sam sang and squealed from his car seat in the back. Max said nothing, and stared out the passenger side window next to me.

"Remind me. What time's your game today?"

"Four," he said in his best Eeyore voice.

"Who's the starting pitcher?"

A soundless shrug was his only response. Max had fallen in love with baseball as a little guy and now played on the varsity school team as well as winter league, fall ball, and majors. By the time he'd hit his freshman year, it seemed our entire social calendar was filled with baseball games. Sam, the youngest sibling of Max's peers, was regarded as the team mascot and was often invited into the dugout after the games.

"Which team are you playing today?" I asked.

Another shrug.

"What's up, kiddo? Everything okay?"

"Yeah. Drop me off here." Every word was the same low-pitched, atonal grunt. It was a statement, not a request.

We were about eight blocks from the school drop-off spot. I ignored his surly tone. He was a teenaged boy. Surly was a staple. "That's okay, honey. I can drop you off closer."

"No!" The sharpness of Max's voice startled me, his Eeyore persona shattered. When I turned to him his face was pinched, his eyebrows crimped. I could see his jaw muscles tighten.

"What do you mean, no? I'm right here. I have to turn around anyway, and—"

"Just drop me off here!"

"What!" I couldn't recall another time I'd ever heard Max raise his voice to me, or to anybody for that matter. "What's up with you today?"

His eyes avoided mine. "I just want you to drop me off here."

Years evaporated in my mind, sending me back to that moment when I insisted that my own mother drop me off several blocks away from a movie theater where a bunch of other kids were already in line. She was wearing curlers in her hair, covered by a pink hairnet with daisies on it, and the ever-present cigarette in her lips bobbed as she spoke. Our car was dinged and smelled like an ashtray. Walking was far preferable to the adolescent scourge of humiliation.

I pulled the car over with a little more of a jerk than intended and shifted into park.

"Uh-oh," Sam said from the back seat.

Max started gathering his backpack and his ball-gear bag.

"Wait a minute."

Max stopped his movement, but did not look at me.

Then I felt it—the seething burn of fury growing in my chest. "Does being seen with me embarrass you?" I asked.

Max shrugged.

I wasn't wearing curlers or smoking a cigarette. The car wasn't a beater. *What the hell does he have to be embarrassed about?*

Other than minor irritations, I couldn't recall ever feeling seriously angry at Max but, in that moment, I felt unappreciated and overwhelmed. I felt the fireball of words rising from my gut. "So I'm good enough to fix your breakfast, wait for you to dilly-dally to the last second almost making me late, and drive you to school. I'm good enough to cart your skinny butt all over the county for games and practices. But I'm not good enough to be seen by your friends?"

I could feel myself cross over whatever imaginary line that forms the boundary between rational thought and ranting. Stopping my rant was a freeway exit I'd already missed. "And just what embarrasses you so much? Is it the four baseball games and three practices a week that I drive you to? Or is it the rides I give to your buddies? Is it my engineering my entire client schedule so that I can get you from school to your games? Or is it all of the team snacks I make the night before games after I've worked all day?"

It was official; I had launched. I was pulling out every mom trick, trying to guilt him into seeing my point. I pummeled him with words, thinking that this would provoke a response. It didn't. Somewhere inside of me, I was bracing myself for something else, though I didn't know in that moment what it was.

Max did not look at me. He said nothing. He just opened the car door and stepped out. To his credit, he did not slam the door.

"Bye-bye, Max," Sam sang, pressing his little hand against his window.

I stewed, watching Max walk toward the school. I thought surely he'd turn. Surely he'd at least say good-bye to his brother. I briefly entertained the idea of laying the heel of my hand on the horn until he turned around. To my credit, I didn't. I watched until he disappeared into the crowd of teens who moved not as individuals, but as a single, multi-legged, hair-flipping, gum-chewing unit.

Fury was the cayenne pepper in my emotional stew, but the main soup was my hurt feelings. I tried to be a cool enough mom. Tried not to embarrass my son. Hurt feelings and anger makes for bitter dining.

After I dropped Sam off, I went straight to my office where I waited for my first client, skipping my tea stop in favor of calming myself. I was furious at Max, but my client deserved for me to be present and available to her. I took deep breaths. I tried to summon my higher self.

At ten minutes past the hour, my client had not arrived. I called my message service and found that not only had she called an hour prior because she'd woken up not feeling well, but my other two morning clients had also called in last-minute cancellations. The frenzy of the morning had all been for nothing. I sent up a little bubble of gratitude to whatever force caused the cancellations. Sam was already settled at daycare so I decided to sit in a café for a while, have a cup of tea, and write in my journal to sort things out.

Enjoying the scent of my ginger tea, I reflected on the hectic morning. My response had been disproportionate. Sure, Max had been rude, but he was doing nothing more to me than I'd done to my own mother at his age, and she'd been no more deserving of my rudeness than I was of Max's. Intellectually, I knew that this was the beginning of Max growing up, pushing away from his dad and me, and charting his own path. His sullen moods and his stubbornness were part and parcel for an adolescent boy. I knew this. I'd majored in human development. I knew the developmental milestones. I'd been working with adolescents for years and recognized the pattern. He was barely fourteen. What fourteen-year-old kid's parents don't embarrass him? But none of what I'd learned in books cracked through to the core of what ate at me.

I wrote in my journal. Scratchy, messy writing. I wrote questions first, then paused and waited for an answer to come. I wrote the questions with my left hand, the answers with my right. It helps when I can separate my thoughts that way. My left-hand writing was barely legible, mere scratches on the page.

Left: *What made you so angry, Betsy?*
Right: *Max was rude. Unappreciative. Disrespectful. I've been busting my butt on his behalf and he acted bratty.*
Left: *What got you so hurt?*
Right: *I was hurt that he was embarrassed by me. I thought he was proud of me.*

Left: *What are you worried about?*
Right: *I'm worried that I've not taught Max
how to express his emotions. I'm worried that
he's so tightly controlled that, as he grows, he
won't be able to let love in. I'm worried that
he won't be happy. I'm worried that we won't
continue to be close as he grows up.*
Left: *What are you afraid of?*

This last question gave me pause. Ink filled a half-dozen pages. It was not a simple answer. I was afraid that the peace in our family had been false and that I'd misjudged our closeness. I was afraid that this was the start of the roaring teenager/mom fights that I knew could be so brutal.

But what are you REALLY afraid of? my left hand asked again.

I allowed the ink to flow without editing my thoughts. After pages of scribbling and scratching the truth came out.

I was afraid he'd say, *'You're not my mother. You can't tell me what to do.'*

My pen lingered on the period of that last sentence, allowing the black ink to bleed. As I watched the ink absorb through the fibers of the page, I knew that I'd feared these words for very long time without ever being aware of it. He hadn't spoken these words. He'd never said them, or anything remotely like them. But I feared that in his silence, he was saying them in a nonverbal way.

I was "all in" with Max. My heart was fully open. He was my son. I had a biological son in Sam, but in my heart I didn't have one son and one adopted son. I was mother to two boys. One grew in my body; both grew in my heart.

Once the gnarly little truth of my fear was uncovered, it lost its power. I relaxed. I was able to see the exchange for what it was—a normal, stupid family conflict during a crazy morning.

It was after nine when we got home that night. Max's team had won their game handily. Max played well at second base, even turning a double play. He'd become so hotly competitive that if his team lost or, worse, if he had made an error during a game, there was no talking to him for the next couple of days.

Once we got Sam put to bed, I knocked on Max's bedroom door. "Hey, Max, can I come in?"

Something akin to a grunt came from behind the door. "Is that *yes*?"

"Yes!" he said with a snap.

I entered his room and sat on the edge of his bed. He sat at his desk, homework in front of him, his profile to me.

"Honey, what's going on?"

"Nothing."

"I wasn't happy with our exchange this morning."

I waited. No response.

"Max, can you look at me? I'm talking with you."

He made a millimeter of a turn toward me, his eyes aimed firmly at the carpet.

I waited. Max is his father's son. They both operate as though they're on a strict word budget and they never overspend. Their silences are long between thoughts, especially during an emotional exchange. Most of the time this is something I admire about Tom, and as Max has grown, I've come to appreciate it in him as well. I like that my husband, and now my son, are thoughtful and unlikely to use words in anger. But there's also a price to a being in relationships with conflict-averse, nonverbal guys. Sure, our house was pretty peaceful, but sometimes the unspoken had its own impact. When I got angry with or hurt by these slow-speaking guys, their reluctance to talk with me only added to my frustration. I was then—and likely am to this day—the designated driver when it came to navigating the emotional landscape and conversation in our family.

Finally, I realized that Max had more waiting power than did I. "Son," I said, calming my voice as much as possible. "You really hurt my feelings this morning. You were rude and disrespectful. That's not okay with me."

"Yeah."

"That's all you have to say? Yeah?"

"Yeah."

"What do you mean, yeah? Yeah, you know you hurt my feelings? Yeah, you remember this morning?"

Max's voice was flat and guttural. "I don't know what you want me to say."

"I want you to talk to me about your side of our experience this morning," I said. Then I waited again. "Do you have anything to say to me?" I finally asked.

"Not really," he said. That carpet must have been fascinating.

"What do you mean, not really?"

"I mean, not really."

"Okay. So let me offer you options then." I'd often had to resort to an emotional multiple-choice question to get such questions answered with Tom. Max was new to the process. "A. You feel badly about your part of this morning and you don't know how to say it. Or B. You don't want to say anything just because you don't want to fight. Or C. You're not sorry at all and you feel like I'm full of it, but you don't want to say that because it'll make me mad."

The digital read-out on Max's bedside clock marked two full minutes passing without a reply.

I drew a deep breath. "Well?"

"I don't know," Max said.

I closed my eyes and allowed my pulse to find its natural, slower rhythm again. I drew another breath to fortify my words. "Max, it's important that we can talk to each other even when we are upset with one another. And it's really important that when we have a rough exchange that we learn how to say that we're sorry to one another. Your dad and I are so proud of you. But this morning, you were unkind, inconsiderate, and you hurt my feelings a lot. I was feeling unappreciated and I got way angrier than I should have. I'm really sorry for that, Max."

"Okay," Max said.

"Okay? Are you saying okay, meaning you're sorry?"

"I can't say that."

"Can't say what? Can't say you're sorry?"

"Nope."

"Why in the world can't you say you're sorry? Because you don't feel it, or because you just don't want to say it?"

Max shrugged, adding a new shade of confusion to the discussion.

"Honey. Everybody occasionally has to say they're sorry for something."

"I can't say it."

"But why not?"

"Can't say it. It makes me sick to say it."

"It makes you sick to say you're sorry?" This one was new. I left a wide space of silence, determined to let Max feel the pressure of filling it before I rescued him.

Finally, he spoke. "If I say I'm sorry, it means I lose."

I scanned Max's room. In perfect order, each of Max's shelves boasted a tidily arranged display of trophies, certificates, and awards from the various teams he'd played on since Little League. Will Clark, his baseball hero, looked down on us from the framed poster over his bed. My competitive son hated to lose any contest.

We talked together for a while longer and I tried to explain how I saw the ability to take responsibility and to care for another person by apologizing as a strength, and not a sign of weakness, and most especially not "losing." I didn't want to wrestle an insincere apology out of Max. I wanted him to understand the value of caring about another person's feelings. I elected to say nothing of the fear I had of him calling me "not his real mother." That felt like my problem, not his. What we had before us—particularly in Max's experience—was a simpler conflict, between a mom and an adolescent son.

"I shouldn't have walked away without saying goodbye," he finally said. "And I didn't mean to hurt your feelings."

It wasn't exactly an apology, but I wasn't going to split hairs. "Thanks. I appreciate that. I'm sorry I got so angry. I sort of lost my mind because my feelings were hurt. Can we have an agreement going forward that we don't leave arguments like that? If you need time to think, that's okay. Just say that. I'll honor it."

"I'll try." My Eeyore had returned in the minor key music of his words.

On the scale of human conflict, our skirmish had been microscopic. But for what it revealed in us, what I'd discovered, it had been a holy war that resulted in deeper understanding and renewed closeness and I was grateful for it.

Those dreaded words—*You're not my mother*—never came from Max's lips, not that day, nor any day since. If he's ever felt them, he's offered no hint of it. After that day, I no longer feared I'd hear them and, without his ever saying so, I believe he has never felt them. I still have to read between the lines with the guys in my house. Now all three of them share the same word budget . . . and they never overspend.

And after that night, I never again heard a crack or break in Max's voice either. He was growing up, and so was I.

DMV Test

It is July 18, 2001. Max is sixteen today and has on his mind one of the two things that are most frequently on every sixteen-year-old boy's mind: driving.

Tom and I have each taken him out for driving practice. Max's calm, cautious nature puts us more at ease than the other parents of sixteen-year-olds we know. Six months ago, within a few tries around the school parking lot and on the back roads of our small town, he showed us he was ready for his learner's permit. Six more months of backseat driving from us and he wants to go solo so badly that it seems to cause him physical pain.

It's fallen to me to take him for his driving test. He drives off with the DMV staffer, a silver-haired man I assume must have nerves of steel to get into the car with so many new drivers. I watch from curbside—parents are not invited to ride along—as Max takes his place behind the wheel and the examiner sits with his clipboard poised.

Max wears a worried look. "It would be so embarrassing not to pass," he confessed to me earlier this morning.

As they roll away I feel a sweet and salty bit of mixed of emotions. I'm proud to see Max growing up. He's given us hints of the man he is becoming. Honest. Hard-working. Responsible. Kind. I've relished watching his every stage, and now I get a second go around, watching his younger brother behind him, blazing his own trail along the path of developmental milestones. But this driving thing is different. This is not just another milestone. Not just another birthday or holiday. This one is the end of one stage and the beginning of another, and I'm awed by this precipice.

I wait on the curb and check the time. It should only be about twenty minutes, I'm told. This particular twenty minutes passes slowly, leaving me lost in reflection.

For every minute of every day since becoming Max's mother, I've either known exactly where he is, or exactly which other adult—Tom, a family member, a friend, a teacher—knows exactly where he is. With a new driver's license, he'll be branching out from us, finding new places and new people. This driver's test is the last of his little-boy steps and the first of the many steps he'll take as he crosses the threshold into manhood. I'm used to providing him with adult supervision and now he is becoming an adult. I think back to birthday parties and baby teeth, Santa Claus notes, and dead goldfish. I think back to bedtime stories and silly string, Halloween costumes, and a tangle of buddies in sleeping bags under a fort of blankets. Sam is at the beginning of these events, and Max, it occurs to me, is coming to the end of them.

I think about Janet and just how many of her boy's

milestones she didn't get to enjoy, and I feel both grateful for what I have and sorry for what she has missed. I've learned in the last ten years to let these two seemingly contradictory emotions coexist. Grief and gratitude are friends in our house. I've learned that this coexistence is the nature of being Max's second mother.

They're returning now. Max sits tall at the wheel. Even from the curb, before they've come to a stop, I can tell that the test has gone well by the way he's holding himself and the relaxed look he wears on his face. It's not *quite* a smile because that wouldn't be cool.

As he drives toward where I stand on the curb, where I've stood the entire time despite the chairs provided in the waiting room, I see a thousand future drives. I see him driving toward his first "guy-trip" with buddies. I see him driving off to college. Driving to the home of his future love's parents when it's time to meet them. Driving to a future bachelor party, to a wedding, to the hospital with his love to welcome a child into the world. I can see it all from that one spot on the curb, all of the past moments and all of the possible future ones, all at once. My chest tightens and my eyes sting as I watch the examiner sign a form on his clipboard and tear it off and hand it to my man/boy.

By the time Max shakes the hand of the examiner, my tears have begun to spill. My face gets hot and my throat tightens into a fist. I'm a redhead with fair skin that betrays my every attempt to hide my sentiments. Though I wipe my tears on my sleeve, I know I look a mess.

For a brief moment, Max flashes a world-class, slightly uncool smile at me, the kind that lets me know that all of those trips to the orthodontist were worth it. For an instant he reveals the excitement he feels before he tucks it away under his understated, too-cool-to-smile persona. I want to run toward him, wrap my arms around him and tell him how much I adore him and how exciting it is to see him grow up. I want to tell him that as he enters this world and goes farther from us, that his dad and I are always here, always waiting for him, always ready to help. I want to tell him that he'll make mistakes and that's okay, that we are there to support him through failures as well as to celebrate his successes. I'm aching to hold him close and let him know what an honor it is to watch him grow and how excited I am to see him cross this new milestone. I want to tell him that his first mother would be so proud of him.

All of this flashes through my mind as he walks the thirty feet to the spot on the curb where I stand. When he gets within reach, I wait, reading how much motherly affection might be appropriate and tolerable to him in this public place, waiting for his cue.

He takes one look at me. His face registers my tear-swollen face. "Are you crying?" he asks. He looks again into my face and shakes his head. "You are so lame." Then he chuckles a little and walks toward the DMV building to file his paperwork.

For a moment I am crushed. All of my mushy love feelings just got dissed, and just when I wanted Max to feel as mushy as I do. Almost as soon as I feel it, that feeling of being crushed dissipates like so much dandelion fluff in a breeze because it dawns on me, in this moment, that I am not a second mom. This has nothing to do with the history of how I came to be Max's mother. In this moment, I'm simply a sentimental mom and I've just been pronounced "lame" by my son. Though the choice of word to describe us may differ, most every mother of every son (and likely of every daughter, though I have no experience in such matters) has taken such a blow, and much worse, as we wistfully watch our children grow and weep as we watch who they become.

I am lame. I am silly and sentimental and ridiculous. I embrace "lame" as the official job description of nearly every mother of nearly every teen. Today, I'm a mom, with a boy who is becoming a man. I'm grateful beyond measure to count myself among my lame, sentimental, ridiculous peers.

Brotherly Love

It's the middle of the night. Sam has risen from his race-car bed and padded down the hall and into the room where Tom and I sleep. He stands on my side of the bed. In the division of labor in our house, middle of the night has always fallen to me. I'm a light sleeper and less cranky than Tom when awakened. Both boys have learned which of us is the softer touch for any given circumstance. I'm good for heartbreaks, owies, play-date requests, and middle of the night worries. Tom fixes flat tires on bikes, builds tree houses, and is the easier mark for pocket money and sweets. I suppose every family has such designations.

I feel him standing there before he speaks, before my eyes are open. "Mama?" Sam whispers.

"Yes, pup."

"I'm worried," he says.

I open my eyes and look into the face of my second son. No five-year-old should worry. I was a five-year-old who worried because I lived in a house full of danger and mayhem. Tom and I have done all we can do to create a home absent those qualities. But the world around us did not honor our efforts. The world is danger and mayhem right now. Sam's moss-green eyes glisten and he wears a pale expression of terror. I pull him close to me and rub circles on his back with my flattened palm. "What are you worried about, pup?" I whisper.

He says nothing. Instead, a small squeak escapes his throat. My little big boy, trying not to cry.

I sit up and glance over at Tom. He faces away from us. His back rises and falls with his sleeping breaths. I take Sam's hand and we walk together into his room. I sit in the rocking chair and bring him onto my lap. His body still fits, but barely, his legs dangling over the side of the chair. He is soft and pliable. Snuggles like this are rare with our busy boy, so I hold him close, drinking in the last sips of the baby he is. He rests his head on my chest and I take in the fragrance of baby shampoo from his downy-soft hair, my secret mommy pleasure that replaced the sweet milky breath of his babyhood.

This is the fifth straight night of these midnight worries. We've tried to shield our little guy from the worst details of what has happened—kept the news off when he's around, limit our talk of gruesome details—but the story is inescapable.

He was in his first week of kindergarten on that Tuesday, the eleventh day of September in 2001. Though we live three thousand miles from where planes flew into buildings, the impact of those human-filled missiles reverberates all the way to California. All the way into our town. All the way into our homes. All the way into Sam's kindergarten class, where he thankfully has a wise and big-hearted teacher. Patty Armanini has created a space for her kindergarteners to talk when they want to, and has helped parents to find simple words to talk to them about something that is anything but simple. I am grateful every day since the attacks that we live across the street from Sam's school. On days when I can work from home, from my upstairs office, I have a clear view right into his kindergarten class where I often see him playing with blocks or clay, playing in the dress-up corner, or sitting in story circle. Days when I must work in San Francisco, an hour away from my sons, are harder to bear than they were just a week ago.

I try not to offer artificial reassurances, feeble attempts to comfort him with words, and instead hold him and wait for him to say what's on his mind. Finally, his head still resting against me, he says, "Those planes made really tall buildings fall down, Mama. What if more buildings will fall down?"

"That's a big worry," I say. "You're safe right here, honey." I wish I could promise him that he has nothing to worry about, that nothing like that could ever happen where we are. But we've all been shaken. My office on Sutter Street in San Francisco has a view of the iconic, triangular TransAmerica building, a view I've always felt so lucky to have. In the last week, I too have imagined that building pierced by an airliner, crumbling to the jammed city street below. We've all been acquainted with our vulnerability and the fact that things will be forever changed because of what has happened. Each time I crossed the Golden Gate Bridge this past week, rather than enjoying its splendor as

I have in the hundreds of times I've crossed it, I see it as a potential target. I see the news footage, yet unrecorded, of the saffron bridge collapsing, crumbling like so much steel and cable into the sea. But I push this aside. I reassure my boy—and perhaps myself at the same time—that most of the people in the world are good, and that only a few are people confused and angry enough to be capable of doing such terrible things. I believe this, I do, under the fresh wound of fear. I try to find words that a five-year-old boy can understand, words that might reassure him and let him sleep. My words are clunky and awkward. Such reassurance has been hard enough to find for myself at forty-one, and for Tom, and for Max, much less for our littlest guy.

"Will an airplane hit our house, Mama?" Sam asks.

"No, sweetheart. I can tell you that won't happen. Those men who drove the planes didn't want to hit our house." It's a tiny promise I can safely make.

"Are the bad guys dead?"

How to answer. I want to tell him the truth, but the truth that a small boy can handle. I'm remembering Patty Armanini's advice for answering questions from our kindergarteners, advice I remember from all of my years in Alanon meetings. *Give them a K-I-S-S,* she'd said. *Keep it simple, sweetheart. Just answer what they ask, without unnecessary elaboration.* "Yes," I say. "The men who flew the planes all died. We don't have to worry about them any more."

"So they can't smash a plane into our house?"

"No, baby. They can't."

After a few moments of silence, our bodies melt into one another with every rock of the chair. I feel Sam's head grow heavier against me. His breaths grow deeper. It seems that's all the reassurance he needs for tonight.

I return to bed, exhausted, but sleep cannot find me, hidden among all of my unspoken worry and sadness.

*

"Look at my punkin!" Sam shouts. "It's a *really* scary one."

Sam's face wears the glow of pride. The day before Halloween is our annual pumpkin-carving party and this is the first year he's been big enough to carve his own pumpkin. Our backyard deck is a jack-o-lantern factory, with newspaper covering tables, mounds of pumpkin guts at each table's center, and an array of tiny saws and scooping tools strewn about. Ours has come to be known as The Pumpkin House in the neighborhood of our small town. Its old wood shingles give the place an eerie look when lit by jack-o-lanterns. Living across the street from an elementary school means we get a ton of eager trick-or-treaters. Dianne's family and mine have made this a joint tradition. Her kids and mine look forward to the carving party each year. My brother, John, and his wife often come down from Reno to join in. The kids sometimes invite their friends to be part of the production. Everyone carves at least one pumpkin and we've had as many as twenty for our Halloween display. On Halloween each year many families take annual photos of their kids in front of our assortment of silly and scary pumpkins. I'm greeted by strangers around town with, "Don't you own the pumpkin house?" My boys love when this happens. It makes them feel a little bit famous.

Max holds up his palm to Sam. "Way to go, Buster," he says. The two exchange high-fives.

"Yours is cool, too," Sam says to his big brother. And it is. Max has chosen a pattern that requires the most meticulous care and has carved an elaborate scene of a creepy graveyard filled with tombstones. Tom has pilfered the last of his summer garden's squashes and gourds to make a free-form display of his own, which he's dubbed "Veggie Man," with a miniature carved pumpkin for his head. We have witches and owls, Frankenstein and Dracula, graveyards and spooky cats.

The carving is done, so it's time for our annual "dress rehearsal." Tom and Jim and John haul all of the pumpkins down to the basement where we can turn out the lights for maximum effect. We all file behind and enjoy the show as they shine a flashlight in one pumpkin at a time. We ooh and ahh each time the flashlight illuminates a new design. Sam's gets voted "scariest," to his delight. Max's gets "Most Awesome" and Tom's gets a unanimous vote for "Most Original." Every pumpkin is awarded a title and we all agree that the best part of them is having so many this year. Sam gets extra accolades for this being his first all-by-himself pumpkin.

The older kids split off with various groups of their friends for trick-or-treating. Max insists on taking Sam with him in his group. Max wears just enough of a costume to legitimize getting candy: one of Tom's sport coats, a tie, and my briefcase. A businessman of some kind. Sam is clad in head-to-toe Batman, his current obsession. The adults stay home to greet the masses and distribute treats.

Hours later, Max returns to the porch carrying a wilted, sleeping Sam in his arms, his full bag of candy dangling from his elbow. Sam's mask has been removed and his sweaty hair sticks to his face. "He's pooped out," Max says.

"Too pooped to pop," Tom adds.

"Do you want me to jammy him up?" Max whispers.

"Thanks, honey," I say. "I think we just let him sleep. His Batman costume just became his new pajamas. Just take off his shoes."

Max holds his brother like the precious cargo he is. "He went potty at the Burtts' house, so he should be okay for the night."

As I watch Max carry his brother up the stairs, I'm touched. Max can sometimes be stiff and surly. He's a quiet guy, serious and meticulous in every task he takes on. It's hard for him to show tenderness sometimes. But Sam brings it out in him like no one else. With Sam, Max is doting and affectionate, kind and patient, silly and playful. With Sam, Max is his softest self and I believe I am now glimpsing the father he may one day be.

That night, some stirring in the hallway awakens me. I wait to see if it is another of Sam's midnight worry visits. But after few moments, there is silence again and I drift back into my unfinished dream. I awaken again a few moments later, this time with a feeling that pulls me from the bed. I have an aching need to see my sleeping sons in order to return to peaceful slumber.

I peek into Max's room and find an empty bed. I step down the hall where Sam's bedroom door is ajar, and see the glow of his nightlight around the door's edges. Through the crack in the door I can see Max's bare feet in front of the rocking chair, and Sam's empty rumpled bed. I can see his Batman cape on the floor. I stand still, listening from the hall, hidden by the door.

Max's voice is just above a whisper. I must stand right at the door to hear. "It's okay, Buster. There's nothing to

*Max and Sam on Sam's first day of kindergarten,
just a week before September 11, 2001*

be afraid of. We're all safe and snuggled in. Here, let me make a baby burrito."

Without seeing, I know what Max is doing. He's tucking a blanket tightly around his brother, making a "baby burrito" just as Tom and I did with Max when he was smaller.

Sam's voice is almost a cry. "But all of those little kids in New York must be really missing their moms and dads. They're probably lonesome and sad. How will they get to school? Who will make their Mickey Mouse pancakes?"

"Yeah," Max replies. "I bet they are sad."

And in that instant my brain begins to calculate. The terrorist attacks of 9/11 took place in the first week of Sam's year in kindergarten. It was just before Max started kindergarten when his mother died. Both of my boys were touched with unspeakable tragedy at the same point in their lives. Max's loss was intimate; Sam's was shared by many. I'm angry and sad that both of my boys had their innocence so disregarded by the fates.

"But even if their parents died," Max continues, "I bet they all have lots of people in their family who love them. That's what happens when a mom or a dad dies. Other people come in to help. Other people take care of them and take them to school and make them pancakes. So they're going to be okay, Buster. You don't have to worry about them."

I swallow, willing myself to be silent. In that instant I am awash in gratitude that what Max has learned from his loss is that there were other people to help him. His grandparents. His mother's sister. Our community of friends. My family. And me.

I slip back into my bed, knowing that both of my boys are safe, and loved, and in the very best hands for this moment.

What a Boy Needs

"First, you have to make a roux," Dianne explains to me as I run the creamy Gruyere through the grater. My sister is the champion mac-n-cheese maker of all time. Decadent and rich, gourmet enough to make the grown-ups moan, it's still mac-n-cheesey enough so the kids all love it, too. Mine is close, but never comes out like Di's. This is not the first, nor will it be the last, mac-n-cheese lesson I request from my sister.

We compare Christmas lists. As the kids have gotten older, it's harder to choose gifts for them. She tells me Megan's clothing sizes and that Matt isn't so much playing videogames any more. Di's kids, and Max, are all in that post-toy, pre-practicality stage of Christmas gifts. Sam's our little guy, the easiest one on everybody's list.

I snitch a pinch of the velvety cheese and pop it into my mouth. "Max is my hardest one this year. As usual, he wants nothing."

Dianne stirs her roux into a golden paste. The air fills with the smell of warm butter. There's something in her posture that says she has something to say, but also doesn't want to say. My sister and I sense these things in one another, know things without exchanging words. "What?" I ask.

"It's just—" She grabs a handful of cheese from the mound I've created and stirs it into the pan. The roux and the cheese say their "I dos." The marriage is perfect. The new fragrance of melting cheese meeting warm butter transforms the kitchen into a warm flannel blanket on a cold night. Di's lips move, but no words come out. She's rehearsing.

"What?" I ask again.

"I think I know what Max really wants, but—"

"But?"

"But he doesn't think he should ask you."

Max has confided in her; this makes me happy. It's why we chose to move to the same town at the same time. We wanted our kids to have their aunties, uncles, and cousins nearby. Di and I don't have secrets from one another. It makes my scalp tingle that she's hesitating to tell me something.

I search my imagination for anything that I would not want to give to Max, anything he couldn't ask for. He's never asked for anything extravagant. He's sixteen. From any other sixteen-year-old, particularly among the mon-eyed kids of Marin County, one might imagine requests for name-brand clothes or expectations of new BMWs with a big bow on top. But not Max. Even if we had the kind of funds for or the inclination to give such things, it's not his nature to ask for extravagance. This is a boy who has saved virtually every nickel he's ever gotten. He has no thirst for things he doesn't need and cares not at all about having the latest, newest anything.

You. He doesn't think he should ask *you.* Di's choice of pronoun is a pebble in my shoe, small but not ignorable. It feels specific to me, not to Tom and me as parents. There's something he wants and he can't ask *me* for it. "What does he want?"

My sister raises one shoulder and tips her head, as if she's softening the next words by making them more of a question than a statement. "He sort of let it slip that he'd really like to have a cat, but that he knows you're not into cats."

Her words, though gently delivered, feel like an arrow to my heart. I'm really not—into cats, that is. I'm an animal lover, but at this point in my life not so much of a *pet* lover and if I had any room at all for a pet, I'm more of a dog person. With two kids, an old house that eats money faster than Tom and I can borrow it, a full-time job, and a commute into San Francisco, I can't imagine having any other living thing that I'm responsible to care for, much less a cat.

When I first moved in with Tom and Max, they had two elderly outdoor kitties. I confessed my cat-reticence to Tom right away and we'd agreed that while I'd co-exist with them, he and Max would be the primary caregivers. "Cats give me the willies," I'd confessed. I felt sheepish and small for saying this, but Tom had commented on the fact that I didn't readily pet the kitties. Given that they were outdoor cats, I was spared having to deal with their "cat-ness" very often. No smelly litter box. No cats climbing on the kitchen counters. No surprise leaps onto my lap. No clawing the furniture or clinging to the drapes. Most of all, no creepy cat noises. I remember barn cats when I was grow-ing up, their eerie mewls and moans emitting from dark corners, their pouncing, how they could sneak up without being heard while clumsy dogs announced their arrivals with their panting and galloping gaits. The sounds cats make always seem like a haunting. Hearing them, when I was little, would make me flee into the house every time.

Critter, the older of Tom and Max's cats, died peace-fully within weeks of my moving in. We'd brought Skee-ter with us to the new house. She and I had established a cordial, if distant, relationship. As her name would imply, she was skittish. She didn't want to be picked up or held. Perfect for me. She had relationships strictly on her own terms, and I respected that. She and I bonded over the small bits of cheese I gave her at the back door each day, a treat she demanded every evening just before our supper. Eventually, I developed an affection for her as a member of the family. I considered her my step-cat, with Tom as the primary pet-dad, and me in a more peripheral role. Skeeter lived with us for several more years before she passed. I'd cried when she died, not because I had been transformed into a cat lover, but because she was ours and because Tom and Max loved her. But truly, I thought I'd paid my dues in the area of cat entanglements and that my obligation had been fulfilled with Skeeter's passing.

Janet loved cats. There's scarcely a photograph of her that doesn't have a cat either in the background or on her lap. She once sent me a thank-you note, the stationery cov-ered with kitties. She would have been that coworker in your office who has a cat calendar, and a cat coffee mug, and maybe kitty paw prints on her Post-It notes.

The pile of grated Gruyere cheese is now mountainous.

"I think that's enough, Bets," Di says, though I barely hear her. Instead there is a harangue in my mind. *Janet would have gotten Max a kitty. If Janet was still here, Max would have had cats his whole life.* Guilt is a boa constrictor around my ribcage, climbing up and wrapping itself around my throat. Max is a teenager. He works hard in school, excels in sports, and is the best possible big brother to Sam. His needs are so simple and he asks for things so seldom. He doesn't date, not since Natalie broke his heart in seventh grade. Maybe he needs something to love. But a cat? Isn't there some other gift that will make my son's eyes light up? Does it have to be a *cat*?

Hours after the mac-n-cheese has been relished by all, I cannot sleep. My mental harangue is now a trio of harping magpies carping in repeated rounds. *Janet loved cats. Janet would have gotten him a kitty to love. Max needs his own creature to love. A good mother gives her children what they need. A good mother isn't selfish. A good mother doesn't let her own neurotic reactions to cats get in the way of her son's emotional development and happiness.*

Tom snores beside me, as usual oblivious to my obsessing. Part of me is jealous of his easy sleep. Another part of me wants to pinch him so he will wake up and feel miserable with me, but that's never worked, not even once. He just tells me it'll all work out and that I'm worrying for nothing. He's a little bit right, but he's also a little bit wrong when he says this. Sometimes my worry, as he says, is just senseless worry. Sometimes it is valid, and I'm aware of something that he's missing. I'm sensitive to things Tom finds unimportant but that I know to be important. His calm is something I love about this man. It's also why I sometimes feel an urge—one I'd never act upon—to pull out his chest hairs one at a time until he sees my point. This is the urge I wrestle in the middle of the night when he snores and I'm agitated.

Tom and I have been married for nine years and this is the first time I've felt the need to compete with Janet. I've always accepted that she was a person very different from myself, that she had her quirks and I have mine, that she had her strengths, and mine are different than hers. I've always considered us a tag team, with her passing the mothering baton to me to run the rest of the race as best I can.

More is going on here, though. I know this much. This is not about the cat, or at least it's not *all* about the cat. What is it that is keeping me awake? Guilt? Comparing myself to Janet and coming up short?

I meditate, as I have for years, to quiet my thoughts. At first my monkey mind generates only criticisms. *You're selfish. All animals are beautiful. You just need to get over yourself. It's time you outgrow this neurotic cat phobia.*

I draw breath into the bottom of my lungs. In and out. In and out. The criticisms finally subside. Like the first drop of rain that hints of a coming storm, the idea pops into my mind. I see Max as he is now. Slim. Taut. Angular. Athletic. A little rigid and stubborn. Highly cautious. His erect posture makes him appear many inches taller than his five feet, nine inches. He is muscle and sinew and has lost any hint of soft little-boy pudginess. He is exceedingly controlled; on any day and without notice, his room would pass any snap inspection by the harshest drill sergeant. He never misplaces jackets or baseball gloves, never forgets his homework. Never back-talks. He is gentle and tender with his little brother, so I know that the sweet little boy is still inside of him, but Max has grown guarded and cautious as he's entered adolescence.

I continue to breathe in and out. In and out. The rain of thoughts is stronger now. Finally the storm comes. Critter and Skeeter were Janet's kitties, alive when she was alive. I know, between breaths, that this part of Max doesn't just *want* a soft kitty to love. He *needs* a kitty to love. He needs the balance. For all of his stiff control, he needs a tumbling, playful kitty. For all of his muscle and sinew, he needs the softness of fur and purr. Max is my son. He is not a step or a half of anything. But he is also Janet's baby boy. The two of them have this thing, this love of cats, in common. I cannot keep my son from this part of his relationship with his first mother, though I'm sure he's not conscious of this connection.

Once this rain shower of ideas is over, I sleep.

The next morning Tom and I share the bathroom mirror. I wash my face while he's brushing his teeth. "So, I decided what to get Max for Christmas," I announce. Tom's relationship to our holiday shopping is to ask people, "Ooh. What did we get you?" as they open their gifts. He tends to leave all gift decisions to me, but this one I thought I should share, given that it affects him.

He rinses and spits frothy toothpaste into the sink. "Yeah?"

"I think he needs a kitty to love."

Tom lifts his head and stares at our shared reflection. His face says, *Really? You?*

"I know," I say, running a brush through my hair. "But I think it's important. I think he needs something for his soft, tender side."

"But a cat. You? You're getting him a cat?"

"I know."

Tom snickers to himself and kisses me on the cheek. "Softy," he says to my smiling reflection.

That day I go to the pet store and buy a collar, a litter box, cat food, and some kitty toys. I wrap them all in Santa paper.

On Christmas morning, Max brings Sam down the stairs to see what Santa has brought. It's stockings first, at our house. Then Di and Jim and the rest of the family come over for presents.

As always there's a note from Santa, letting the boys know that they're, as usual, on the Nice-list. Santa is a pretty effusive guy, praising Max for his grades, congratulating Sam on helping with chores. But this year Santa has a special announcement. He lets the boys know that his biggest present to them could not be put into a box, that it is up to them to find the gift and that they will be doing so on December 26th at the animal shelter, where Santa knows that the perfect kitty is waiting to be adopted. Santa leaves two new ornaments for the tree—one for each boy's future holiday collection—each a kitten with a bow around its neck. Santa is careful in his note to let the boys know that they'll need to take special care of this kitty, and that adopting pets comes with a big responsibility to love and care for them, to keep them safe, and to give them a happy life. Santa is smart this way. He knows about adoption.

After he reads the note, Max finds my eyes from across the room. He tilts his head like the RCA Victor dog and asks a silent question. Once we lock eyes for a few seconds he seems to have the answer to his unspoken question and he breaks into a wide grin. "We're going to get a kitty tomorrow, Sammy."

Sam squeals, but his focus is on the candy cane in his stocking. Santa knows that the kitty was more for Max than for Sam.

The next day we go to the shelter. Christmastime is not the most ideal time for kitties, we're told. Not so many babies this time of year. I didn't know that cats had a season for babies. My ignorance about cats is vast.

We step into the room where the kitties are housed. I walk behind Max, carrying Sam on my hip as we scan the rows of kitties in crates. There are a few that appear to have been through a war. One missing an eye. Another with a mangled tail who hisses at us when we pass. Sam's thighs tighten around my waist and he hides his head. I feel the same way.

"Don't worry, Samsta," Max says. But he's looking at me. "We're going to pick a really nice kitty." Max peers into each of the crates.

"If there's not one that's just right, we can come back another day," I say. "Or we could drive to Santa Rosa. There's a shelter there also. You don't have to rush. It's a big decision."

Max shakes his head. "No. Our kitty is here." He walks farther down the row and stops. He leans in, peeking into one crate. He is still for a long time. "What about this little one?" he asks the kind attendant. "Can I look at her?"

Soon Max is seated with a kitty in his lap. She's not the kitten I'd imagined, but a nearly full-grown cat, fat, white with a smoky gray mask, gray patches, and a gray tail and two gray socks. Her bright apple-green eyes do not blink. She is frozen with fear, but doesn't scratch or bite. Max holds her without saying anything for a long time.

The staffer at the shelter tells us that this kitty is about six months old and she's been at the shelter for several months. She was rescued alone and when she came in she was skinny and frightened, but she's mellowed a lot. They don't know if she was feral or if an owner had abandoned her. They'd been worried about her for a while, but she seems to be coming around. They've fattened her up and she lets people hold her now, though only for a few minutes at a time. "She likes her groceries," the attendant says. The gray and white kitty seems never to want to leave Max's lap.

Max strokes the purring cat and invites Sam to touch her too. Sam puts his hand out, but retracts it. "It's okay," Max reassures. "Our kitty won't bite you."

The picture is complete. I had thought he wanted a cat that would give him affection, show him love. But that was only part of the picture. He needed this kitty so that he could show love to her, a place where he could show his unguarded tenderness. This is the tenderness he will need to welcome love into his life. This time, my late-night worry was telling me something that I needed to tune into.

Watching Max with that kitty in his lap, I see every photograph I'd seen of his first mother. Janet's angles are Max's angles. Her quirky nature is Max's quirky nature. Her tidiness and sense of order is just like his. And, like his first mother but unlike his second, he is most at home with a kitty in his lap.

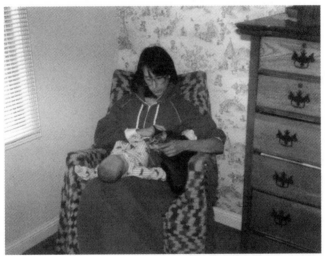

Max's baby books are filled with pictures like this one of Janet with her new baby and a kitty very nearby. Fall 1985.

Soundtrack

It was a tough ball game. Max's team should have won; they were the better team. Though he played well at second, unforced errors by his teammates cost the game in the final inning. Our drive home is silent. A black cloud hangs in the car. At fifteen, he's been my son for eight years. I've learned that he cannot be consoled after a loss and one can put him into a rotten mood for days. I turn on the radio and keep my mouth shut.

Simon and Garfunkel's braided voices beckon us to feel more "groovy," but the mood cloud still hovers. Max's athletic body is taut and rigid, his uniform's knees dirt-stained, his face smudged with black grease-paint patches that he's explained are for preventing sun glare. Now is not the time for me to ask why he's worn the war paint for a night game.

As we approach a stoplight, neither Max nor Mick Jagger can get satisfaction. The light is long and traffic is oddly heavy in our small town. Max sighs his impatience. We inch up bit by bit and wait through several slow rounds of green-yellow-red before we're at the intersection.

The Stones's rock ballad gives way to an acoustic guitar melody and Eric Clapton's soulful voice. I recall the story behind this song. It is a record of Clapton's aching grief after his four-year-old son fell off a balcony to his death. He wonders if his boy will know his name if they meet in heaven and as the melody drifts, I too wonder if the babies I lost would recognize me. Would they hold my hand? Would they even know I was their mother if I met them in heaven?

My throat tightens as I think about others I've lost. I don't know if I believe in a literal heaven, but I've wondered if I'll meet my father on the other side of this life and if his transition from life to afterlife freed him from the history that broke him and made him into the cruel man he was. I wonder if he'll tell me he's sorry for all the harms he caused to my siblings and our mom and me. I hope I get to thank my grandpa for being a good man, and to hold my mom close one more time, and then for forever. I recall the early death by suicide of my nephew, Brian, his quick smile and beautiful face that will remain young forever. When I think of Brian I feel the sting in my eyes, and a single warm tear spills.

Finally, we're near the intersection. As I move my foot to the gas pedal, I glance at Max. The song and the memories have transported me to another plane—I nearly forgot he was in the car. I catch a glimpse of a shimmering tear stream on his cheek that reflects the headlights as cars pass. It's as though he's crying light. I'm surprised the game has upset him this much. Tears are rare for my son. He gets broody and angry over losses, but I don't remember him ever crying over a game before.

"Honey, it's okay. You still have a chance at the championship," I say in my most soothing mom voice.

Max must've have forgotten I'm in the car as well, because he startles at the sound of my voice and wipes his tears with the heels of his hands, a gesture I recognize as Tom's. I see his Adam's apple bob and hear his tight swallow. His voice is low, his eyes downcast. "This song always makes me think of my mom," he says. "I wonder if she'd know me."

He turns his face toward me. His eyes are red, his cheeks are now both streaked with silver rivulets. My heart is a flock of sparrows, fluttering inside my ribcage. Every molecule of me wants to comfort Max, tell him how much his mom loved him, how proud she would be of him, and that I'm sure that if there's a heaven, she will certainly know him.

My better instincts tell me to stay silent and let him have the room to feel what he feels without interference from my verbal acrobatics. This is a moment between Max and his first mother. It is not mine to intrude upon. They've had so few moments together; I've had so many, and will have so many more. As I drive toward home, I reach across the car and rest my hand on top of his. He weaves his fingers with mine. I know that the father who sings his pain is telling us the truth, that somewhere beyond there would be peace. And that he is sure, there'd be "no more tears in heaven".

Joni Mitchel's *Blue* is the soundtrack of Tom's and my love story. Tom Petty's *Full Moon Fever* is the music of my relationship with Max. I'm happy that my first son and his first mother have a song of their very own.

Time Travel and U-Turns

September 15, 2011, is a normal Thursday that will become the worst day of my life. In the last few days the TV has played nothing but the horrific images for the tenth anniversary of September 11. How memory warps our idea of time. That day's shock and horror seems to have happened just yesterday and a thousand years ago all at once.

The phone rings in our Nevada City, California home in the middle of the afternoon with an unfamiliar number on the caller ID. Recognizing the Reno prefix, I assume it's my brother, John, calling. Maybe from work or from a friend's house.

Max is at his part-time job, and Sam is at school when the phone rings. The recession has brought Max back home for a while as he searches for a job and makes decisions about where he wants to live. Tom is out in his wood shop a hundred yards away from where I sit at my desk in the house. The Reno call is not from my brother. It is Joe, his boss. I've met Joe a few times over the six years since we moved from Marin County up to the Sierra Foothills.

"John didn't come to work today. You're on his emergency contact card," Joe says. His voice is somber. "Do you know where he might be?"

My desk clock reads 3:28. "No," I say. "I talked to him yesterday afternoon. But not today."

It's not like John to not show up for work without calling. He's had some health challenges, including being diagnosed with diabetes and high blood pressure a few years ago. I instantly soar to high-altitude worry that he's had a heart attack or diabetic seizure and is unable to reach a phone. I'm an hour and forty-five minutes away.

"Would you like me to drive out to his house and check on him?" Joe asks. "I can get there in about thirty minutes."

"Please, please," I say, my heart filled with both worry and gratitude.

"His buddy Jimmy knows the place," Joe says. "He'll go with me."

In the next seconds after I hang up the phone, I imagine my brother lying motionless on the floor after trying to reach a phone. I imagine hours spent clutching his chest or bleeding if he's fallen and hit his head on the sink. I pace. I freeze in my tracks. Then I pace some more. Seconds seem like hours, so I have no idea if I'm alone for ten minutes or thirty seconds. My mind generates a hundred options for what might have happened. I'm terrified to step away from the phone and decide to carry it with me. I walk, zombielike, out to Tom's shop and tell him about the call. "It's probably just a mix-up," he says. I read worry in his eyes. Time slows.

I use my cell phone to call John's number. No answer. I text. *Where are you? People are worried.* A few minutes later. *Johnny, call me. I'm really scared. If you've gone out of town without telling anybody, I'll kick your butt. We're freaking out here.* With every second that passes without a reply my belly roils and my muscles stiffen. My eyes are dry and itchy. My jaw clenches so hard that it feels I could crush all of my teeth into dust.

It's 4:05 when the phone rings again.

"His truck is in the driveway," Joe tells me. "But the place is locked up and all of the curtains are closed. Jimmy tried the back door. What do you want us to do?"

My panic finds new, uncharted altitudes. I've got a key to John's house, but it's here. There's a key code pad on John's front door, and I used it once years ago, but can't recall the code. *Shit. Shit. Shit!*

Tom stands beside me, and I read him puzzling, trying to surmise the unheard half of this call. The concern in his eyes gives me clarity. Tom seldom worries unnecessarily. "Call the police," I say to Joe.

I hang up the phone. When I tell him what's up, Tom looks as though he just got slapped. He too was on the phone with John yesterday, as he has been every day for the past few weeks. He's been fixing up John's RV and they talk about one mechanical detail or another. If I hear Tom laughing on the phone, I know he's talking with John. I realize in that moment that John is not just my brother and Tom's brother-in-law. He's Tom's friend.

It is twenty agonizing minutes before the phone rings again and my mind has played a hundred options. A pair of sheriff's deputies has arrived and Joe tells me they are unwilling to break down the door. He hands his phone to one of the officers.

The deputy introduces himself and asks, "Do you know if he has firearms?"

This question opens a whole new world of worry I haven't allowed myself. "A hunting rifle," I say. My mouth tastes of metal as I speak the words. I hated seeing that damned rifle in John's coat closet every time I visited. The deputy explains to me that because he has weapons, he's considered armed and unless John has made a threat to his own life, or unless we have direct knowledge that he's in danger, or a danger to someone else, they cannot enter. *Armed! I've just told a sheriff's deputy that my gentle brother is armed!* "I can't risk the lives of officers without cause. I'm sorry, but this is our protocol. You have to understand," he says. I don't understand. I tell him about John's diabetes, his high blood pressure. I tell him that John has never been violent to anybody, that he's one of the gentlest men I know. None of this is enough.

John's pal Jimmy takes the phone. "Hey, Betsy," he says. His voice is dry and flat, not the friendly guy I know. "If his truck is here and the place is closed up, I can't figure how he'd not be in there."

Terror dislodges whatever has been blocking my memory and I suddenly recall the door code, my brother's year of birth. "I remember the code," I tell Jimmy. "It's 1-9-6-1."

"Call you right back," he says.

During the next moments, Tom stays with me in the living room next to the phone. My body is there with the man I love, but it is a hollow, vacant shell that I no longer occupy. I feel cold, though the day is hot. I can barely breathe. Tom holds me and I want to take comfort from the embrace, but there is none to be found. I am absent, floating somewhere on the highway, over the pine ridges and the desert sage brush between my home and my brother's.

The phone blasts. Though I've been waiting for it, it sounds like a scream and sends shudders through me.

"We're in the house," Joe says. "His bedroom door is locked. The sheriff won't go in. John's dog is here. She was in her crate." Joe clears his throat. "She's okay. Jimmy took her outside."

My old skill of freezing time clicks in. What plays in my mind is not a movie, but a series of still photographs revealed one at a time. I see John's dog, Samantha, a stone-deaf boxer he adores. She's been a comfort and a companion, a clown of comic relief for him since John's wife left a few years ago. *He'd never do anything to harm Samantha.*

In the miniscule gaps between my mental images, I remember a conversation I had with my brother four years ago. We sat on his couch together. He'd been broken-hearted by his wife's infidelity and sudden departure. He was sad and struggling and I'd driven to Reno to be with him. After a couple of days together, I worked up the courage to ask, "Are you thinking of killing yourself?"

It may seem an odd question in most families, but my family had already lost Brian, my sister Jan's son, to suicide when he was eighteen, twenty-five years before. In our family, we ask the questions others dare not speak because we know of dark possibilities that some people can't imagine. John's reply to my question is etched word-for-word in my memory. *I won't tell you I've never thought of it.*

But honestly, after what happened with Brian, I'd never do that to you guys. I linger on the memory of the words *I'd never do that*, trying to squeeze a drop of reassurance from them.

Then I remember what Joe said. *The bedroom door is locked.*

John lives alone. If he was ill or had fallen, his door would not be locked. And he would never have Samantha in a closed crate while he was home.

"What do you want me to do?" Joe asks.

I've been giving Tom the information as it comes in and I've never seen him wear this kind of shock on his face.

"I don't want anybody to get hurt," I say to Joe.

"Your brother wouldn't hurt *anybody*," Joe says. His words are simple and sure. "I know he wouldn't hurt me. I could kick in the door."

Silence hangs and I hear only the electronic whir of the phone line for a few seconds, or maybe an hour. "Just say the word," Joe tells me.

I look at Tom. He's my touchstone. "Kick it in," I say.

In the moments that follow, Joe has handed the phone to someone else. I hear scuffling, then an ear-splitting crash. Then silence.

I hear Joe's breath before his words. In the seconds of his exhalation, I know. Every molecule of me knows even before he says the words, "I'm so sorry, Betsy. He's gone."

Tom is beside me, his hand rubbing my back. My body crumples like a wounded bird. I tilt the phone so Tom can hear, too. He listens just long enough to hear what happened then pulls away, his palm over his mouth. He collapses beside me on the couch and I listen to Joe and then the deputy and then Joe again. The words they speak are not sentences to my ears; each phrase is a searing hot coal, a missile that pierces my heart and ricochets within my ribcage. *I'm sorry. Gun shot to his chest. Died instantly. No note. I'm sorry. No sign of struggle. Apparently suicide. I'm sorry. Coroner investigation. Autopsy. I'm so sorry.* As I listen it feels as though my warm blood has left my body. My skin is ice cold, but my chest is full of burning embers. I feel the heat of Tom's body wrapped around mine, but I shiver. I may never feel warm again.

Someone other than me speaks, pushes my voice past the knuckles in my throat. She is polite and clear-thinking. She thanks Joe and tells him how sorry she is that he had to find John that way, asks if Joe feels safe to drive. "We've had enough tragedies today," she says. She asks about John's dog, and then asks Joe to thank Jimmy for taking her with him. She asks the deputy if there's any possibility of John's death being anything other than suicide, as though any alternative would be better. There is no indication of foul play, but they'll investigate to be sure. My cool-headed inhabitant provides details to the deputy, John's history, his health, his recent moods, my contact information. My calm proxy gathers the deputy's name and telephone number and inquires about procedures to follow.

As this other woman gathers inadequate answers to her questions, she files them away for me to sort later. While she completes the phone conversation in my stead, the *me* that I know disappears into a bloodless place of disbelief, a place devoid of life and light. I tremble. My lungs cannot pull in enough air.

With the click of the phone receiver in its cradle, I am

reunited with my body as a singular thought comes to me. "Oh god. How are we going to tell the boys?"

Tom and I hold each other. "They'll be okay, baby," he says.

I want this to be true. I've severed whole branches of my family tree, unwilling to expose my sons to the addiction and abuse and general craziness that clawed at the tender flesh of my own childhood, rabid with my desire to preserve their innocence and safety. My once very large extended family has been reduced to a small handful of those closest and most trusted family members, a small limb of what was once a huge tree. Max knew tragic loss far too early. It's been my mission to protect him. But now, despite my every effort for the twenty years of my marriage, the tragedy of my family history has swiped its ugly claws into the tender flesh of my present life. Into the flesh of my sons. Max and Sam adore John. There are no words that will make this any less cruel. My body is rebelling, threatening to vomit.

After a few moments, or maybe ten years of Tom and me holding each other, Tom remembers that he's supposed to pick Max up from work. "Are you going to be okay, baby?" he asks. "You can come with me. Or I'll be back in about twenty minutes. I don't want to call Max and—"

Tom is struggling to find words. We entertain the idea of calling Max to get a cab, but Tom vetoes it. "I want to get him," he says. He wants me to go along, feeling like I shouldn't be alone.

"Go," I say. "I'll be okay. I want to be by the phone." Somewhere in the recesses of my mind, I am thinking John is going to call me and I can't leave. It's absurd, but I can't think my way past it.

Tom is gone for no more than a minute when panic rises from my gut and I'm racing to the bathroom, heaving. My throat burns as I vomit the last of the hot coals and my shivering becomes violent. In a rash moment, I call my sister's house. I can't stop myself. It's not quite 5:30. I don't want to call her cell. She could be driving home from work. I should wait, but I can't. I am so charged up I could throw sparks. I call their house and Jim answers the phone. I instantly wish I'd waited. He's alone until Dianne gets home. *Stupid. Stupid.* Jim and Di got married when John was just ten years old. He's been Jim's little brother almost as long as he's been mine and now I have to tell him that John has shot himself. Jim keeps repeating, "No. No. No."

Now I've passed the hot coals of this to Jim. *Dammit! What's wrong with me? Stupid. I'm usually calm in a crisis.* Jim is alone with this now and I can't believe I've done this to him. *Shit!*

Another yearlong ten minutes pass until Dianne calls. Her voice is barely above a whisper. Her throat has been scalded now. "I can't believe this," she says in strangled words. Hearing Dianne cry grips my heart. And still, I shiver. I shiver hot. I shiver cold. Every morsel of me wants to protect those I love from this kind of pain, and yet I must tell her and Jim all I know, all the while knowing that my words are incendiary missiles traveling across the phone lines to their hearts. We begin our feeble attempts to assemble this morbid puzzle without all of the pieces. Di says, "Again. Here we are again, Bets. I can't believe it." Our duet of sobs is an atonal fugue, a dirge of sorrow and agony. "But he just told me that he was brewing a special holiday beer for Thanksgiving," Di says. "He asked Megan what flavors of beer she likes." We do this for a while, this verbal autopsy of all of the things John has said in recent days and weeks and months, all of the things he's said that did not hint at what would be the horror of today.

"Are we sure?" Jim asks. "Sure that this is not something else? Sure that this is suicide?"

The only other option is murder. I wonder why we are all thinking in this moment that this option would be better than suicide?

My mind flashes back to our childhood house in Indiana and John's little body airborne over the coffee table, propelled by my father's kick to his backside. The legacy of our father's cruelty and abuse has wreaked havoc. Not everyone in my family has made it out alive and my baby brother is now among the casualties. How much higher will the body count go? My imagination climbs the twisted trunk of our family tree, past the gnarled roots and the knots, to the broken branches. My nephew Brian's death, and now John's, are the bitterest fruits that diseased tree has borne.

I hear Tom's truck in the driveway. Dianne and I exchange our words of love before we hang up the phone. We will talk many more times before either of us finds sleep and for hours at a time in the following days.

When he walks in the house, Max takes one look at me, freezes, and says, "What?" Tom has wisely waited to talk to him until we are together.

Tom and I sit him down and tell Max what's happened. His face drains of color. Our son has become a man of twenty-seven in another distortion of time, because in this moment he is seven years old to me. He says nothing, but stands and walks toward me. He cradles me in his arms and we rock together. For the first time since I became his mother, my son rocks me.

Max and I began being mother and son because of a tragic loss and it has felt like my duty to protect him from sustaining another. I've always thought of John as part of a dowry I brought with me to my marriage, a gift I could share with my son. This son of mine lost his mother, his unborn twin brothers, and now his beloved uncle. But rather than being broken by this, he has become my comforter in a way I could never have imagined. It will be weeks and months and maybe years before I fully appreciate that Max has this capacity for compassion not despite the losses he's sustained, but because of them. In this moment, all I can do is let him rock me while I weep.

Sam gets home at 10 pm after an evening class. His eyes scan our faces. "What?" he says when he comes through the door, just as his brother did. Sam at sixteen looks just like John did at this age, with his long limbs, thick, unruly brown hair, mossy green eyes, and a spray of freckles across his nose. Sam is affable and funny, a dreamer, a slob around the house, and generous to a fault, as John has always been. It is both consolation and torture to see my brother's face on my younger son.

My proxy has left me, and words now fail. For once, Tom is the messenger because I cannot force words through what is now a fist in my throat. As Tom explains what's happened, I watch Sam's sweet face twist into an expression that looks as though he has taken a bullet himself, and my broken heart breaks once more. He and John have always shared a special connection and now that's forever broken. I watch Max. He is still and silent, his face a picture of shock and befuddlement. He rises and sits down on the arm of Sam's chair and puts his arm around his brother. In that embrace, I find just enough bittersweet solace to make it through the night.

In the next days we all function, but like zombies. Joe and his staff at work have kindly arranged the memorial service in Reno, where most of John's friends are. Jan and Rich, my sister and brother, fly in for the memorial. The nieces and nephews are with us. The age span is wide in my family, my older brother nearly twenty years older than my younger, and Jan and Rich live three time zones away. We have rarely been together, all five of us at once, and I realize at John's memorial, with his ashes there, it is the last time the five of us will ever be together again. The room is filled with a couple hundred of John's friends and coworkers, all wearing the same stunned faces. I called most everyone in John's cellphone contacts to let them know what happened. This hot coal has seared us all now. We will forever bear the scars.

Organizing the comings and goings of so many family members, thinking of food and lodgings, calling people with this horrible news, all of these tasks have provided structure to the days that followed John's death. After the memorial has passed and everyone goes home, the structure collapses. All I want to do is sleep, but sleep is a vixen, flirting with me, seducing me to near-slumber, then leaving me wide awake and stranded, tangled in the thorny briars of my thoughts. Tom, Max, Sam, and I deal with each other tenderly, all of us avoiding the minutia of the little squabbles over wet towels on the floor and shoes left in the living room that usually pepper everyday life. I cling to every bit of evidence that my boys are coping, that they'll be okay. In my darkest moments, when I alone lay awake in the night, I imagine a future where one of my boys is ripped from me because he died at his own hand. These imaginings, unfounded as they are, send me into panic attacks and sleeplessness that no amount of logic will soothe.

Dianne and Jim and I talk on the phone several times a day. The distance between our homes seems like light years and I ache for our old house in San Anselmo, just so that we can be nearer.

I cannot make ravioli at Christmas. It would break the small pieces of my broken heart into even smaller pieces. John and I have been making the ravioli together for so long. I cannot do it without him. The holiday feels twisted, but we decide to use the time to be together, to honor what remains of our treasured family and to celebrate the love we share. If we've learned nothing else from the horror of losing John—and Brian before him—it is to stay closely connected to one another, to say how much we mean to each other, to bathe each other in love and adoration because we know how quickly a life can end. The holiday is a mix of happy memories and tears.

On a January evening at dusk Tom finds me, huddled in a blanket, sitting on our backyard swing, watching the towering cedars and Ponderosa pines change hues in the melancholy twilight. My breath forms clouds with each exhale, but I don't feel cold. I am numb. I wonder if my body's thermostat will ever function correctly again. In the four months since John's death, I've felt like a stranger to myself. My usual comforts offer nothing. I can't read. I can't write. Sleep eludes me. I can't concentrate. My skin feels as though I've been scoured with lye—raw and vulnerable. Friends and loved ones have revealed the depth of who they are with their kindness, with phone calls, and letters, and gifts certificates for massages, and pots of Mexican wedding soup.

Tom sits close to me on the swing and we stare off into the forest of conifers in our yard, watching evening fall. Our dopey salt-and-pepper doodle dog, Edgar, wanders over and puts his head in my lap. He is the animal that Sam needed to love when we moved to Nevada City. Edgar's hardly left my side in the past weeks.

"I have an idea," Tom says. "But don't say no before you really think about it."

Instantly I am tense, but say nothing.

"I've done some calculating," he says. "If we think really modestly, and we use the life insurance money that John left you as a part of the down payment, we might just be able to move back to Marin. I've been looking at listings online and we might be able to swing it if we downsize a lot."

We came to the Sierra Foothills more than six years ago in a move prompted by financial necessity rather than desire. Though I've made a beautiful handful of what will be treasured lifelong friends here in Nevada City, it's never fully felt like my home.

Tom goes on to explain that with the housing market crash, home prices are depressed. If we think small, we might be able to afford a short sale, or foreclosure property.

I study Tom's face, praying that he wouldn't tease me about something like this, but unable to believe what he's saying. Though I have a few dear friends here in the foothills, since John's death, rather than feeling halfway between my sister and brother, I've felt only far away from those I love in the Bay Area. The distance has been torturous.

As if hearing my thoughts, Tom says, "I know you want to live closer to Di. I'm pretty sure we can do it." Being a beneficiary on John's life insurance has felt like such a bitter inheritance—blood money. I close my eyes to absorb what Tom has just told me. The thought that rises in me is, *John would be happy that his money helped us.*

For all of the words Tom doesn't say every day, he demonstrates his love for me in a thousand ways. He's been secretly researching, protecting me from false hope, not sharing it until he'd figured it all out. Tom is a man who fixes things, repairs broken items to their former function. I am broken right now in a way that I've never been broken before. His customary tools have been useless against my brokenness, so he utilized imagination and his secret search to restore me.

Today, I hear Tom's unspoken love words all at once in a grand symphony. For the first time since that horrible Thursday afternoon four months ago, I feel shimmering bubbles of happiness erupting in my heart. I throw my arms around Tom's neck and squeeze. I give an explosion of grateful kisses.

"I guess we'll be making a U-turn," Tom says. "Back to Marin it is."

"Back home," I say.

We sway together on the swing for another few minutes, my arms around Tom's neck because my gratitude will not allow me to let him go. Edgar's tail wags as though he understands it all. After a few minutes, Tom brings his hands to his lips and blows on his fingers. "Let's go in the house," he says. "I'm freezing my ass off out here."

For the first time since I came outside, I actually feel the cold.

John and his dog, 2010. I'll always remember his sweetness and gentle nature with babies and animals.

I See Dead People and Gratitude

Moving is a bitch. It just is. Even under the best of circumstances the process is tedious and exhausting. When you add layers of sorrow to the task, it grows from a list of wearisome jobs to heart-wrenching excavation.

Though our move from Nevada City back to Marin County feels like a huge blessing and I'm grateful every day as I look forward to it, to pack up a household, clean up behind ourselves, and downsize to a property less than half the size of this one is a process that's taken weeks. It is part boring packing, part archeological dig. Tom's sold some of his biggest shop tools and furniture that wouldn't fit in the new place; he'll be back to just a garage for his tools instead of the dream shop he's enjoyed in Nevada City. Our slim budget allows for a modest house in the burbs in the Bay Area, but not the land and outbuildings we have here. Were it not for the small inheritance from John and the housing crisis, we'd not be able to consider the move at all. Tom's sacrifice of his shop so that I can live nearer to family and friends is one of his biggest acts of generosity in our marriage.

We've had one garage sale already, but somehow our two-car garage is still packed to the gills. The house is packed up, all but the barest necessities for the remainder of our days here. The task can no longer be avoided. I must take on the garage.

As I begin to make my plan of attack, it seems insurmountable. We've lived in this house nearly seven years. Our garage has become the repository for everything we don't use but can't bring ourselves to part with. It is a dust-covered mountain range of memories.

Tom's on yet another run to get more boxes. I sit on the cool cement step inside the garage and examine the neat piles of furniture and trunks and boxes that form a labyrinth on the garage floor and the shelves full of labeled boxes, stacked to precarious heights. Almost none of these boxes have been opened since we moved them here. Many of them haven't been opened since we moved them into the basement of our San Anselmo house twenty-one years ago. And a few, some from my trail of apartments and some from Tom's, likely haven't been touched in even longer than that. *Does everybody do this?*

From that cool cement step I spy a box on a high shelf, labeled *Grandma's Punchbowl.* I let my eyes scan the other labels on other boxes. I see my own writing, *Mom's recipe books.* A set of hooks on the wall cradles several dozen fish-

ing poles, below them three different tackle boxes and large
fishing nets given to us after Karl's passing two years ago.
Forming the foundation for the labyrinth's walls are three
old steamer trunks I remember moving from Tom's house in
Pacifica to San Anselmo, and again to where they sit now.
I've peeked in those trunks over the years. I know what waits
for me there. Nope—not quite ready for those yet.

Tom arrives with a stack of flattened boxes. "Hey,
baby," he says with more cheer than I can fathom in this
final stage of packing. He comes toward where I sit. Reading my slumped body and what must be my sour expression, he says, "What's up, buttercup?" His mood is buoyant. For Tom, this is just a move. Moves excite him. He
always looks ahead to where we're going; I look back at
what we leave behind.

"I see dead people," I say.

Tom looks over his shoulder as though there might be
a zombie sneaking up on him.

"This garage is full of all of the stuff that belonged to
people who have died."

"Just get rid of it all," Tom says, and part of me is
jealous for his unsentimental practicality. He's right, sort
of. We should get rid of nearly everything in this garage.
I've carted my grandmother's punch bowl to every place
I've lived since I moved out of my mom's house at seventeen. I remember my grandma making punch, serving it at
baby showers and special events at the Sons of Italy halls
of my early childhood. I've carted this box like it holds
Waterford crystal, when I know that my grandparents
never had anything of such monetary value. I keep moving
it out of affection and sentiment, but never once in all of

those years have I served punch from it. *Does* anyone *serve punch any more?*

I've intended to sort through my mom's haphazard stacks of recipes since she passed thirteen years ago, just as I've meant to sift through the boxes of John's things that I've been unable to look at since his suicide nine months ago. The garage is not a storage place. It's a museum of unfinished projects, heartbreaking loss, and memories. It's a death museum.

I stand, brush off my numb backside, and put my hands on my hips as I survey the task before me.

"Look out, world," Tom says.

"Okay," I say with fortified dedication. "Here's how this is going to go."

Tom steps back. He knows what I'm like when I get like this. After avoiding a task for too long, once I dedicate myself to it, he's right. *Look out, world.*

"I'm calling the family and giving them a week's notice on anything they might want while I sort out wheat from chaff, then chuck the chaff. We've held on to a bunch of this crap because we thought somebody else might want it sometime. Those days are over. It's now or never."

Tom pumps his fist. "Go get 'em, baby!"

"Anything not claimed by that time is 100 percent my discretion. If we want it, we keep it. We toss what's broken or not working. We keep only what we absolutely love, no matter whose it was. It's a waste and a crime that this has all been sitting in here for so long."

"This garage doesn't stand a chance," Tom says. He unloads the boxes from his trunk and disappears down to his shop where he's continuing to sort and select his own collection. Sam's already boxed up his room.

Over the next five days, I sort. Dust and grime cake on my skin and I sweat it off in muddy rivers in the summer heat, but I am undeterred. I make trip after trip to the local Goodwill, donating mountains of clothes and books and camping gear and linens and lamps without shades and generic flower vases. Surely my grandmother's memory is not served by my carting that punch bowl one more time. I decide she's better honored if it's being used by people celebrating than if it's stacked in my garage. I hope it finds its way to a Sons of Italy Lodge or a church kitchen to be used at weddings. She'd have liked that.

When I open boxes that contain my mother's belongings, I'm greeted with the surprise odor of cigarette smoke. *How can that linger for this many years?* I close my eyes and remember. Near every memory I have of my mom includes her smoking and the smell of it feels like a visitation. From my mom's belongings I salvage her handwritten recipes and toss the dozens of old magazines with recipes from another era: a veritable rainbow of Jell-O salad, enchilada casserole, tuna surprise. I laugh a little that I ever felt the need to hold onto such things. Letting go is getting easier.

My boys have chosen from among Karl's fishing poles and tackle boxes; the rest go into the donate pile. Karl managed to live to his eighties without ever having had a surgery, and it was only in his last months that he ever entered a hospital as a patient, something I can imagine him bragging about were he still with us. As I move this stack, I recall Karl's surly exterior, and the sweetness when he called me his daughter, and when he said that Sam, yet unborn, would be his grandson at their fiftieth anniversary. Verna is alone now, living in an assisted-living facility, her memory only a gossamer hint of what it once was. In one of the boxes, I find the recipes she's written down for me over the years. Her recipe for chocolate chip cookies has the words, *Max, No nuts,* written on top. I know that Max and Jim will share a laugh about that. I recall Verna so often arriving at my house with a batch of these cookies. I see her pumpkin pie recipe, the one she made for every Thanksgiving we've shared in the last twenty-one years until she could no longer safely cook on her own. "The secret of pumpkin pie is you can use butternut squash and no one will ever know," she once told me. I hold the recipe against my heart and remember Verna's quirky ways, and her utter adoration of Max and Sam. With her memory all but gone, it seems my sons have nearly lost the last of their grandparents. With my mother's death, I feared Sam would have no grandparents at all, and mine had been so important to me. I'm so grateful that Karl and Verna took him as their own. Since marrying Tom, I've continually redefined the word "family."

ℓℓℓ—ℓℓℓ

It's ungodly hot during our packing ordeal, and even with fans blowing on me all day, the garage is nearly unbearable. The shelves are empty. The furniture and most of the boxes that formed the maze in our garage are all gone and I can see the floor for the first time in years. I'm left with only one stack of items and three steamer trunks to sort. I decide that the remaining tasks are to be done in the cooler evening hours. And a bonus: I get to drink wine while I tackle these last two projects. I decide I deserve wine.

That night, with good Pinot Grigio poured into a

mason jar and the yellow glare of the floodlights Tom set up for me, I start the last of my tasks.

First, I sort through the detritus of John's belongings. I've distributed mementos to each of my siblings and our kids. I have his silver baby cup carefully preserved. I have kept what I need. I pick up the things that Tom and I rescued from John's house before it all went to probate, silly things that for some reason I couldn't leave behind that day. His ostrich-skin cowboy boots. His tattered Birkenstocks. His Reno Rodeo belt buckles. These things that felt so important to me a few months ago have now become an anchor, holding me down. The ostrich boots sag with the wear of years, but still have good life in them. Somebody will think they're cool, so I put them into the donate pile. The Birkenstocks are another matter. I saw my baby brother wear these so frequently, they feel like part of his body to me. They bear the perfect print of his feet on their insoles. I run my fingers over the timeworn surface where my brother stood. Shoes seem so personal somehow, but no, I can't keep these and they're beyond their usefulness to anyone else. I take a look over my shoulder and see no one, so I indulge my urge and kiss each tattered shoe before I toss them into the trash.

With the last of his belongings sorted, I find myself talking aloud to my brother. I sweep the newfound floor I've just cleared in angry strokes. "Damn you, Johnny. You sure left a shit pile for us to sort." As soon as the angry words leave my lips, tears spill.

Leaving this house, I'll be moving to the first place I've ever lived where my brother will never visit. "It's not right," I say as I sweep. "You should still be here."

Finally, I'm left with one last task: the steamer trunks.

Those three steamer trunks are the repositories for all of Janet's belongings. I've asked Tom if he wants to sort them out. He has skirted the task with the grace of a martial arts master. I asked Max if he wanted to go through them with me. He too declined. At first I'm angry with my guys for shirking this task, but then I realize that the task is best in my hands anyway. They'd avoid the whole thing and chuck the lot of it without searching through the flotsam and jetsam for the gems I know I want to find. As much as I want to thin our belongings, I have a promise to keep. I promised Max on the day that I married his father that I'd preserve Janet's memory for him. This job is about keeping my word. It is my job to do.

Well past midnight, I sift through one steamer trunk at a time. I've set aside one box for those special few items of Janet's that I want to preserve for Max. Each trunk greets me with the smell of old paper and dust when I open it.

The first trunk is filled with mementos of Janet's childhood. There is a collection of stuffed animals, bears and monkeys, chicks and puppies, and one unidentifiable form that I think might have once been Humpty Dumpty. I select one small plush cat to keep, and put the rest into the bags I'm donating to the local women's shelter. I hope they give comfort to the children who come there. Humpty is too tattered to save. I toss the faded construction-paper school projects and the bags of hair barrettes. I box up the costume jewelry and the romance novels, the old Kodak Instamatic camera and the square flashcubes that go with it all for one last donation run. I know Max won't care about any of these particular items.

The second trunk is filled with school yearbooks and photo albums of Janet's adolescence. I flip through the pictures, feeling as though I'm watching her grow up, seeing Max's face on every page of her youthful photographs. Her yearbooks are inscribed with the silly quips of high school friends with messages like *2-Sweet 2-B 4-gotten*. I find half a dozen journals and part of me feels that I should just put them into Max's box without reading them. I feel like an intruder. But then my imagination and curiosity get the better of me, and I worry that there might be something in there that might trouble him. I swallow and open the first journal. It's a travel log of a driving trip that Janet and Tom took. She's only filled two pages with her tiny, block printing. Rather than the romantic notes or outpourings of her heart, I find that Janet has written only lists of their stops, of what they bought at each stop and its price. There is nothing personal on these pages. When I read that they bought Lays Potato Chips and Pepsi for $3.45, it makes me laugh. Janet never tried to be anything she wasn't. She was simple and straightforward, blunt in her words. As I sort through her journals I realize that she was the female version of her dad Karl, and Max is so very like them both.

The third trunk is the hard one. Among other things, that contains a fat bundle of nearly a hundred sympathy cards sent to Tom and Max after Janet died. I recognize the names of some of the friends we still hold dear, along with many others from people I don't know. I sit on the cement step and read each card. I decide to discard the ones that are simply signed, but elect to preserve the ones where the senders chose to include a fond memory of Janet or affections for Tom and Max. Max deserves to see how so many people loved his first mother. As I get to the bottom of the stack, I spot my own handwriting on an envelope.

I open the card, a photograph of a beautiful meadow full of blossoming wildflowers. Inside, in my own hand I see these words that I don't recall writing:

Dear Tom:

There are no perfect words to comfort you right now. I can't imagine how hard this has all been for you.

I will always recall Janet with the expression I saw on her face the first time I saw her with Max in her arms. She wore pure joy looking at him. Her life was too short, but if her face that day told me anything about her life, it was that she was happy in the family you created together. I hope that offers comfort.

Please know that you have a wide circle of friends who care about you and that circle includes me. I make a pretty good babysitter, if ever you need a night to yourself. Ask for anything . . . any time.

With love and sorrow, Betsy

I tuck this one card into my pocket and I'll store it with my own mementos. It seems as much a part of my love story with Tom as it is a memory preserved for Max.

With the cards sorted, I face only two more small boxes at the bottom of the trunk. The first is a small red jewelry box. Inside is Janet's simple wedding band. I set this aside. In the last box, nestled in the tissue paper I wrapped them in, is the collection of ceramic Beatrix Potter figures I put into this chest myself. I unwrap each small rabbit and frog and goose, recalling my animating them with the question that troubled me so many years ago. I once used these figures to ask myself aloud if I was up to the task of mothering Max.

I peer into the painted faces of the figurines. "Yeah," I said. "I think I did okay."

※

Max and I stand together in the kitchen of our empty living room in Nevada City. The single box I've made with the collection of Janet's mementos sits between us on the counter. The Pod containers have been loaded and will be taken to our new home back in the Bay Area.

I've explained to Max why I made the choices I did on his behalf and I've given him the option of opening the box alone or with me. He's chosen this. He lifts the lid of the box and peers inside. My heart beats fast, not quite knowing how this will be for him.

I've tied the collection of sympathy cards together and wrapped them in tissue. I explain what they are and he sets them aside for later viewing. He laughs as he sifts through some of the photos and pulls out one of Janet's school pictures from middle school.

He holds it up.

"It looks just like you, but with glasses and a girl's hairdo," I tease.

Max grins. "Yeah, I guess it does look like me."

"Looks like Grandpa, too," I say.

Max presses his lips together and digs into the box.

All grown up. Tom and me with Max and Sam with our ham of a dog, Edgar. Thanksgiving, 2014.

He pulls up the small box of ceramic figures. "Hey," he says, brightening. "I remember these."

I show him one of his birth announcements that also bears a Beatrix Potter watercolor illustration. "She really liked this kind of thing, didn't she?" he says.

"Yeah," I say. "She was sweet that way. I thought maybe you might want to set these figurines aside. Maybe if you choose to have kids some day, you could use them in the nursery. Your dad told me that he thinks that's why your mom bought them in the first place. You had Beatrix Potter wallpaper in your first baby bedroom."

Max nods, his eyes glued to the figures in his lap. His voice is soft. "Thanks for going through all of this stuff," he says. "I bet that was kind of hard."

"That's okay, honey. I'm glad to do it."

"I know, but—"

Finally, he finds the red box. "It's your mom's wedding ring," I say. "I don't know if you want to wear it or if it would even fit you, but I put a chain in there and if you'd like, you could wear it as a necklace."

Without looking up, Max pulls the silver chain from the case and threads it through the ring, then places the necklace over his head. He fingers the new item where it hangs in front of his heart. In his perfect Eeyore voice he says, "Thanks a lot. That really means a lot to me."

I reach for him and we exchange an embrace. It's a pretty sweet feeling when you're locked in the arms of your son and you can't tell who's hugging whom.

In this instant, Max is a man, but no matter how old he gets, he's preserved forever as a little boy in my eyes, a little boy whose mother left big shoes for me to fill.

Last Laugh

Whenever I break a rule or tell a lie, I get caught. It's been like that since I was a kid. There's just something about my luck or my demeanor that doesn't let me get away with shady things. My mom used to tell me that my face always ratted me out. For the most part, this has served me well in life, keeping me from getting into the kinds of trouble that more successful sneaks create in their lives. But occasionally a rule is meant to be broken.

On the first anniversary of John's death, Dianne and I decided that we wanted to release his ashes to the sea at a nearby Marin County beach. It had been a year of extraordinary sadness and we felt the need to release some of our grief with this ritual and to remember our brother after the sharp edges of the shock of his suicide had dulled a little. I also brought a bag of rose petals from our garden to release with his ashes, my way of saying *Thank You* for his posthumous help in our moving back to Marin County.

After our mom died, twenty years before, we had wanted to release her ashes to the sea but were given all kinds of prohibitions by the funeral home at the time. There are regulations against releasing human "cremains" at the coastline. Out of grief and exhaustion, and perhaps too little questioning of authority, none of us examined the validity or necessity of these warnings at the time, nor did we use our imaginations to come up with a more pleasing plan, so we paid the Neptune Society to release her ashes some sixty miles off the coastline as per regulations. I've since heard of friends who buried their loved ones' ashes in their yards or scattered them at a beloved fishing hole. I've always regretted that we didn't rebel a little with Ma's ashes, because I felt so detached from the experience and it seemed such a pathetic good-bye. While I'm glad there are regulations that people don't just get to dump human remains wherever they feel like it, the laws against putting ashes into an ocean seem kind of stupid. Campfires get swept into the sea all the time, right? Dumping a couple of pounds of nontoxic, organic matter into the biggest body of water on the planet had neither a negative environmental impact nor did it seem like a high crime.

Jim didn't feel the need to go along—everyone has his own way of honoring those passed—so Di, Tom, and I drove, ashes and rose petals in tow, the forty minutes on winding roads to where the Pacific meets the Marin County coastline. We'd picked a beach where no one was swimming. It would be icky to get coated in human ashes, after all. We searched for a spot where the wind wouldn't blow John's ashes back into our faces. Much as I loved him, I didn't really want to *wear* my brother on my face and in my hair. This was trickier than one might imagine, given the capricious nature of ocean breezes.

We stopped at five or six different beaches, finding each one inappropriate for one reason or another: crowds, too windy, swimmers in wet suits. Finally, we found the perfect spot. It was a secluded cove with only a gentle breeze blowing parallel to the coastline. There were no swimmers and very few people on the beach: a guy walking his dog and a couple in the distance who clearly wanted to be undisturbed. We set our sights on a spot toward the opposite end of the beach. This was working out splendidly.

Just as we walked onto the soft sand with our Safeway grocery bag containing the container full of John, a series of cars started arriving and spilling their passengers into the parking lot. Within moments park rangers arrived and signage appeared. How had we missed that this was California Beach Cleanup Day? It seemed my lifelong pattern of not getting away with things would remain intact.

"Well, that's just perfect," Dianne said, exasperated.

"What do you think, guys?" Tom asked. "Should we go someplace else?"

"This is probably clean up day on every beach in California," I reasoned.

We talked for a few more minutes and considered our options. Teary-eyed, Di and I decided that we'd just have to be quicker than we'd planned, but that we were eager to have this private memorial behind us on this sad anniversary day. We decided that rather than tossing the ashes and making a conspicuous scene of things, we'd pour them onto the sand at the water's edge and let the fingers of the sea claim them gradually, along with the rose petals.

The vision of it was clear in my mind. We could be there together, reminiscing as we watched as our brother's ashes being pulled out to sea, with rose petals marking their swirling path to the mysterious beyond. A romantic image and a fitting memorial.

"Look out," Tom whispered. "There's a ranger just over there."

I felt like an idiot for how nervous we all were about getting caught. We were like kids on a caper, worried about getting busted while we toilet-papered the principal's house. Soon the ranger walked toward the other end of the beach and we had our window of opportunity.

While Tom watched over our his shoulder, I poured the soft gray ashes onto the beach near the water's edge, then topped the mound with the flower petals.

The prankish nature of the moment passed and the solemnity of it hit me. The three of us stood together and looked out over the water. The sun in the distance wore a gauzy layer of fog, offering a mercifully soft light. Gulls screeched in the distance. Di and I linked arms. "Just doesn't seem right that he's gone," she said.

"I'm not as mad at him anymore," I said. "I guess if he was in that much pain, I wouldn't want him to suffer with it. I guess my lifelong pro-choice stance now means I believe in someone's right to die, too."

"I feel the same way," Di added. "Just seems like if he'd have let people know what was going on, he might've felt a lot differently."

"It still makes me sad that he didn't leave a note behind, some kind of explanation," I said. "I feel a little selfish wanting that, though."

Suicide creates a jigsaw puzzle that will forever be missing pieces. Those left behind spend weeks and months and years sorting through the memories, dissecting old conversations, discovering new details to try to complete the picture that would give us answers to how such a horrible thing could have happened. The answers for why John took his life will always be, at best, a hypothesis. We fill in the gaps with our best guesses and our assumptions. We write new stories to fill in the holes. Living with this blurred, incomplete picture is part of the agony of losing someone you love to suicide.

With John's ashes and the rose petals at our feet, we waited for the sea to reach forward and take our brother away, meanwhile sneaking peeks to see that the ranger and the trash gatherers didn't wander through our spot. We waited.

"He'll always seem like that skinny little kid to me," Dianne reminisced, teary.

"He'll always be my baby brother," I said, through the tightness in my throat.

As our stories meandered from recent years to those long ago, from funny stories to sad ones, I looked down at the mound of ashes and flower petals near my feet. "Um. Does it seem like the water is getting farther away?" I asked.

"Crap!" Tom said. "I think the tide is going out."

At just that moment the horde of beachcombers began making its way toward us.

"What are we going to do?" Di asked.

"We can't just leave this pile of ashes here," Tom said.

My perfect, romantic vision of this memorial was obliterated. After a quick exchange of panicky ideas, we determined that our only option was to scoop the ashes

into the water ourselves. Tom pulled out the plastic urn
from the Safeway bag and started scooping. I used the liner
bag from the urn to push the ashes along. Di kicked at
the flower petals. After a few moments of this Di began
to laugh. It was contagious. Soon we were all laughing
and cursing and kicking at the sand while we watched the
beach cleaners and the rangers make their way toward us.

With all of us breathless, the task was finally done.
We stood together again, snickering and watching the pink
and yellow flower petals float on the foamy surface of the
water, accompanied by the mournful calls of gulls over-
head and the whooshing sound of the breaking waves.

During all of our ridiculous scrambling, I'd secretly
snatched a small bit of ash from the mound, not quite
ready to let all of John go. As we watched the last of the
petals disappear into the current, I ground the bit of ash
into my palm with my thumb. John and I were the stragglers in my family, born much later than my older three
siblings, with Di as the bridge between the two batches
of us. He and I shared a bed until I was ten and he was
seven. We shared a room with bunk beds for another three
years after that. He'd always felt like part of me. I wanted
to grind that little morsel of him into my skin, into my
blood, and make it part of my own body. I found a small
cut on my palm and pressed the ashes into it, recalling a
time when we were small and we'd used a pin to poke
both of our thumbs, then we'd rubbed them together to
make us blood brother and sister. It was an unnecessary
gesture, of course, because we already shared blood. But
in that moment on the beach I felt the same urge to create
some tangible way to experience our bond.

This would be the last speck of my brother's earthly body that I would ever touch. We wept a little and laughed a little more.

Each year since, I've commemorated John's birthday by bringing rose petals from our garden to wherever we are, and releasing them. I went back to the same beach spot one year. The following year we released petals from home off of an ancient wall in Siena, Italy, after Dianne and I had lit candles in a chapel near the Vatican in honor of the loved ones in our family that we'd lost to suicide.

"He had to give us just one more laugh on his way out," Di said. "He couldn't just have made this one easy on us. Somehow I feel like he's laughing with us."

"He'd have laughed his ass off watching us kicking his ashes into the surf," I said. I was happy to have finally gotten away with breaking a rule.

Tom folded the grocery bag and tucked it under his arm. "I guess that's what they mean when they say 'last laugh.'"

"You had it, Johnny," I said. "You got the last laugh."

I Know You

Our family watched helplessly as Verna slipped into the murky depths of dementia. Karl had preceded her on the same course just a few years before. When he died, her decline was rapid and undeniable. I've always felt that Verna's sheer will and devotion to Karl kept her own condition at bay until the moment he no longer needed her.

Verna had always been feisty, opinionated, and strong-willed. She and Karl both prided themselves for their independence and self-sufficiency. Into their eighties, their headstrong natures had served to keep them independent for much longer than most can manage. They walked every day, stayed fit, lived modestly and, despite humble means, saved their nickels for a tidy nest egg so that they'd never have to rely on anyone for financial assistance. Frugal. Proud. Stubborn. The qualities that made them both admirable also made their advanced years harder on others, especially their daughter, Karen—one of my dearest "outlaws".

As young women, Janet and Karen had a sister pact about caring for their parents should the need arise. When Janet died, Karl and Verna were still healthy and strong. But Janet's early passing unexpectedly made Karen an only child, alone to manage her parent's care. Karen turned her life upside down to provide all the care to her parents that she and her sister had agreed to share.

When it was obvious to the family that it was no longer wise for her to live alone, Verna dug in her heels. She, like so many of her generation, rejected all ideas for alternative living situations, particularly if it meant moving anywhere that resembled what her peers called "the home," or "being a burden" on her daughter by living with her. Verna began to exhibit the "sundowning effect" that so many with dementia suffer. She would function fairly well in the morning, the times she usually saw doctors, so it was hard for them to see the degree of her impairment. But as twilight appeared she'd become disoriented, forgetful, and frightened. She started having hallucinations about little children dancing in her house at night. She began to burn food and misplace items, and became unable to care for her basic needs. We all feared the worst, that she'd start a fire or take a fall while she was alone. Tom and I lived two hours away and it wasn't clear she'd know how to call for help. It was clear she was afraid to stay alone. And still, she rejected every notion of someone staying with her or moving to a safer environment. Eventually, as her small accidents grew more frequent and the fog in her mind thickened, no choice remained. Karen made the difficult, role-reversing decision that so many adult daughters are called upon to make, and overruled her mother in service of her best interests. She also called upon the two people to assist her that her mom would never argue with: Verna's twin brother, and Max.

Under the guise of a Sunday drive, Karen and her Uncle Vern drove her mom to what would be her new accommodations at a skilled memory center in a nearby town. When they got there, Max, now in his late twenties, stood waiting at the curb to convince his grandmother that this step was one she must take. "We all love you, Grandma," Max said to her. "We all think it's best that you stay here for a while." He ushered his frightened and confused grandmother into her new residence. She followed him without the fight that all of us had feared. I could see that it broke his heart to deceive her.

For so many years it had been I who felt the need to fill Janet's shoes, to mother Max when she could no longer. But now it was Max stepping into the role his mother had left behind, partnering with his aunt, as his mother would have, to care for his grandmother. I've never been prouder of my son and I'm sure Janet would be, too.

As her memory further faded in her assisted living residence, Verna grew more docile and less resistant to the help she required. As hard as it was to watch her decline, Karen told me many times how grateful she was to have this time with her mother. With her memory dimmed, Verna mellowed, and what emerged were the sweetest aspects of her nature. She grew cooperative, appreciative, and calmer. Except, that is, toward me.

While Verna had always treated me with kindness and affection for the twenty-plus years after Tom and I were married, the more demented she became, the more pleasant she became to others and the more hostile she became toward me. If I was in the company of anyone else, particularly Max, Verna was nothing but sugary-sweet as she'd always been. But when I was alone with her, it was an entirely different exchange. Several times I stopped in unaccompanied at the memory center to visit her. On each visit she would take one look at me, stare right at me and say, "Nope. I don't want to see *YOU.*" Then she'd turn heel and walk away.

I assumed she didn't recognize me that day. She had good days and bad, so I decided to come back another time. After a couple more rejections, not wanting to upset her, I elected not to visit her alone, seeing her instead only at gatherings with the family.

When Verna and her brother, Vern, turned ninety, Karen and her cousins arranged a celebration of their shared birthday. At a local community clubhouse, relatives and friends gathered to toast the elderly twins. Vern, still vibrant and memory intact, was a gracious escort to his sister, who smiled blankly and accepted the well wishes of others. I wasn't quite sure how many of them she still recognized or how much of the hoopla she understood. But she seemed happy that day, and that was all that mattered.

Midway through the party I encountered Verna in the ladies' room with the caregiver Karen had arranged to assist her mom that day. From behind the door of a stall I heard Verna ask her aide for a breath mint. I let them know that I had some with me. They emerged from the stall and I watched as the gentle woman helped Verna wash her hands and apply lipstick. Always a tiny woman, in her later years Verna was even smaller, her head barely reaching the height of my shoulder. Her hair remained in the same beauty-parlor shape it had always held, but very little else about her seemed the same.

I took two tins of mints from my purse and placed them on the counter. "Here you go, Verna. I have spearmint or peppermint."

Verna looked up into the mirror for the first time, and her eyes locked directly onto my reflection. I'd greeted her earlier with Max and she'd worn a pleasant, if vacant, smile. When she spied my reflection, the placid expression she'd been wearing withered into a suspicious, angry scowl. She squinted at my reflection and raised her pointed finger. "I know you," she said.

Visions of a certain movie witch and a certain girl from Kansas popped into my mind, but I decided to ignore her expression. "Of course you know me, Verna. I'm Betsy. Tom and I wished you and Vern a happy birthday earlier. Here are the mints you wanted."

Her finger still raised, she pursed her lips. "I know who *you* are," she said with extra bitterness.

Verna's caregiver tried to soften the exchange. "Look here, Verna. Betsy has a mint for you." She took a candy and offered it to Verna, who accepted it readily and popped it into her mouth. Like a child distracted momentarily by a shiny toy or a lollipop, Verna's tranquil expression returned. Her assistant started gathering Verna's things and headed to open the door.

Thinking the encounter over, I relaxed a bit until Verna once again found my reflection in the mirror. Though frail and likely no more than ninety pounds, her expression made her appear formidable. She raised her finger again and her mouth twisted into a grimace. Her gaze was full of fire. Her lips worked for a moment, as if trying to articulate words that she could not quite conjure.

When the words assembled themselves, she tilted her head and spoke in harsh staccato, her finger wagging. "You are not Janet. They can't tell me, I know. I know!" Her lips worked some more until they found the next sentence with more exaggerated staccato. "You. Are. Not. Janet."

I stood in stunned silence for a moment, then fashioned my face into a smile I didn't feel like wearing.

With that, Verna stepped toward her caregiver, who looked at me with sympathetic eyes. "She doesn't mean it," she said.

"Thanks. I understand," I said. "Here." I gave the woman a tin of mints. "She might want one later."

Alone with my reflection, I watched my eyes turn red and I swallowed to try to shrink the lump in my throat. I knew Verna's anger was born of her dementia and she couldn't help what she was doing, but somehow the words *You. Are. Not. Janet.* felt like arrows, shot one at a time, straight at my heart. Though the caregiver was trying to be kind, I knew that Verna meant exactly what she'd said.

Verna passed away only a few months after that exchange in the ladies' room. Karen was with her as she drifted away. Since then, I've thought a lot about that moment reflected in the bathroom mirror. To me, this encounter with Verna at the end of her days always seems inextricably linked to our first meeting more than twenty years before. It has always fascinated me that the exchange took place in the mirror . . . a place of reflection. The day I first met Karl and Verna, she had been so afraid that I might come between her and Max, that I might prevent her from seeing her beloved grandson. Of course, I never had any such intentions, and Verna's fear wasn't personal to me because she feared it before we'd even met. After Alzheimer's robbed her brain of its regular function and perspective, that dormant terror still lurked in a dark corner of her mind and erased the twenty years of pleasant encounters, shared holidays and Little League games, graduations, and camping trips. What was left after those memories were stolen was the fear she'd had when we first met.

And in the end, the words she spoke to me in the mirror weren't personal either. There was nothing more I could have done to allay her fear or to show her love. None of what was within my power changed the fact that I had stepped into the shoes of a daughter that had been cruelly taken from her mother. Perhaps my very presence reminded Verna of Janet's absence. In the end, after she'd forgotten my name and what relationship I had to her family, Verna knew only one thing about me: I was not Janet.

I choose to look at my relationships with all of my "outlaws" as a gift, another aspect of my vast inheritance. As a result of Janet's early passing, I inherited not only a husband and a son, but an entire family. Karen is my bonus sister, her daughters my adored nieces. Karl and Verna were grandparents to both of my sons, and I'll be forever grateful to them for that. Family relationships are seldom simple. Just as I've learned that grief and gratitude necessarily live side-by-side, I've come to believe that love and resentment often coexist in family relationships. To Verna, at least in one corner of her mind, I may have always been "not Janet," but I know she and Karl loved and appreciated me and were happy for my loving relationship with Max; they said so often. For all of their quirks and stubborn ways, I loved them, too.

Verna at 90, surrounded by some of my favorite "out-laws."
Back row, my bonus sister Karen, Max in the middle, and
Verna's 90-yo twin, Vern. Front row, Karen's daughters, my
bonus nieces with Alison on the left and Simone to the right.

Mixing Metaphors

* an epilogue *

When I moved from Indiana to California's Central San Joaquin Valley as an adolescent, I met our neighbors, Mr. Seavers and his family. Mr. Seavers was a professional grafter working for California's orchard industry. My brother John and I played with Mr. and Mrs. Seavers' son, and so we had occasion to hang out at their house. I'd never heard of grafting and was fascinated to learn about it. I was that kind of kid, insatiably curious and perhaps a little strange. While the other kids played ball or Kick the Can in the empty lot next to the Seavers' house, I hovered around Mr. Seavers asking him about grafting and he showed me the most magical trees I'd ever seen.

In their back yard, Mr. Seavers had grafted 52 different kinds of citrus onto a single tree and dozens of stone fruit varieties onto another. New to California, I'd never before even seen an orange tree, much less anything like the spectacular fruit rainbow in his yard. He called them his "Frankenstein Trees." The enormous trees boasted separate branches of individual varieties of familiar fruits, and other branches chock-full of varieties and hybrids I'd never heard of. I loved their exotic names—tangelo, lime-on, pomelo, limorange, pluot, apripeach, nectarine—and wrote them down in the notebook I kept even then. I was especially intrigued when cross-pollination within the tree resulted in individual fruits that seemed to be of one variety, but had a single wedge, sometimes just a sliver, of another within the same fruit. I recall an orange with a single yellow slice, as if a wedge of the orange had been cut out and replaced with a a smaller slice of lemon. Another was a green lime with a single, larger insert of a slice of bright lemon yellow, with perfect lines of demarcation between the colors. These fruits looked artificial, but I picked them and sliced them open, and tasted the sweet and tart of every one. Mr. Seavers reveled in my unusual fascination. The other kids couldn't have cared less.

In the decades since first seeing those trees and their peculiar fruit, I've come to think of my family tree like Mr. Seavers' trees, embellished with all that he taught me about his techniques. We had the normal "graftings" with marriages and arrivals of children by birth or adoption. Mr. Seavers also taught me that not all grafts take; branches wither because of disease or mismatching, while others are selected for surgical removal for the ultimate health of the tree. All of this has happened in my family as well. We had our share of divorces, deaths, estrangements, and decisions to sever some ties that were unhealthy. Often geography alone caused a severance, with no hard feelings attached.

Other severances were by design. Given the violence, addiction, and abuse that took place in my original family, I was a ferocious defender, unwilling to let any such influences into my home to touch the tender buds I was dedicated to nurturing. In my youth, I thought the only way avoid perpetuating what had plagued my own family was to eliminate any possibility of having children at all. I'm grateful that I was given the chance to learn how wrong I was.

After the trauma of losing his mother at such a young age, I was determined to protect Max (and later Sam as well) from any trauma, abuse, or chaos that was within my control. Though there are beautiful individuals in my father's extended family, there were also others who, like my dad, suffered the same maladies that made him what he was. I've allowed the geographical distance between the West Coast and the Midwest to remove those limbs. It is a costly severance. I went from having a very large extended family to having a small, select group, which today consists mostly of my sister Dianne's family and my own with occasional sweet encounters with the families of my other surviving siblings who live across the country from me. My mother's family was loving and safe. Those who remain of my Graziani relatives are dear to us, with only geography as a limit to our contact. Theirs are trees of a beautiful variety, but in groves far from our own. Our visits are treasured, if too rare.

This book is also treelike, requiring pruning of what's not necessary to tell in service of the story. The stories I've included in this collection are, by intention, a tight focus on those events that marked the moments of stepping into motherhood by marrying a widower with a son. That means a lot of events and people—both of the "in-law" and of the "out-law" varieties, from both Tom's vast extended family in Indiana and Ohio are barely mentioned, and the long limbs of my own extended family tree—are not included, not because they're not important and dear to us, but because that isn't what this particular story is about. After losing so much of it, I've developed a new definition of family and am fortunate to have some friends that are family to me and some family members that are my dearest friends. I call this treasured group my "FRamily." They too are absent from this story, but not from our lives, and certainly not from our hearts.

Neither have I included chapters or scenes in this book where Tom, Max, Sam, and I have the petty arguments of daily life. It would make for pretty boring reading, I assure you. Like any couple, Tom and I have arguments, of course: hurt feelings, misunderstandings, stupid disagreements. I often say that Tom and I have had the same four fights over and over again over the course of our long marriage. I get mad when he interrupts my writing to have me help him fold a painting tarp—as he did this very morning as I was wrote these last pages. He gets cranky when I push him to express himself with words rather than with the loving and affec-tionate deeds that are his more fluent language. He declines more invitations than I'd like. I accept more than he'd like. He forgets most things, I remember everything. At the time that I write this, our twenty-fifth anniversary is a few months away and we must both still strive to learn the love language that the other speaks. Over the course of our lives we've had a handful of big blow-ups that shook us to our roots, but the union has survived the blasts. Of late, our biggest fights are when I try to convince him that he needs a hearing aid and him telling me that I mumble. Our waistlines have thickened, we spend too much on dining out, too many vegetables go unused—the stuff of riveting storytelling.

Tom, of all of the "characters" in my story, is the hardest one to write. He's a man of deeds rather than words. He lives in an uncomplicated way, satisfied by the simple pleasures of life. I've known him to lie exactly once in our marriage. It was a small fib he told on a DMV form. Tom sold a pickup and the guy who bought it asked if we could declare he'd bought it for $2,000 instead of $4,000 so that he could pay lower registration fees and we would have to pay less tax. Tom agreed in the moment, but was up most of the night fretting, with a bellyache. He took the next morning off work, and went to the DMV to correct the amount and pay the proper fee. He called the buyer in the morning and apologized, but said he just didn't feel right about not telling the truth. Bad guys make more colorful characters on the page, but this good guy is plenty colorful for me. He's easy with a laugh, whistles every day, and always puts the needs of our sons before his own pleasures.

This book started out as a mother/son story, but as I wrote, it became clear that it was also our love story, mine and Tom's. I end these pages more keenly aware of the enormity of losses we have sustained together, but more deeply appreciative of how we've loved each other through those losses.

We've never used the terms "step" or "half" or "adopted" in our family. I don't remember once being called Max's stepmother, or our sons referring to one another as half-brothers, though there'd be nothing wrong with those terms, of course. I don't know that this was ever a conscious decision; it just seems to reflect how we feel toward one another. We were spared some of the challenges that many blended families face. We never had to fight over custody or visitation, child support, or different rules in different houses. Though we had the conflicts that any family has, the biggest fights in our lives have never been with one another, but with grief and loss as our adversaries. Maybe because the entire existence of our family is built on a foundation of loss, we have a special appreciation for how fleeting life can be. So many things seem unimportant when you measure them against losing the ones you love most. We know how easily that can happen. Loss has cost us much, but has also given us plenty.

When I look at Max and who he has become as a man, I recall the most extraordinary fruits on Mr. Seavers' tree. Max was made by Tom and Janet, and I see both of them and their family members in both his appearance and his character. I see his grandpa Karl in Max's athleticism, his love of baseball, and his determination. I recognize Verna's frugalness and sense of order in how he operates his home and financial life, and I recall her so often saying, "Little acorns make big trees." Max is steady and truthful like Tom, tidy and a little stubborn, and disinterested in food as recreation, as Janet was. Now and then I recognize a wedge of myself and of my family members as part of the fruit of Max's character. He laughs the biggest when he's with Sam, Dianne, Jim, and his cousins, Matt and Megan as well as Karen's daughter's, Simone and Alison. He has developed an appreciation for rituals and traditions that our two families have shared over the years. I like to think I've helped him to add tenderness to his qualities. My simple hope is that my addition to his life has added more sweet than sour and that he knows how much I adore him.

Most of this story takes place before our younger son, Sam, was even born. His absence from the bulk of these pages is merely a function of the storytelling, not a reflection of his place in our lives, of course. He is on the brink of adulthood at the time of this book's publication. The story of who he will be as a grown man is yet to unfold. Having Max as our first son gave us little preparation for Sam as our second. Where Max is practical and steady, introverted, highly organized, and occasionally too rigid for his own good, Sam is gregarious, impulsive, disorganized, generous, imaginative, and a giant slob, a great deal like his late Uncle John. Despite this, he and Max seldom argue. Perhaps having eleven years between them eliminated the rivalry most brothers have. When they are together, our sons play hard, laugh loud, tease mercilessly, and shake their heads at one another's eccentric differences. Max was, by far, the strictest parent in our house when it came to Sam. Sam will toe the line for his older brother much more easily than he will for Tom and me. I consider each son the best present I've ever given to the other. Cross-pollenating worked out pretty well.

Mr. Seavers taught me that you know that a graft is successful when new blossoms appear. It's exciting to watch the newest buds begin to form and bloom as our kids, and our adored nieces and nephews grow up, forge their individual paths, and welcome friendships, and loves, and for some, families of their own into their lives. I recalled Max's broken heart in middle school and how he wouldn't welcome more goldfish after his died. As a teenager, so cautious, so averse to risk, I feared that he might have a hard time risking his heart to welcome a love into his life. I wondered if he'd let himself be soft and tender, if he'd learn to say he was sorry. In recent years, I've watched Max with his friends and with his love. I've seen him show his affection, his loyalty, and his protective nature. I've seen him love, really love someone, and maintain close friendships from childhood to adulthood and there's nothing that makes me happier. Watching both of my sons love others, witnessing their gentleness with the women they care for, and their tenderness toward children, elderly people, and animals is the most extraordinarily beautiful blossom to me. They are gentle men, untouched by the menace that I grew up with. We've sheltered them from the harms that are within our control. This is the sweetest fruit I could imagine. I've made my share, perhaps more than my share, of mistakes as a mother. When I see my sons love one another, their friends, and their partners, I also know that Tom and I did a few things right.

Of course, the first and most obvious of the broken limbs in our family tree was Janet's death. Losing someone so young, with so much living left to do, was shocking and sad beyond words. Virtually everything that I cherish in this life, I have because of the scorching menace of loss. I live on a vast love inheritance. I have Tom and Max only because Janet was lost to them. Sam exists only because we lost twin babies before him. John's death allowed us to return to the community we call home. While I'd never have asked for the fires, and thought at the time that each one might consume us, I'm grateful now for the fertile loam left behind in the ashes from which so much beauty has thrived.

It's a switch of metaphor that I'll indulge here, but at the start of the assembling of these stories, I knew that the book would be called *Filling Her Shoes*. In the earliest days in our family, I felt that it was my job to take up where Janet had been forced to leave off, to step into the shoes of a loving mother and to walk in them as she might have. Over time, I learned that my stride was different than Janet's, that the style of shoes I wore needed to be my own. As my gait grew more confident, I needed to remove her shoes and put on a pair that fit me better and was more suited to the journey that I chose to walk. Tom and I needed to design our own shared path. As much as I value the inheritance Janet left behind, I could not extend her life by walking her journey for her. But Janet is never far from my thoughts as I walk mine.

I've now been Max's mother for five times as many years than his first mother was given, and am hoping that I'll be here to enjoy many more. I've outgrown the new shoes I put on early in our lives together. My gait is slower than it once was. I have stumbled and fallen, taken thousands of missteps. I didn't always know my way. As I look to the future of my life, of getting older, and sooner or later taking my own leave from this earth, I strive to bequeath my vast inheritance of love to those I leave behind. Writing these pages is my attempt to bequeath to my family all that I have been given.

It's only right that I should pass on this love story of my inherited family.

*Tom, Max, and Sam . . . my three loves, all in one boat on a lazy
summer day. 2006.*

Author's Message about Suicide

It is my family's tragedy that we have lost three of our most beloved men to suicide. I'm convinced that all three of these beautiful, smart, funny, generous, amazing men somehow lost their ability to see beyond their pain and came to believe that the world would be better off without them. If I know only one thing after losing them, it's this: They were wrong. The world is not better off without them. Their funerals were packed with people who'd have done anything to help each of them, if only they'd been asked for help.

If you have feelings that life is not worth living or that the only way for your pain or heartache to stop is for you to leave this world, please stop. Ask for help. Ask friends. Ask family members. Ask coworkers. Ask therapists. If you're a person of faith, ask your clergy member. If you can't bring yourself to talk to someone you know, call the National Hotline for Suicide Prevention at 800-273-TALK (8255). Your life is worth this effort. You are utterly unique, and the world would miss you. In this time of despair, you likely cannot imagine a time when life will be easier and more joyful, but it is there, waiting for you to create it.

If you have lost someone to suicide, I know that your pain is unimaginable. My family members and I are forever changed by our losses, but though we are changed, please know this: we are not ruined. It takes a long time and this loss never leaves completely. But joy finds its way into your life again. Hope and heartache learn to live together. And love is the most renewable of all resources.

I wish you all love, joy, and comfort. With fond affection,

—Betsy

Gratitudes

This book is just part of the story of how my family became a family. Many loved ones and dear friends whom I adore make only slight appearances or are entirely absent in this book, but my appreciations are vast to those I name here, and to many unnamed others who've loved and supported my family and me. We've been celebrated in great times and comforted in our darkest moments. My gratitude is boundless.

My "family" includes many not connected by blood or marriage, most especially including our dear friends and my tribe of writers. The other three members of my long-lived writing group, *Bella Quattro,* are Amy Peele, Linda Joy Myers, and Christie Nelson. Ladies, not only would I not be the writer I am without you, I'd not be the woman I am without you. Hollye Dexter and Linda Shreyer read and reread these pages, helping me to shape them into a story. I'm grateful to you, my beautiful Frenchies, and so happy that the fates brought our paths together. Special thanks as well to dear friend and skilled writer/editor Joan Keyes. I didn't think I could love you more than I already did, but once again I was wrong. Julie Valin has offered undying support and the deepest kind of friendship. Thank you, sister-friend. Suzie Zupan operates as a personal cheerleader for my every step, it seems. Just how did I get so fortunate to find you, darling? A special thank-you bubble rises from my studio in California and floats to Pennsylvania to glisten its appreciation to Amy Ferris. Amy encouraged me to be braver than I am because she is braver than I am. You've changed my life, dear one. Julie Barton's gorgeous memoir *Dog Medicine* inspired me in the editing of this story to share the hard parts of family along with the beautiful parts. For your generous support to this virtual stranger, I thank you, Julie, and look forward to the full blossom of this bud of a friendship.

If you're a writer and you have Brooke Warner as your champion, editor, mentor, and friend, you can count yourself rich indeed. Thank you, Brooke, for your keen mind and your big heart and for confessing that a couple of my stories made you cry. It was just the validation I needed. In a sea of books written (or likely ghost written) by pop idols and reality stars, SWP welcomes good stories well told, and I'm honored that they felt mine was worth telling. Thanks to the designers and proofers, and to Cait Levin, who was my personal usher through the SWP process this time. Thank you to Julie Metz for bringing her immense talent, heart, and intuition to the design of this book's cover. And thank you to so many of my fellow She Writes Press sister writers for your generosity and encouragement. It sure is nice not being alone out on this trail. Special affections to Susan Boggs of SW Media for being such a calm and steady support for all things tech and marketing, and being such big fun while you're doing it. I have Eva Zimmerman to thank for taking the scary out of having a publicist and for her kind and gentle coaching through the process.

On the family front, I owe immeasurable gratitude to Tom's sister, Joyce Kirschner, his brother John Fasbinder, their late brother Bob Fasbinder and their loving family members for the love and adoration (and a confessed amount of spoiling) that they gave to their littlest brother. You and your parents helped Tom to become the partner and father he is. My sons and I are the most appreciative beneficiaries.

Big love and appreciation to my "bonus sister" and favorite outlaws, Karen Lundgren and her daughters, Simone and Alison. How grateful I am that you, along with Karl and Verna Lundgren, were part of the package deal I got when I married. I treasure you all.

The oldest of my siblings, Rich House and Jan Burr, make only fleeting appearances in this story. The gap of years and the distance of miles between us have made our lives more separate than it would seem they should be. Regardless of how many miles exist between us or how infrequent our contact, we are survivors of the war zone of our home life, occupying the same foxhole in different decades, and will be forever united for what we endured. My wishes for your happiness, health, and joy know no bounds, and it thrills me that you've found loving, devoted partners to share in your journey. I wish you every comfort for the losses you've sustained and every joy that life has to offer. I only wish we still had John, Brian, and Rob here among us.

Michelle Colvin, Megan Shell, and Matt Grubb, while not children of my body, are certainly children of my heart. There is no scale to measure my love for you, or my delight in watching your lives unfold and the layers of love you're creating in your life and families.

I'm grateful to Mel and Bette Gardner and their family for offering me early glimpses into what a safe and loving family could be. You were silent mentors in the design of my own family and I'll be forever grateful.

Huge affection to Andrea Chao. All any mother really wants for her children is that they find partners who love them as much as we do. It's a joy to watch you love Max and to see how much he adores you in return. I count you among my fondest blessings.

Dianne Grubb has played many roles in my life: mother, sister, protector, companion, role model, and most of all, friend. Without her just ahead of me in the birth order, I might not have survived the family we shared. Not all of us did. How fortunate I am that in the safer, more secure, and more joyful environs of our adult lives we share a sisterhood I never could have imagined. Thank you is a paltry, inadequate phrase for what I feel for you, but thank you, thank you, thank you, sweet sister mine. When Di married Jim Grubb, she brought into my life a brother-from-another-mother. Watching Jim and Di love their children allowed me to envision having my own. I owe a debt to you both, and my love for you and your family is immeasurable.

When I'm on the other side of this life, if I'm offered a chance to look back, choosing Tom Fasbinder as a father for my sons will be the choice I'll be proudest of. Tom partnered with me to break a generations-long cycle of paternal violence. Our sons have reached adulthood never once fearing their father. They've grown up in a cocoon of their father's devotion. If our sons choose to become fathers themselves, I'm confident that their children will know only love, protection, and kindness from their fathers. My humble, quiet husband, did you know that you are changing the world with your silent revolution? Thank you, my love, for your devotion, your gentleness, your deep honesty, and your kind heart. Thank you for loving me. My beautiful lover, dear friend, partner in life, co-parent, home handyman, supporter . . . you're all that AND a side of happily ever after.

I say often that I have two sons, one who grew in my body, both who grew in my heart. When Sam was born to us, he brought sheer delight and became the final piece that made our small family complete. Sam, as you stand on the brink of adulthood, we are so very proud of your huge heart and your big dreams. We cannot wait to see those dreams come true. If there is love bigger than what I feel for you, your dad, and your brother I cannot imagine that I could contain it in this mere mortal form.

Max, thank you for the instant trust you granted when I asked your consent to publish these stories. For this, and for thousands of other ways you've trusted me, I adore you. Your first mother was loved by many and disliked by none, and is missed by all who knew her. You are so like her. Honest. Kind. Hardworking. Loyal. Modest. A little stubborn, and utterly your own person. Her legacy is you. I'm grateful to Janet Lundgren Fasbinder for the beautiful beginning she gave to you, *our* much-loved son. I'll be grateful for the remainder of my days for the vast inheritance she left behind and that I had the good fortune of being your second mother and trying each day to fill her shoes.

About the Author

Betsy Graziani Fasbinder is the author of the critically acclaimed novel *Fire & Water* and the founder of The Morning Glory Project, which celebrates those who have not only survived tragic loss and trauma but who have turned their heartbreak into heroism and their history into inspiration. Betsy has been a licensed psychotherapist in California since 1992. She lives with her husband in their intermittently empty nest in Marin County, California. Learn more at www.betsygrazianifasbinder.com.

Selected Titles from She Writes Press

She Writes Press is an independent publishing company
founded to serve women writers everywhere.
Visit us at www.shewritespress.com.

*Loveyoubye: Holding Fast, Letting Go, And Then There's
The Dog* by Rossandra White. $16.95, 978-1-938314-50-6.
A soul-searching memoir detailing the painful, but ultimately
liberating, disintegration of a twenty-five-year marriage.

*Breathe: A Memoir of Motherhood, Grief, and Family Con-
flict* by Kelly Kittel. $16.95, 978-1-938314-78-0. A mother's
heartbreaking account of losing two sons in the span of nine
months—and learning, despite all the obstacles in her way, to
find joy in life again.

*Warrior Mother: A Memoir of Fierce Love, Unbearable Loss,
and Rituals that Heal* by Sheila K. Collins, PhD. $16.95, 978-
1-938314-46-9. The story of the lengths one mother goes to
when two of her three adult children are diagnosed with po-
tentially terminal diseases.

Splitting the Difference: A Heart-Shaped Memoir by Tré Miller-
Rodríguez. $19.95, 978-1-938314-20-9. When 34-year-old Tré
Miller-Rodríguez's husband dies suddenly from a heart attack,
her grief sends her on an unexpected journey that culminates in a
reunion with the biological daughter she gave up at 18.

*The Butterfly Groove: A Mother's Mystery, A Daughter's
Journey* by Jessica Barraco. $16.95, 978-1-63152-800-2. In
an attempt to solve the mystery of her deceased mother's life,
Jessica Barraco retraces the older woman's steps nearly forty
years earlier—and finds herself along the way.

Fire Season: A Memoir by Hollye Dexter. $16.95, 978-1-63152-
974-0. After she loses everything in a fire, Hollye Dexter's life
spirals downward and she begins to unravel—but when she
finds herself at the brink of losing her husband, she is forced to
dig within herself for the strength to keep her family together.